CW01024631

THE PIONEERING LIFE OF
MARY WORTLEY MONTAGU

SCIENTIST AND FEMINIST

THE PIONEERING LIFE OF
MARY WORTLEY MONTAGU

SCIENTIST AND FEMINIST

JO WILLETT

PEN & SWORD
HISTORY

AN IMPRINT OF PEN & SWORD BOOKS LTD.
YORKSHIRE - PHILADELPHIA

First published in Great Britain in 2021 by
PEN AND SWORD HISTORY
An imprint of
Pen & Sword Books Ltd
Yorkshire – Philadelphia

ISBN 978 1 52677 938 0

Typeset in Times New Roman 11.5/14 by
SJmagic DESIGN SERVICES, India.
Printed and bound by CPI Group (UK) Ltd, Croydon CR0 4YY

Pen & Sword Books Limited incorporates the imprints of Atlas, Archaeology,
Aviation, Discovery, Family History, Fiction, History, Maritime, Military,
Military Classics, Politics, Select, Transport, True Crime, Air World,
Frontline Publishing, Leo Cooper, Remember When, Seaforth Publishing,
The Praetorian Press, Wharncliffe Local History, Wharncliffe Transport,
Wharncliffe True Crime and White Owl.

For a complete list of Pen & Sword titles please contact
PEN & SWORD BOOKS LIMITED
47 Church Street, Barnsley, South Yorkshire, S70 2AS, England
E-mail: enquiries@pen-and-sword.co.uk
Website: www.pen-and-sword.co.uk

Or
PEN AND SWORD BOOKS
1950 Lawrence Rd, Havertown, PA 19083, USA
E-mail: Uspen-and-sword@casematepublishers.com
Website: www.penandswordbooks.com

Contents

Characters

Achmet-Beg - the writer and thinker with whom the Wortley Montagus lodged in Belgrade. He and Mary became soulmates. He almost certainly died in the Siege of Belgrade soon after they left.

Addison Joseph - Wortley's best friend. Together they did the Grand Tour as young men. Founded *The Spectator*, and commissioned Mary. Instrumental in recalling Wortley from Turkey. He died in 1719.

Algarotti, Francesco - Mary fell hopelessly in love with this Venetian culture-lover when she was 47 and he was 24. She followed him to Italy, hoping for a life with him.

Anderson, John - young Edward Wortley Montagu's tutor and 'governor' who travelled abroad with him.

Ansbach, Caroline of (Princess of Wales and later Queen) - fell out with Lady Mary over the *Town Eclogues* but they later became great allies over smallpox inoculation.

Arbuthnot, Dr John - a friend of both Mary and Pope, he eventually sided with Pope against Mary in their quarrels. A Conservative, he nevertheless supported the campaign for inoculation against the smallpox.

Argyll, 3rd Duke of - Bute's powerful elderly uncle.

Astell, Mary - Twenty-three years older than our Mary, Mary Astell was the first English feminist. She encouraged Mary to write her *Embassy Letters* about her time in Turkey.

Augusta, Princess - Prince Frederick's wife and mother of George III. False rumours circulated that she and Bute had an affair.

Baglioni, Dr - Mary's doctor in Lovere, known as 'Miraculous Man'.

Ballini, Francesco - Mary's banker in Brescia.

Barlow, Mr - Mary's landlord at Middlethorpe Hall, York.

Bathurst, Baron Allen - a friend of both Mary and Pope. He remained loyal to Mary after the split. He had his six children inoculated but his young servant then died from the smallpox.

Blunt, John - the key figure in the South Sea Bubble crisis.

Bonnac, Monsieur and Madame de - the French ambassador to Turkey and his wife. They became friends with the Wortley Montagus.

Bowes, Eleanor - Mary wrote a poem about Eleanor who had been married off at fourteen and died promptly afterwards. Her husband owned a colliery near Wortley's. Her mother, Mrs Verney, wrote gossipy letters about Mary.

Bristol, Lady - older friend of Mary's. John Hervey's mother.

Burnet, Bishop Gilbert - Mary sent the bishop and his wife her translation of *Enchiridion*.

Bute, John Stuart, 3rd Earl of - married Mary's only daughter in a love match. Although Mary did not initially rate him, he rose to become Prime Minister by the end of her life.

Bute, Lady Mary - Mary's only daughter. The first person to be inoculated in the west. She married the Earl of Bute (see above) - a marriage her parents did not support - and had a large family.

Caldwell, Sir James - an Irishman Mary met first in the Languedoc. She came across him again at the end of her life, in Rotterdam and London, and lobbied for him to be given an Irish peerage.

Cheyne, Aunt - Mary's father's sister, Lady Gertrude, married but without children. She took on guardianship of Sister Gower when Mary's grandmother died, and the children were split up. Later she brought up Frances Pierrepont.

Chiswell, Sarah - a childhood friend of Mary's. Her father had managed Mary's old family seat of Holme Pierrepont. Mary tried in vain to persuade Sarah to come with her to Turkey. She wrote to Sarah all about the 'engraftment' used against the smallpox there. Sarah herself was never inoculated and died from the disease.

Congreve, William - playwright. He first met Mary at the Kit-Cat Club. She wrote to him from Turkey. He had a long affair with Henrietta, the Duke of Marlborough's daughter and heir.

CHARACTERS

Conti, Abbé Antonio - a Venetian thinker who lived in Paris, an ex-priest, whom Mary met in London as a young woman. They became great friends and she wrote to him often during her Turkish trip. Conti introduced Mary to Rémond. They met again later in Venice.

Craggs, James - a courtier like Mary. He was involved in the South Sea Bubble Crisis. Craggs owned a house in Twickenham. Died in the smallpox epidemic of 1721. His death inspired Mary to take action.

Crosse, Mr - the Wortley Montagus' chaplain in Turkey. He opposed Mary's inoculating young Edward.

Curll, Edmund - notorious publisher. Responsible for publication of *The Town Eclogues,* including Mary's poems. Pope ensured he drank an emetic in revenge for the harm he had caused.

Dashwood, Lady Catherine - a Lady of the Bedchamber who asked Mary to help her write a poem rejecting the advances of a younger, impecunious suitor.

Denbigh, Countess of, Mary - Mary's mother's stepmother. She brought up Mary's mother and remained a powerful role model for Mary.

Erskine, Fanny - Sister Mar's only daughter. She had an older stepbrother, Thomas Erskine. Fanny was caught up in the conflict over her mother. She married her cousin.

Eugene, Prince - leader of the Austrian troops at Petrovardin. The Wortley Montagus met him in Vienna.

Fatima - wife of a Turkish dignitary, whom Mary met in Turkey.

Feilding, William - an Uncle (related to Henry Fielding) who supported Mary in her elopement with Wortley and who repaid her some money when she was in Turkey. His daughter, Lady Hester, died of smallpox in 1721.

Feilding, Mary- Mary's mother who died when she was three.

Fielding, Henry - a distant cousin of Mary's. He was a playwright and novelist. Mary was his literary patron and he wrote poetry supporting her in her row with Pope.

Fox, Stephen - Hervey's lover of many years.

Frederick Lewis, Prince of Wales - George II's son, inoculated at Mary's suggestion. Mary wrote a lewd poem about his affair with Anne Vane. He would form a strong and valuable friendship with Lord Bute.

Frederick the Great (Frederick of Prussia) - Algarotti's patron and lover.

Fribourg - Mary's French man-servant.

Garth, Dr Samuel - a friend of Addison's. He attended Mary's brother and Mary herself for smallpox.

Gay, John - a poet and playwright. A friend of Mary's and Pope's in London. He wrote *The Beggar's Opera.*

George I - the first Hanoverian King. He came to the throne in 1714. Mary found his court dull but visited him in Hanover on her way out to Turkey.

George II - Prince of Wales until 1727. King until 1760. His wife was Caroline of Ansbach.

George III - Bute was his tutor and it was due to his influence that Bute became Prime Minister once George ascended the throne.

Gibson, John - one of young Edward's tutors and 'governors'.

Gower, Lady Evelyn - (referred to here as **Sister Gower** after her marriage). The sister to whom Mary was never close. She married John Gower and had a brood of children, one of whom died of smallpox, his mother having refused inoculation.

Graeme, General William - leader of the Venetian military forces and an ally of Mary's there.

Grange, Lord - Earl of Mar's brother who managed his exiled brother's estates and crossed swords with Mary over the fate of Sister Mar.

Grimani, Pietro - Procurator of St Mark's, Venice, later Doge and then Pope.

Grizell, Lady - Scottish aristocrat, mother of Griselda Murray, a friend of Sister Mar's.

Hale, Dr Richard - Sister Mar's doctor in London when she became insane.

Halifax, Lord - Wortley's cousin, First Lord of the Treasury under George I.

Hamilton, Colonel William - General Graeme's subordinate in Venice.

Hervey Lord, John - a great friend of Mary's. Bisexual, 'amphibious thing' as Pope called him. Involved in Mary's falling out with Pope. Had relationships with both Stephen Fox and Anne Vane during Mary's Twickenham years. Unbeknown to Mary, he started an affair with Francesco Algarotti at the same time she did.

CHARACTERS

Hill, Aaron - like Mary he had travelled to Turkey. He later became an eloquent admirer of Mary's struggle for the acceptance of inoculation.

Hinchingbrooke, Lord - Wortley hoped to inherit his title, as they were cousins, but Hinchingbrooke produced an heir, dashing Wortley's hopes.

Irwin, Arthur Ingram, Viscount - a hint of Mary's being romantically interested in him in 1724.

Jenner, Edward - the scientist who later in the century hypothecated that material from cows - ie vaccination - would work just as well to protect humans against smallpox.

Jervas, Charles - Irish portrait painter. Pope lodged with him in London. Not as good a painter, so Mary thought, as Kneller.

Johnson, Robert - the captain of the *Preston,* the ship which brought the Wortley Montagus home from Turkey.

Jurin, James - Secretary to the Royal Society who set about compiling data to prove the effectiveness of inoculation.

Keith, Dr James - physician who observed the inoculation experiment in Twickenham and quickly had his own only surviving son inoculated.

Kingston, Duchess of, Isabella - Mary's stepmother.

Kingston, 1st Duke of, Evelyn Pierrepont - Mary's father (referred to here as **Kingston**). He resisted her marriage to Wortley and their relationship never recovered. He married a second time to Lady Isabella Bentinck and had two further daughters.

Kneller, Sir Godfrey - society portrait painter. Owned a large house and grounds in Twickenham and rented Savile House to the Wortley Montagus. German in origin.

Law, John - responsible for the French Mississippi Company financial crisis.

Lepell, Molly - John Hervey's wife.

Lincoln, Lord - young man on his grand tour, who met Mary in Florence and then in Genoa. Joseph Spence was his tutor.

Loudoun, Lady - a Scottish aristocrat caught up in the struggle over Sister Mar. Mar hoped to marry off his only daughter to Lady Loudoun's son to raise funds.

Mackenzie, James Stuart - Lord Bute's younger brother, he met Mary in Venice and they struck up a close friendship.

Maitland, Dr Charles - the surgeon who accompanied the Wortley Montagus to Turkey and oversaw young Edward's inoculation there. Back in England Mary sent for him to inoculate young Mary. He then became the public face of the inoculation campaign.

Mar, Countess of, Frances - Mary's favourite sister (referred to here as **Sister Mar** after her marriage). Had an arranged marriage with John Erskine, Earl of Mar, who was a Jacobite and forced into exile. She succumbed to mental illness as a result and Mary spent years fighting her cause.

Mari Anna - Mary's French Huguenot maid. She entered Mary's employment in Avignon and stayed with her for the rest of her life.

Michiel, Chiara - a great Venetian friend of Mary's. They enjoyed a long correspondence.

Montagu, John, Dean of Durham - Wortley's uncle, his father's brother.

Montagu, Edward - Wortley's wealthy cousin who helped their son get a commission in the army.

Mora, Dr Bartolomeo- Mary's secretary. She hired him in Lovere and he stayed with her for the rest of her life.

Mundy, Philippa - a friend of Mary's when they were teenagers.

Murray, Griselda - a friend of Mary's in London. Griselda was reportedly raped by her butler in 1721 and she and Mary fell out over Mary's writing about the incident.

Murray, John - the British Resident in Venice. He and Mary disliked each other intensely.

Oxford, Lady Henrietta, (earlier Lady Harley, born Henrietta Cavendish Holles) - a distant cousin of Mary's who remained a close friend for their entire lives. She married someone her family disapproved of. Mary's daughter complained she was not clever or interesting enough to be Mary's friend, but her mother disagreed. She left Mary a generous legacy on her death.

Oxford, Lord - Henrietta's husband, who sided with Pope against Mary and his wife.

CHARACTERS

Palazzi, Count Ugolino - a conman who escorted Mary from Avignon to Brescia and ensured she stayed in the area for ten years, defrauding her.

Palazzi, Countess - the count's mother.

Peterborough, Lord Charles - the lover of Claude-Charlotte, Countess of Stafford, he then secretly married the singer Anastasia Robinson, who had lodged at Mary's house.

Pierrepont, Elizabeth - Mary's grandmother, who brought her up from the age of three to the age of nine.

Pierrepont, Evelyn, 2nd Duke of Kingston - Mary's nephew and heir to the family estate.

Pierrepont, Lady Frances - Mary's niece, only daughter of her brother William who died of smallpox. Mary assumed guardianship of Frances, who then eloped with Phil Meadows.

Pierrepont, Gervase - Mary's wealthy great-uncle.

Pierrepont, William - Mary's beloved only brother who died from smallpox, leaving a young widow, a son and a daughter.

Pomfret, Lady Henrietta Louisa, Countess of - a friend of Mary's who like her lived abroad. Her eldest daughter, Lady Sophia, met and wrote about Mary too. Mary visited her second daughter, Lady Charlotte, on her return to England.

Pope, Alexander - illustrious poet at the time, hunch-backed, Catholic - a great friend of Mary's in her youth but they fell out spectacularly in middle age.

Raitt, Alexander - Lord Grange's agent in the complicated machinations over the Mar estates and financing Sister Mar, her husband and their daughter Frances (Fanny).

Rémond, Nicolas-Francois - a French friend of Abbé Conti's, he had a crush on Lady Mary and as a result she started giving him investment advice. When the South Sea Bubble Crisis blew up, he started blaming her and blackmailing her to recoup his money.

Roberts, James - printed *The Nonsense of Common Sense,* to which Mary contributed nine articles.

Roncadelli, Madame - Palazzi's aunt.

Skeffington, Clotworthy - the suitor Mary defined as 'hell'.

Skerrett, Maria - daughter of a London merchant who became a companion to Lady Mary. Through Mary she met Sir Robert Walpole, many years older than her, and became his mistress and later his wife.

Sloane, Sir Hans - royal physician, a very wary supporter of inoculation. Only many years later did he acknowledge Mary's true role.

Smith, Joseph - the British Consul in Venice and an enemy of Mary's. A friend of John Murray's.

Spence, Joseph - a friend of Mary's. He met her in Rome in 1741 when he was there as a tutor to Lord Lincoln and wrote home with news of their various, wide-ranging conversations.

Stafford, Claude-Charlotte, Countess of - older, French friend of Mary's during her Twickenham years. Her lover for a time was Lord Peterborough.

Stanyan, Abraham - ambassador to Austria who conspired with Sir Robert Sutton to get Wortley recalled.

Steele, Richard - an older friend of Wortley's and Addison's.

Steuart, Sir James and Lady Frances - Jacobite-supporters who came to Venice in 1758 and became Lady Mary's greatest friends in her final years.

Stuart, Lady Louisa - Mary's grand-daughter, her first informal biographer.

Sultan Ahmed III - ruler of Turkey when Wortley was ambassador.

Sutton, Sir Robert - Wortley's predecessor as ambassador to Turkey. He had had his own children inoculated. He conspired against Wortley from Vienna.

Thistlethwayte, Anne - a friend of Mary's to whom she wrote letters from Turkey.

Tichborne, Wilhemina -Mary inoculated Wilhemina as a young woman and struck up a pen-friendship with her in later life.

Timoni, Dr Emanuele - celebrated physician who attended young Edward's inoculation in Turkey and wrote about the process to the Royal Society.

Townshend, Lord Charles and Lady Dolly - political ally of Sir Robert Walpole's and his wife, whom he had quickly married to avoid a scandal. Dolly (née Walpole) was a teenage friend of Mary's.

Turner, William and Mary - Lady Mary's servants in Europe. Mary Turner gave birth in Venice. They later gave in their notice and returned to England.

Vanmour, Jean-Baptiste - portrait painter based in Turkey. His portrait of Lady Mary hangs in the National Portrait Gallery.

Voltaire, Francois-Marie Arouet (known as) - a literary friend of Mary's. Supported her inoculation campaign.

Walpole, Horace - a writer and aesthete, Robert Walpole's youngest son, he was an enemy of Lady Mary's, probably due to her support for his aunt Dolly and for her part in her father's relationship with his mistress and second wife, Maria Skerrett. Mary came across him in Italy.

Walpole, Lady - Sir Robert's daughter-in-law, whom Mary met in Italy where she was living with her lover, Samuel Sturgis.

Walpole, Sir Robert - first English Prime Minister. A friend of Lady Mary's. She was instrumental in his relationship with his mistress and second wife, Maria Skerrett (see above). Walpole's political success damaged Wortley's career in public life.

Wharton Duke of, Philip - unstable, scandalous friend of Mary's during her Twickenham years. Pope was jealous of their friendship.

Wortley, Anne - Wortley's sister and Mary's friend, who died young.

Wortley Montagu, Edward - Mary Wortley Montagu's husband (referred to here as **Wortley**).

Wortley Montagu Edward - Mary and Wortley's renegade son (referred to here as **Edward)**, whom she said broke her heart.

Wortley Montagu Sidney - Wortley's father, Mary's father-in-law. Lived just north of Sheffield with his mistress. Involved in family mining business. Died 1727.

Yonge, Mary - Mary wrote a poem about Mrs Yonge, whose husband divorced her for having an affair and profited financially by doing so.

'she shines like a comet; she is all irregular, and always wandering. She is the most wise, most imprudent; loveliest, disagreeablest, best-natured, cruellest woman in the world.'[1]

Introduction

Changing the Course of Science

'the private satisfaction of having done
good to Mankind'[1]

A 3-year-old cradles her wooden doll as she makes her determined way across the hallway of the family home in Twickenham, and tenderly, gently, puts her to rest on the rug. Two adults stare down at her - a 53-year-old Scot, grey-haired, travel-soiled, weary, nervous, and a 32-year-old woman, the little girl's mother, stylishly-dressed, restless, swelling with maternal pride but at the same time focused on her adult guest and the plans for his visit. Blissfully unaware of the two pairs of eyes, the child lovingly tucks up the doll and begins to hum a lullaby. Dr Maitland brushes away a tear. He has not seen the little girl since she was a baby, a few months old. "She is a very great credit to you, ma'am."[2] Lady Mary Wortley Montagu, aristocratic, mistress of her domain, smiles back at him. "She is so very different in character from her brother Edward. You remember Edward, Dr Maitland? His swollen joints? All the cold baths I was constantly giving him? His milk teeth took an age to come through and he made us all suffer so. Not like this one. She is so robust. So self-contained. Nothing troubles her."[3]

Edward himself wanders into the room, a tall 8-year-old now, brushing off his mother's habitual criticism, interested to see who has arrived. Not his father, as he had hoped, but a tall gentleman, felt travelling hat in hand, who speaks with an unfamiliar Scottish burr. His father is in London on important parliamentary business. His mother interrupts his thought-process. "You recall Dr Maitland, Edward? From our time in Constantinople?" Dr Maitland shakes the boy's hand, admiring his grip. "You are grown so tall and strong since I saw you last, young Master Edward." Edward has a vague, hazy memory of the man standing before him three years ago. An unidentified sharp pain shoots through his left arm. This man holds him tight, calming him, soothing him, settling him into a dark wooden bed in their house far away in Turkey. Mary smiles. Young Edward's half-understood memory binds the three of them together. It is the reason she has written to Dr Maitland.[4]

It is spring 1721 and the latest smallpox epidemic is raging in England. Dr Charles Maitland has risked his own life to travel from his home in Hertford to the small town of Twickenham, just outside London. Earlier in the spring Mary's great friend and neighbour, James Craggs, has died from the disease, as has her lively young cousin, Lady Hester Feilding. Now, with her husband Wortley away, Mary keeps the doors to their Twickenham villa locked and bolted, sending her servants out to neighbouring houses to glean the names of the dead. When Mary's grandparents were alive an outbreak of smallpox did not cause this degree of alarm. Back then smallpox was seen as a childhood disease. Parents even encouraged their children to catch it early in life. But over the past fifty years the situation has deteriorated. Every time there is an outbreak it feels more severe and the gaps between the outbreaks are narrowing.

Six years previously Mary herself had contracted smallpox. She had been a court beauty at the time, recently married, beginning to make her way as a writer, the prospect of a glittering life ahead of her, friends with the poet Alexander Pope and the playwright William Congreve. She had fought the smallpox for several weeks and had then emerged in January 1716, weakened, to a snow-covered London, her eyesight severely impaired, the white glare temporarily blinding her, and her face disfigured by the disease's characteristic weeping pock marks. Her husband Wortley had been distraught at the transformation in his wife. Her career at court was now over. Her eyes were no longer fringed by their distinctive dark lashes but rimless and red. Her friends and foes had remarked on her new, disconcerting 'Wortley stare.' She had been lucky to survive. Her only brother, heir to their father's titles and himself a young father of two, had died the previous year, aged 19.

Just a few months after Mary's brush with death, Wortley had been named His Britannic Majesty's Ambassador to the Turkish Court in Constantinople and Mary had found herself travelling out to his posting as a diplomat's wife. Among their entourage had been the surgeon Dr Charles Maitland. Originally from Methlick in Aberdeenshire, Dr Maitland's reason for agreeing to accompany the couple and their young son Edward had been that he had heard the rumours that the Turks knew how to protect themselves from the smallpox. They reportedly used a process known as 'engraftment', a simple form of early inoculation. Outbreaks there were supposedly still far milder than they had become in the west. Maitland was not a member of the prestigious all-male Royal Society, where new thoughts and ideas were debated and evaluated, but he knew that a certain Jacob Pylarini had written to the society in London a year earlier, describing 'engraftment' in detail.

Every autumn, once the soaring summer temperatures had abated, groups of fifteen or twenty people got together to be 'engrafted'. For several weeks they isolated themselves from their friends and families. The predominantly Muslim Turks employed a Christian woman, usually Greek or Armenian, often elderly and almost certainly illiterate, to carry out the process. As a Christian, her life was expendable. She was required to find someone nearby who was suffering from smallpox and to visit their sick bed. She extracted a small amount of smallpox matter from their sores, transferring this liquid into a clean glass vessel. She quickly transported this back to the waiting group of Turks, storing it in her armpit or bosom to keep it warm. Next she used a three-edged surgeon's needle to open up some small wounds, normally on the arms or legs of each of the people gathered together. Although she was treating Muslims, sometimes out of Christian superstition she would make cuts on their foreheads as well, so the wounds on their heads, arms and legs made the shape of a crucifix. She carefully transferred the smallpox pus she had collected from the glass vessel into walnut shells, one for each patient. Using her three-edged needle again, she introduced a tiny amount of the liquid from the nutshell into each person's bleeding wounds. She strapped the nutshell to the small cuts, so as to use every last drop of the precious smallpox matter. The group of Turks would then wait patiently together for several days. Typically, on about the eighth day they all started to run a fever and would be put to bed. A few red and yellow spots appeared on the patients' bodies. Had they contracted smallpox naturally the number would have been far greater. A week or so later they would all be well enough to go their separate ways, protected from smallpox for the rest of their lives.

Once Mary had arrived in Constantinople with Wortley and Edward in May 1717, she had settled her family into their new home, a seventeenth-century palace in the suburb of Pera. She had thrown herself adventurously into experiencing Turkish life. Soon she had taken to wearing Turkish clothing, delighting particularly in her distinctive baggy trousers. She had crossed the Bosphorus to see the sights. When the wives of the Turkish dignitaries had invited her to dine alone with them, she had become the first Christian woman to accept their invitation. There she had taken the opportunity to ask them about the practice of 'engraftment'. They had reassured her that it was totally safe. They had never known of anyone dying from its after-effects. She had learned that the previous ambassador, Sir Robert Sutton, had decided to have his two sons engrafted before returning to London. She had reported this to Dr Maitland.

Next door to the Wortley Montagus lived the French ambassador, Monsieur de Bonnac, and his wife. The two couples had soon become friends. They too had heard of the Turkish practice of protection against smallpox. Monsieur de Bonnac had joked with Mary that the Turks inoculating themselves was a little like westerners taking the waters in a spa town. No one in the west thought that spending time at a spa could be dangerous, just as here in Turkey no one questioned engraftment, let alone feared for their lives in agreeing to have it done. Madame de Bonnac was a far more cautious character than her new friend, never once even venturing across the Bosphorus. Later in the century Voltaire would comment that, had she been as brave as Lady Mary, 'she would have done the nation [of France] a lasting service'.[5]

In March 1718, Wortley had been away for several months travelling with the Turkish sultan. Mary had realised this would be a good time to take action. She had consulted with Dr Maitland, who had agreed with her that they should have the 5-year-old Edward privately 'engrafted' at their home. Mary's household in Pera also now included a Dr Emanuele Timoni, an Italian whom Wortley had employed as their private household physician, a more prestigious role than that of a humble surgeon. Dr Timoni had lived in Turkey for several years and so had been wholly at ease with the idea of engrafting a child. He had been elected a fellow of the Royal Society in England whilst he was studying at Oxford in 1703. It was he who had arranged for Sir Robert Sutton's sons to be inoculated. He had written an article for Sutton to take back to the Royal Society called *De peste Constantinopoli grassante*. Surely, Mary had reasoned, her own son should have the same protection as Timoni had given Sir Robert Sutton's boys. Her household chaplain,

Mr William Crosse, had not agreed. She would be acting against the will of God, he had warned her, by deliberately infecting her son with a life-threatening disease. Mary's response had been simply to ignore him. She and Maitland had arranged for the customary little old Greek woman to come to the house in Pera with a tiny amount of smallpox pus contained in the walnut shell. There the old woman had made a couple of scratches on young Edward's legs. When he had begun to cry at her blunt, three-edged surgeon's needle, Maitland had stepped in and opened a couple of the boy's veins more gently. Mary and Maitland had been pleased that Edward had stopped crying. The pus from the walnut shell had been mixed into Edward's bleeding wounds, which had then been bound for several hours, the walnut shell strapped to them.

All had gone well, as planned. Edward had played happily for the rest of that temperate March day and had continued well for seven more. Then, as expected, he had been seized with a fever and a few yellow spots had appeared on his body, which had gradually turned red. His mother had ensured he was confined to bed for a couple of days. Some eight days after his fever, he had made a full recovery. Mary had written confidently to the still-absent Wortley that she prayed God their son would continue well. Edward had at most twenty or thirty of the infamous pock marks on his body, she had reported, and was already singing and playing and calling out to the servants to bring him his supper. She felt sure the engraftment would grant him full protection for the rest of his life. Maitland and the servants had known the truth, that Wortley would never have agreed to the experiment if his headstrong wife had consulted him beforehand. But when Wortley returned Maitland had made sure he avoided the subject with his employer.

Mary had given birth to her only daughter, also called Mary, three months before Edward's inoculation, in January 1718. She had considered having her baby daughter inoculated at the same time as Edward but had eventually decided against it. The baby's Armenian nurse had not been engrafted. As a Christian she had probably never been given the opportunity for inoculation by the Turks. Nor had she ever contracted the smallpox naturally. Mary had liked her and had valued her services as baby Mary's nurse. On balance she had decided it would be too risky to expose the Armenian nurse to catching it from her daughter. The baby had already proved herself easy-going and sunny - very different in nature from her demanding and often sickly older brother - but nevertheless at three months she was very young to be engrafted.

Mary had written to her old friend Sarah Chiswell about the whole process, about Edward's reaction to inoculation and about her wondering whether or not to have her daughter engrafted as well. In England Mary had tried to encourage the unmarried Sarah to accompany them on their adventure to Turkey, but Sarah's family had felt it was too risky and so Sarah had stayed behind. In her letter to Sarah, Mary had found herself speculating as to whether the doctors at home would necessarily be enthusiastic about introducing the idea of general inoculation against the smallpox. They might have heard about it from the learned papers delivered to the Royal Society, but actually trying out the process itself in England would be a step none of them would be inclined to take. After all, Mary pointed out, their bank balances would be sure to suffer as a result. 'Perhaps,' she wrote to Sarah, 'if I live to return, I may, however have courage to war with 'em.'[6] If having young Edward inoculated in Turkey had been brave, then to have her second child inoculated back home in England under the noses of the medical establishment would be something on a totally different scale. To do so, she knew she would have to make war with the medical establishment. But she also knew that she would make history.

Back in England this spring, Mary's summons to the cautious Scottish doctor can only mean one thing. Both of them are acutely aware of that fact as he arrives in Twickenham and greets her and the two children, despite her having kept her letter deliberately vague in case it is intercepted. Maitland already realises that Lady Mary is 'reserved to set the First and Great Example to England of the perfect safety of this practitude, and especially to persons of the first rank and quality.'[7] He can feel the potential of future repercussions. He fears something going wrong. And even if all goes smoothly, he understands that he risks his profession punishing him for striking out on his own in this way with a woman who has never received any medical training. He himself is only a surgeon after all, not a member of the prestigious College of Physicians, let alone the Royal Society. Three years ago, back in Pera, Mary's confidence had emboldened him. Now it makes him nervous. There Dr Timoni had overseen everything they did. Here they are to act alone.

Maitland hesitates. "The cold weather concerns me, Madam. You remember the temperate climate in Pera? Was that not more favourable to what you propose?" Doctors in England ascribe the fact that smallpox is less virulent in Turkey to its warmer weather. "Maybe we should wait until the weather improves?" Mary gives him her 'Wortley stare'. Her fringe-less eyes accentuate her hostility to this delaying tactic. She has not summoned him to Twickenham to have obstacles put in her way. "Do you not remember, Dr Maitland, the stories of the peoples on the banks of the Caspian Sea who practise engrafting with no ill effect? Their climate is surely far colder than ours in Twickenham?" Maitland cannot disagree, but he is reluctant to proceed, nevertheless. Maybe the weather will change for the better?

He tries another line of attack: "You recall Dr Timoni, Madam, who was with us back then in Pera?" She remembers Dr Timoni's reassuring presence all too well. "Could we perhaps invite a couple of London physicians as witnesses to our actions?" Mary is implacably opposed to this idea. What can their inviting doctors as witnesses do to help? Doctors will only block them from proceeding. Stubbornly, Mary stands her ground. Far better to keep their actions secret. No one needs to know until the inoculation has taken place. And then if they fail and it all comes to nothing, or if the worst happens and little Mary suffers or even - Maitland dares not say the words - if she does not survive, then no one will be any the wiser. Maitland doubts that the independent-spirited Lady Mary has consulted her husband on her plan. As usual, Maitland decides it is best to say nothing to her on that tricky subject.

The days pass slowly. Mary and Maitland circle each other while the children play happily, unawares. The socially assured Lady Mary makes sure her guest has every comfort, plying him with a large fat capon and veal sweetbreads, using her considerable charm to keep him with them.[8] They sit together at mealtimes, reminiscing about their time together in Turkey, studiously avoiding the topic of inoculation. Each day Dr Maitland looks to see if the sun is shining. Every day for a whole week it continues cold and wet. Every day he considers whether he should insist on a witness or two. Surely Lady Mary can see this would protect his reputation? Every day he decides his best course of action is just to bide his time. For her part, she knows exactly the game they are playing. She is someone who is accustomed to getting her own way, and this is no exception.

Eventually Dr Maitland ventures out to take a sample of smallpox matter from someone nearby who is suffering from the disease.

He returns with a walnut shell containing the precious liquid. Yet again at their simple supper of bread and milk nothing is said on the subject of whether other doctors should be present when they carry out the experiment. Lady Mary and Dr Maitland eat their evening meal and retire to their separate bedrooms in silence. On the seventh day, biblically, the sun breaks through from behind the clouds and the two arrive at a compromise. Dr Maitland will inoculate young Mary, they will wait for the pock marks to appear on the little girl's skin, and then and only then will physicians be allowed in to examine her.

They decide against bleeding young Mary, or purging her, or putting her on a special diet before her engrafting. After all, this is not part of the process in Turkey. Instead, on the second sunny day of Dr Maitland's visit, the confident Lady Mary takes her daughter in her arms and the cautious Doctor opens up a few shallow wounds on her wrists and ankles and mixes the pus with them. The little girl cries a bit, but not as much as her brother had done when he was confronted with the old Greek woman's blunt needle. Soon she is playing happily again. The fever duly starts, and the pock marks appear. Maitland stays with them, the tension now dissipated. On the tenth day - not the usual eighth - little Mary starts to run a high fever and is put to bed. Her mother summons a local apothecary, without telling him that she and Maitland know exactly why little Mary is unwell. "My thinking, sir, is not to give her any medicine but to wait until this fever abates of its own accord." Deferential before the formidable Lady Mary, the apothecary readily agrees.

Now and only now, three venerable members of the College of Physicians are invited by Dr Maitland to come and examine the patient. Lady Mary remains mistrustful of the medical profession in general. She will only agree to them visiting her daughter's sick bed one at a time. During each of the three visits she keeps a protective guard at the nursery door. The examinations pass off without incident. Next 'Several Ladies and Other Persons of Distinction' as Maitland terms them, society friends of Lady Mary's, are also invited to visit the sick room and inspect the patient.[9] The little girl smiles contentedly at all of her visitors and allows herself to be examined, showing off her spots, sticking out her tongue, letting them check her forehead for signs of a fever.

One of the physicians who visit the sick room is particularly impressed. Dr James Keith, a Scot who like Maitland has been educated at Marischal College in Aberdeen, observes the state of little Mary and listens carefully to Dr Maitland and Lady Mary's accounts of their actions. Dr Keith lost his two eldest sons to smallpox, back in 1717. He has a third son, Peter, now nearly 4 years old, born just after the deaths of the two older brothers. Will Dr Maitland consider inoculating Peter as well? Dr Maitland is honoured by the trust the eminent Dr Keith has put in him. He readily agrees. Young Peter is 'of a pretty warm and sanguine complexion' and Dr Maitland is aware that Peter's father is a well-regarded physician and he himself only a surgeon.[10] So he follows the usual practice whenever any medical intervention takes place and bleeds Peter before inoculating him, taking five ounces of blood. Ten days later the smallpox matter from the walnut shell is introduced and eight days after that, as predicted, young Peter starts to run a mild fever and a few pock marks appear. Peter is soon completely recovered and safely protected for the rest of his life.[11]

The pioneering Lady Mary's inoculation of her daughter with the help of her ally Dr Maitland and his subsequent inoculation of young Peter Keith will go on to become the subject of enormous controversy. Clergymen will preach from their pulpits on the evil of tampering with nature, pamphlet writers will rail against the likely dangers and physicians will resist a practice they have not officially endorsed. Lady Mary had not been the first westerner to have her child engrafted in Turkey, but she will be the first person to try out the process back in the west. She will have risked the lives of both her children, but she will have successfully calculated that risk. When she goes on to face opposition, she will use her own particular skills to face down her opponents. She is a superb networker and so she will set about gaining approval at the highest level for the action she has taken - from the Royal family itself and specifically from the Princess of Wales, who will have her own children inoculated just like Lady Mary's.

Next Lady Mary will begin to spread the word among her friends and acquaintances that engraftment is something worth doing. Over the next few years she will spend her time travelling between aristocratic households throughout the country at their invitation, inoculating patients against the disease. At times the demands for her services will feel overpowering. She will occasionally have to seek refuge back home in Twickenham just to give herself some well-earned rest. Her daughter, young Mary, who will often travel with her on these inoculation trips, will later remember the 'looks of dislike' from those who disapprove of her mother's actions and 'the significant shrugs of nurses and servants' when mother and daughter arrive.[12] Even Lady Mary's family and close friends will disagree with her and doubt her methods. Lady Mary has two sisters and one of them, Lady Gower, will refuse to have her own young son William inoculated. He will then die from smallpox. Lady Mary's friend Sarah Chiswell will also refuse protection. She too will die from the disease.

The College of Physicians will gradually come to accept that the groundbreaking Lady Mary and Dr Maitland are right about engraftment, but they will insist on medicalising the process. Patients will have to be bled and purged before the inoculations take place, contrary to Mary's advice that none of this medical preparation is necessary. When patients who have been engrafted then go on to die - in two to three per cent of cases - doctors will refuse to believe that this may be to do with the bleeding and purging rather than the inoculating. As Lady Mary will cynically recognise, there are 'some Fools who had rather be sick by the Doctor's Prescriptions than in Health in Rebellion to the College'.[13] In Turkey, after all, she had seen untrained, illiterate old women taking charge of the process, and doing so wholly successfully. As an amateur scientist, Lady Mary had seen with her own eyes the simple folk practice of inoculating against mild smallpox. She had correctly thought through the implications of using this process to protect volunteers against the much more dangerous strain of smallpox back in England. She and Maitland had then carried out a successful clinical trial on her daughter Mary. Lady Mary's achievements as a medical pioneer will go largely unheralded during her lifetime. Only later will she come to be recognised for what she is: a scientist who changed the course of history.

Lady Mary's mistrust of the establishment and her determination to work things out in her own way over the question of smallpox inoculation are characteristic of her entire approach to life. Her default position will always be to question and to disrupt. She will become a feminist, a hundred or so years before the word has even been invented. She views women as equal to men and will argue in her writing that women have the right to be educated and to participate fully in public life. She will never be conventional. She will write about marriage and the financial dependence of women on men from her own personal experience. She will marry someone she does not love, then fall in love with someone half her age and as a result set off to live in Europe for over twenty years.

Inevitably she will always attract passionate controversy, vilified by many of her contemporaries and adored by others. As her friend Joseph Spence will put it: 'She is the most wise, most imprudent; loveliest, disagreeablest, best-natured, cruellest woman in the world.'[14] Although she becomes famous in her own lifetime as probably the most intelligent woman of her generation and the friend of some of the greatest politicians, writers, artists and thinkers in her day, Lady Mary is now largely a forgotten figure. This biography, on the anniversary of her scientific breakthrough, seeks to redress that balance.

Chapter 1

Childhood

'from the lap of one…to the arms of another'[1]

Mary Pierrepont was born into a world of immense privilege. Throughout her life she both rebelled against and simultaneously celebrated this heritage. Her paternal ancestors, the Pierreponts, had arrived in England with William the Conqueror in 1066. By the thirteenth century they were significant landowners in the county of Nottinghamshire. In the sixteenth century Henry Pierrepont married a daughter of the famous Bess of Hardwick and built the first of the family houses at Thoresby. His descendants continually rebuilt and improved it until, by the time Mary lived there, it was one of the greatest aristocratic seats in England. Through the generations the Pierreponts increased their wealth, largely through well-planned marriages with heiresses who added to their fortunes. Mary's great-great-grandfather, Robert Pierrepont, married the heiress to the seventh Earl of Shrewsbury and was made the first Earl of Kingston in 1616. Mary's great-grandfather, 'Wise' William, married the heiress to Tong Castle, Shropshire. Her grandfather Robert married Elizabeth Evelyn and inherited through her the estate of West Dean in Wiltshire. A line of powerful women who brought their inherited wealth to their marriages led directly to Mary herself.

Not that her maternal ancestors were any less illustrious. Her mother, Mary Feilding (sic), was the daughter of the third Earl of Denbigh. The Feildings, who originally hailed from Warwickshire, had been elevated to the peerage around the same time as the Pierreponts. Mary's cousin was the novelist and playwright Henry Fielding (he joked that he was the first member of the family who could spell) and she would take pride in later life at the success of his novel *Tom Jones*. Both Mary Feilding's parents had died before she married our Mary's father, Evelyn Pierrepont, in June 1687. The young couple continued the family tradition of lucrative arranged marriages. The orphaned Mary Feilding's dowry was the princely sum of £60,000 (over £13.5 million today), although her groom probably never received the money that he was due. Mary Feilding had been brought up by her stepmother, Mary, Dowager Countess of Denbigh, who ensured the bridal couple received a 'voluntary gift' in compensation of £1,000 (approximately £230,000 today). In middle age Lady Mary was to praise the Countess to her own granddaughters as 'retaining to the last the vivacity and clearness of her understanding, which was very uncommon'.[2] Again, here was a powerful, dynamic female of a previous generation whom Lady Mary both admired and celebrated.

Both Mary's parents' families were united in defining themselves as Whigs. Mary would think of herself as 'Whig to the teeth - Whigissima', a keen supporter of the more forward-thinking of the two political parties, just like her forebears. During her great-grandparents' lifetimes deep political divisions had emerged in England. Different generations took opposing positions in the Civil War which followed. Mary's paternal great-great-grandfather, Robert Pierrepont, prevaricated over which side to support but eventually decided for the king, on the opposite side from his son, 'Wise' William, who sided with parliament. When Robert was then killed by a cannon ball, family history had it that this was divine vengeance. The story was matched on the other side of the family. Mary's maternal great-grandfather was also a parliamentarian and fought in the battle of Edgehill against his royalist father, who then died in the battle. The younger, free-thinking, pro-parliamentary generation gradually won through.

Not only did they win the Civil War, but they also emerged with their wealth and social position largely intact. They were members of the new establishment, prepared to challenge the divine right of their monarchs and confident that they had the power to shape their own destinies. As parliament began to form itself into two opposing parties, the Whigs and the Tories, they defined themselves as the more forward-thinking Whigs. Mary wrote that she was brought up steeped in 'the true spirit of Old Whiggism'.[3] When Mary's great aunt foolishly married a Tory, her father disowned her and made Elizabeth Evelyn, Mary's grandmother, sole heir to the family home of West Dean. When in 1660 parliamentary rule came to an end and Charles II was crowned king, Mary's great-grandfather 'Wise' William Pierrepont opposed the move. But this was a time for pragmatism rather than principles. There was no question that 'Wise' William's views would require him to forfeit any of his own wealth or power. He simply withdrew from public life and continued to work behind the scenes to ensure law and order were maintained in his particular corner of England. Lady Mary was justly proud of him, even though her own style would be far less pragmatic and far more confrontational. Her family, she wrote, had 'produced some of the greatest Men that have been born in England.'[4]

No record remains of the exact date of Mary's birth. She was christened on 26 May 1689 at St. Paul's Church in Covent Garden. Her young parents had travelled to London for King William and Queen Mary's joint coronation, intent on improving their social prospects. Charles II had died childless and the crown had passed to his brother James II. But when James married a Roman Catholic the political establishment acted quickly to have him swiftly and painlessly removed. Mary's family, both Pierreponts and Feildings, supported this 'Glorious Revolution,' where not a drop of blood was spilt. The crown was handed instead to James II's daughter by his first marriage, the protestant Queen Mary II, and her husband and cousin, William of Orange. The birth of Mary's parents' first child would not hold them back from being close to power at such a moment. Mary's father Evelyn would soon inherit the title fifth Earl of Kingston. Later he would be made Marquess of Dorchester and then first Duke of Kingston-upon-Hull. He would also hold a plethora of significant public offices: member of parliament for East Retford, Knight of the Garter, Lord Privy Seal and even Regent of the Kingdom.

Whilst their public life flourished, tragedy struck the couple's private life. Mary's mother gave birth first to her two sisters, Frances in 1690 and Evelyn in 1691, and then to her only brother, William, in 1692. But a couple of months after William's birth she died from post-birth complications. Inevitably, the psychological effect of this loss on the 3-year-old Mary would prove to be enormous. For the moment Mary's father was left with four children under the age of three when he himself was only in his twenties. He acted quickly, placing all four of his children in the care of his widowed mother, Elizabeth Pierrepont, and his married sister, Gertrude, Lady Cheyne, who was financially secure but childless. He dispatched them all to live at Elizabeth Pierrepont's home, the Jacobean manor house of West Dean near Salisbury in Wiltshire, where he himself had grown up. Meanwhile he continued his own life in

London and managed his estate at Thoresby in Nottinghamshire, finishing building a magnificent new house which his older brother, the fourth Earl of Kingston, had begun there. His household accounts show that he spent his time fulfilling every cliché of the eighteenth-century rake, betting on racehorses, drinking copious amounts of wine and brandy and fathering illegitimate children. In the portraits he had commissioned of himself in middle age he looked portly and self-congratulatory, someone accustomed to living life exactly as he liked, never challenged or (heaven forbid) contradicted.

Only the stable block at the 3-year-old Mary's new home, West Dean, survives today but it feels a pretty spot, rural but remote, just as it must have done to the young siblings growing up there. All that remains of the parish church which once stood by the house is the Borbach Chantry, the chapel where regular prayers were said for the souls of the dead. In church every Sunday as a little girl Mary would have looked across the nave to the chantry, with its dominant, life-size statue of her squire grandfather, Robert Pierrepont, grandmother Elizabeth's late husband, who had broken his leg and died from the resulting complications. His splint was carved into the marble. He had fought for his country without injury in Italy, France and Spain but suffered a fatal accident back in Wiltshire. His monument served as a powerful reminder - if young Mary needed it - that life could be snatched away in a moment. A female angel descended to bring her grandfather safely up to heaven. The marble inscription praised his wife and their happy marriage: 'Both great examples never to refuse, / In matches what wise parents chose.'[5] Parents, the message was clear, knew best when it came to the important decisions in life such as choosing a spouse. Mary's own parents' match had been arranged, as had her grandparents'. She would break the rules.

When Mary was 7 years old, she had a day she would never forget. She and her siblings were in London, visiting their childless Aunt Cheyne in Chelsea. To their surprise, Kingston's carriage appeared at the door with the order that Mary be dressed and sent up immediately to a house in Temple Bar in the City. Kingston was an active member of the gentleman's club, the Kit-Cats, a Whig stronghold, where a group of like-minded friends and acquaintances wined and dined, gossiping about the news of the day. Each year members of the club nominated the most beautiful woman in England to be chosen for their annual toast.

This year Kingston had suggested not a beauty in her twenties but his 7-year-old daughter instead. When his fellow members reminded him that according to the rules of the club they would need to evaluate her looks first before agreeing to toast her, his response was simple: 'Then you shall see her!'[6] The little girl was ushered into the dining room where the club members were gathered, braying 'Mary, Mary, Mary!' stamping their feet and banging the table in the middle of the room. She made her way steadily through the crowd, a nervous smile playing on her lips. She had never in her life received this amount of attention and she found to her surprise that she loved it. Kingston took hold of her, hoisting her onto the long, oak table, like 'a human candelabra', to be admired by his drinking-group friends.[7]

Mary would always recall the heightened drama of the moment, the delight she felt at being the centre of attention in the stuffy, panelled room. Her grand-daughter Lady Louisa, in the account she wrote of the day, explained that among those present were some of the most eminent men in England: 'She went from the lap of one poet, or patriot, or statesman, to the arms of another,' all stuffing her with sweetmeats and stroking and caressing her.[8] Her chief memory of the experience was of the sound of their voices loudly proclaiming her to be both witty and beautiful: '(N)ever again, throughout her whole future life, did she pass so happy a day.'[9] Through today's lens the image of this little girl being handed around and caressed by the group of men has very different, potentially abusive connotations. The members of the club drank their toast in praise of little Mary as the most beautiful lady of the year. Her name was then engraved on a drinking glass, alongside those of others the members had previously honoured.

Certainly, this attention from her usually distant father was extremely flattering to the little 7-year-old. Yet as soon as Kingston had achieved his aim, Mary was put back into the carriage and trundled by herself to Aunt Cheyne's house in Chelsea while her father 'carried on the frolic'.[10] She had been summoned, used, and discarded. The relationship between Kingston and his oldest daughter would never again feel particularly close. She often strove to please him, even when he was uniquely displeased with her. In her twenties, when she decided to defy his wishes, he would cut off all communication with her. His conditional love must have left her with the sense that at some fundamental level she had done wrong. And all this then translated itself into her spiky relationships with her own husband and children and also into the rich vein of irony which runs through nearly all her writing.

The safe haven of West Dean was lost to Mary when she was 9 years old and her grandmother, Elizabeth Pierrepont, died suddenly. The children could no longer stay there. Elizabeth left the handsome sum of £12,000 (£1.5 million today) to Evelyn, the youngest of the three sisters who was then sent away from her siblings to live with their childless aunt, Lady Cheyne. Mary would never again feel the same way about Sister Evelyn as she did about Sister Frances. Mary's grandmother would have rationalised to herself that her two older granddaughters were likely to fare better on the marriage market than Evelyn, so her plan provided protection for her youngest granddaughter at the same time as giving Aunt Cheyne a daughter figure. Frances, Mary's second sister, received £1,000 (£130,000 today) in her grandmother's will which would help her secure a good husband. But Mary, the oldest sister, received nothing. Mary was expected to inherit a large sum from her father's uncle, the wealthy bachelor Gervase Pierrepont; hence a seemingly harsh decision on her grandmother's part. But this legacy never materialised. The different ways in which the sisters were treated inevitably left their scars.

Perhaps there was a logic to Grandmother Elizabeth's will, but nothing indicates that there was any affection from the grandmother towards her oldest granddaughter. The move to West Dean had been an expedient one, after all. Elizabeth and Mary seem disarmingly similar, dynamic certainly but at times insensitive to other people. Perhaps they rubbed up against each other in those early years. No one could ever replace Mary's dead, hardly-remembered mother in her affections, after all. Later in life Mary wrote her allegorical fairy tale *Princess Docile*. Docile's mother, the Queen of Contrary, feels like a portrayal of Grandmother Elizabeth. She commands a new tutor 'to spring clean her daughter's [ie Docile's] Brain.'[11] Perhaps this was how it felt. It would be twelve years after Elizabeth's death before Mary would return to Dean. She was exiled there for two short stretches while her father banished her from the complications of finding the right husband. At that point she found the place unbearably lonely and tedious, seeing 'nothing but trees in a wood'.[12]

After their grandmother's death the two eldest girls, Mary and Frances, and their brother William were dispatched to live at Thoresby, their father's grand estate in Nottinghamshire. The splendid mansion would have felt very different from the manor house at West Dean. The household included two chaplains, a housekeeper, a steward, a bailiff and even a pheasant-breeder. Kingston himself remained a distant figure, busy with his properties and public life.[13] The children were left to their own devices, roaming around the grand house and parkland. They must have felt proud at having such an important man for a father but at the same time unsure as to what they meant to him. One of Mary's early poems described someone carving the names of his lovers into the bark of nearby trees. It feels a detail inspired by real life. Perhaps the Thoresby pheasant-breeder came across the children carving words into the trees there.

William had his own tutor and Mary and Frances were given a series of governesses. Back at Dean this role had fallen to the elderly Mrs Roper, who had first served the family as nurse to their own dead mother, Mary Feilding. Mrs Roper was undoubtedly loyal but her educational skills were not developed. She would have simply taught the children to read and write, add and subtract. She was left a legacy in Grandmother Elizabeth's will, so she did not accompany the children to Thoresby. Instead new governesses were hired to replace her. Mary retained no fond memories of any of these women. They were taken on not as teachers but as companions. Unlike William's tutor, they were relatively uneducated. Their main role was to prevent their charges from learning too much. Mary always blamed them for filling her head with 'superstitious Tales and false notions' and angrily accused them of teaching her 'to believe I was to treat no body as an Inferior, and that poverty was a degree of Merit.'[14]

In 1705 Mary's brother William, aged 13, headed to Cambridge, leaving the two sisters alone to set about the serious task of getting themselves an education. Thoresby housed one of the country's foremost libraries with thousands of books and manuscripts. Mary and Frances began to spend all their time in it, teaching themselves Latin. Mary was determined to read Ovid in the original and found a Latin dictionary and grammar to do so. To avoid detection by their disapproving governesses, the sisters pretended they were reading romances. The governesses did teach the two girls more practical skills such as embroidery, cookery, dancing and riding, all of which Mary enjoyed in later life. As the eldest, she was also taught the art of carving meat, courtesy of a specially procured carving master. She began taking her meals separately from the others, so she had more time to practice using her knife. Impressed by his daughter's intelligence, Kingston encouraged her to study Italian and engaged a master to teach her drawing for which she developed such a passion that her eyes suffered. The teacher was dismissed.

Mary fell in love with literature at Thoresby. She prioritised and devoured books by female authors. She adored the romances by Madeleine de Scudéry, whose heroine Sapho was a beautiful, noble orphan who became a writer, rejecting marriage and choosing to live happily unmarried with her lover Phaon. Mary took note. She read works by Aphra Behn, by Anne Dacier, by Margaret Cavendish, Duchess of Newcastle, and by her future friend, the first English feminist, Mary Astell. Like Mary Astell, the 15-year-old Mary longed to be the lady abbess in an 'English Monastery', well away from the distraction of men.[15] The library had been stocked as part of the refurbishments her late uncle made to the house. It is unlikely anyone else there had ever read these books. It feels a remarkable stroke of good fortune that Mary had access to this exceptional collection, that her governesses were disinterested and that she read these women writers at such a receptive age.

With no one to direct their reading, free to think for themselves, the sisters soon began writing. At first, the poems and prose they wrote were simply a game to amuse themselves. Gradually young Mary developed her own style. By the age of fifteen she had filled two notebooks with ambitious romances, largely pastoral in tone, heavily influenced by Ovid, Virgil and Horace. She set about rewriting all the stories she found in her father's library from the point of view of the women characters, seeing Julius Caesar through Cleopatra's eyes and Alexander the Great through his two queens'. Romantic love was a common theme. She imagined herself as 'the beauteous Hermensilda', who fell in love with the female Clarinda and carved her lover's name into the bark of trees.[16] She soon took the imaginative leap of writing in the voices of male protagonists as well. In her romance *The Adventurer* she created her first hero Strephon, who suffered at the hands of various female admirers before he rejected love for good. She later dropped hints that someone punished her for writing these early stories, probably one of her despised governesses: 'But oh my Punishment exceeds my crime.'[17]

Mary and Frances were not always at Thoresby. They often visited friends and relatives living nearby and attended the races at Nottingham and probably at York. A distinct group of female friends began to feature in their lives. Lively, witty letters went backwards and forwards between them all. A distant cousin, Lady Henrietta Cavendish Holles, who lived at the beautiful Welbeck Abbey nearby, became a lifelong friend. An only child, Henrietta was often criticised as not being Mary's intellectual equal, but her friendship proved precious for the rest of Mary's life. Sarah Chiswell, on the other hand, was a friend who did not have Mary or Henrietta's prestigious social position. She was an orphan, but her father had worked for Kingston at the old family seat of Holme Pierrepont, which often served as a base when the Pierreponts attended the Nottingham races. Philippa Mundy, another friend, was the daughter of a local squire in nearby Derbyshire. Mary, Frances and Philippa wrote each other letters full of gossip and shared jokes but also increasingly about the different men they were beginning to meet. They devised a code. Men were divided into three categories: 'paradise', the man you dreamed of spending your life with, 'hell', the man whose attentions you dreaded and 'limbo', the man who fell between these two extremes.

Mary and Frances spent every winter in London at their father's house in Arlington Street near St. James' Park. They visited their sister Evelyn at Aunt Cheyne's in Chelsea, but she felt like a distant stranger. They began to take part in the social season and were both formally presented at court. A letter to Philippa Mundy described the elaborate outfit Mary wore to attend Queen Anne's birthday celebrations in February 1711. Their time was not totally taken up with social engagements. A family called the Brownlows lived next door and Mary and Frances would climb over the garden wall at night to gossip with the Brownlow daughters. Eventually they were discovered, and the practice banned.

Young Mary Pierrepont was small, slim and dark. A friend remembered her as having 'beauty greater than I ever saw', but noted that it was her personality and her mind which truly distinguished her.[18] Quick, intelligent, with an infectious sense of humour, she would not find it hard to make the sort of dynastic marriage her family expected. As yet Mary, Frances and their friends did not know many eligible men, but they still speculated. Although they had some sense of their own powerlessness in the game, they still anticipated their future with enormous excitement. Their letters were full of giddy expectation about the adventures on which they were about to embark.

Dolly Walpole, sister of the future prime minister Robert Walpole, served as a salutary early example of the perils ahead. Dolly had fallen in love with a man her family deemed unsuitable. To make matters worse she then sought help from a scandal-ridden older woman. She teetered close to the edge of total social exclusion, from which there could be no recovery. At the eleventh hour her brother, Robert Walpole, saved the day by hurriedly marrying her off to his best friend, Lord Townshend. Mary remained supportive of Dolly throughout, watching events as they unfolded and gossiping about them in letters to her girlfriends. Robert Walpole's first wife, Catherine, would never forgive the young Mary for supporting Dolly, and the rift between these two women would play out in the next generation.

For the moment, as she approached her twenties, Mary was preparing to start playing the marriage game for herself. Mary, Frances, and their friends would have very little power, as Dolly's story graphically illustrated. Marriages for families such as the Pierreponts were above all dynastic alliances and love did not play a part in the choice of suitors. The unions formed were simply a means of protecting and increasing a family's wealth, the financial transactions negotiated between the couple's parents. The system was a brutal one. Not one of Mary's single female friends would emerge from the experience unscathed.

Henrietta Cavendish Holles, who was a significant heiress, dismissed her first suitor because he stank of alcohol. She was initially wary of the second but grew to like him just as her mother cooled towards the idea, causing an irreconcilable rift between mother and daughter. Mary's friend Philippa Mundy was encouraged to be brave when the man she saw as 'paradise' went off with someone else and she was forced into marriage with a man she felt nothing for. Mary's own sister Frances was hurried into a match with the wrong suitor by her father, keen to be rid of his final unmarried daughter, so he himself could pursue the young heiress he had his eye on. Other friends such as Sarah Chiswell were not wealthy enough to have any value in the marriage market and so remained vulnerable spinsters. By the winter of 1708, Mary was nineteen. Kingston settled on her, as his eldest daughter, an allowance of £200 a year (£32,000 today). He bought each of his three daughters a fan to mark the occasion. His intention was clear. Mary was ready to embark on the quest to find the husband whom her family deemed suitable. She would play the game in her own fashion: unconventionally, mercurially, passionately and courageously.

Chapter 2

Courtship

'I am entirely yours, if you please'[1]

The word elopement evokes something sublimely romantic. Couples are so much in love they throw caution to the wind, risking the disapproval of those around them, and run away together to marry in secret. The poet Robert Browning eloped with his fellow-poet Elizabeth Barrett. Lydia Languish, the heroine of Richard Sheridan's play, *The Rivals,* dreamed of all the trappings of a romantic elopement with its 'ladder of ropes - conscious moon - six horses'.[2] In Jane Austen's *Pride and Prejudice* Lydia Bennet ruined the social reputation of her entire family by eloping with Mr Wickham. None of these examples feel like feminist acts on the part of the women involved. And yet Mary Pierrepont's elopement with Edward Wortley Montagu in August 1712 was just that. The 23-year-old Mary decided to reject the marriage system she had been born into and to forge her own path with someone she realised she did not love, whom she classified as neither her 'heaven', nor her 'hell', but her 'limbo'.

The couple had met some three years beforehand. In June 1709, Mary wrote a giggly, school-girl letter to her new friend, Anne Wortley, who lived in a village outside Sheffield, forty miles from Mary's Nottinghamshire family home of Thoresby. There was a rumour that the young bachelor Lord Herbert had stolen the chamber-pot of a beautiful married lady as some sort of love token. This was perfect material for the correspondence that had grown up between Mary and Anne. What a pity Herbert had not had the chamber-pot engraved, like the Kit-Cat Club toasting glasses, Mary jested. Soon afterwards Mary met Anne's brother, an already-distinguished lawyer and member of parliament some eleven years older than her, Edward Wortley Montagu. Wortley was immediately struck by Mary's slight, dark looks with her pale skin and brown eyes, fringed with their distinctive eyelashes, but above all by her intelligence and erudition. Soon Wortley was reading Mary's letters to Anne over his sister's shoulder and writing out drafts for Anne to use in response. His words still survive along with the letters themselves, praising Mary for having 'wit joined with beauty', and plotting a meeting at the nearby Nottingham Races.[3] Mary knew exactly what was going on and wrote back, equally flirtatiously. The game was on.

The Wortley Montagus came from solid Yorkshire stock. Though not quite as aristocratic as Mary's family, they were nevertheless from within the same social circle. Wortley's father was Sidney Montagu, the second son of the Earl of Sandwich, and his mother Anne Newcomen. Although Anne bore Sidney five Wortley Montagu children, of which Edward was the second son, the marriage was not a happy one, and after a time Anne sought to end it. Following a standard procedure at the time among the aristocracy, an act of parliament sorted the terms of her children's maintenance. Anne converted to Catholicism and fled abroad alone, where she entered a convent. Wortley, like his future wife, had an absent mother.

The children were brought up in the village of Wortley, while Sidney built a big house nearby for his mistress. Sidney Wortley Montagu was a gruff, distant figure, pre-occupied by his business deals as he began to amass a fortune from his ownership of mining stock in Newcastle and the north east. Wortley had a disinterested father, as again did his future wife. Unlike her though, he had a formal education. The young Wortley was sent to Westminster School and Trinity College Cambridge and then on to the Bar. He did the customary grand tour of Europe, where he was accompanied by his best friend, Joseph Addison (who was to go on to found the *Spectator* and who had met Mary when she was toasted by the Kit-Cat Club aged 7). While they were abroad news reached them that Wortley's older brother had died. He was now the heir to his mother's 'entailed' Wortley estates, although not necessarily to his father's self-made fortune. The process of 'entail' meant that as the oldest son Wortley would inherit all his mother's wealth when his father died, an agreement that had been written into his parents' marriage contract. This was a relatively standard procedure of the time. From Wortley's point of view, he was a strong marriage prospect for the 20-year-old Lady Mary Pierrepont and she for him. She had captured his heart, but his head could also see the advantages of the potential match.

The first blow to the couple's prospects was the sudden death of Wortley's sister Anne in February 1710, cutting off their only means of communication. Undeterred and with characteristic boldness, Mary took the potentially scandalous step of writing from London direct to Wortley. This was the first letter she had ever written to a man, she explained, and it would be her last, so he must burn it once he had read it. Ignoring her request, he made a careful copy and kept it along with the original. He wrote back to her declaring his love: 'there has not yet bin, there never will be, another L.M..'[4] The secrecy and subterfuge of their correspondence alarmed him, though. They immediately fell into what became a familiar habit of sparring with each other by letter, weighing up whether or not they were really suited. They were two very different people, he wrote. He was 'a reasonable man', unlike her. He suspected that 'you can never suit', but as a challenge he set her the task of persuading him that a relationship between them might indeed work[5]. Warning bells should perhaps have rung for her even then - or maybe this was simply flirtatious games-playing on his part - but before she had time to write back, she went down with the measles and the correspondence between them was again threatened. There was no way of smuggling letters out to him, since she could not trust the servants in the new family house her father had bought in Acton, just outside London.

Both fathers - Wortley's father Sidney and Mary's father Lord Kingston - then discovered that their son and daughter had been writing to each other, though crucially Kingston only learned that Wortley had been writing to his daughter, not that Mary had compromised herself by writing to Wortley. It was decided that a match might be acceptable in principle to both the families and Kingston opened marriage negotiations with Mary's suitor. Almost immediately these negotiations stumbled. The problem was 'entail'. Kingston was adamant that Mary's wealth must automatically pass to her eldest son. Wortley, following the line of his enlightened contemporaries, argued that this rigid system left no flexibility at all if the eldest son proved himself unworthy. As things turned out, Wortley's mistrust was to prove to be correct. The only son of the Wortley Montagus' marriage did indeed grow up to be someone his father deemed unworthy of receiving a large inheritance. But Wortley was ignoring the fact he himself was due to benefit from the system of entail. He would inherit his mother's wealth, bypassing his own father. The arguments for and against the system were finely balanced. Wortley wrote a piece in the new *Tatler* magazine laying out his views. Kingston refused to budge and so the marriage negotiations reached an impasse.

At this Kingston sent his two daughters to West Dean, so as to get Mary out of the way, asking Frances to keep an eye on her sister and report everything back to him as his own personal spy.

Wortley continued to write Mary love letters and she continued to respond. He was ardent in his protestations: 'All the services of my life would be too small a return. The Adding a part of my Fortunes to yours will make you rich and happy, me rich and easy.'[6] She was more wary, accusing him of distrusting her. For Wortley, the emotional strain of feeling such overpoweringly strong emotions for Mary but being mired in intellectual argument with both her and her father proved overwhelming. He decided to travel to the town of Spa in Belgium to restore his health by taking the waters there, while he continued to write long letters to Mary back in England.

Exiled in rural West Dean with just her sister Frances for company, who was charged with reporting back to their father on her sister's actions, Mary thought she would set herself the challenge of translating into English the *Enchiridion,* a piece of Greek prose by the stoic classical philosopher Epictetus. He wrote that whatever pain and ill-treatment the soul endured it must remain untouched. This message doubtless resonated with Mary. Stoicism such as this would not necessarily serve Mary well in her own life, although feminist thinkers of the time such as Mary Astell were big advocates. Mary later confessed 'that she never was in so great a hurry of thought', as at this time of her life.[7] She then sent her translation to Bishop Gilbert Burnet, the local Bishop of Salisbury, and his wife Elizabeth, eager for some praise. Her letter to them had all the hallmarks of a bright, young bluestocking trying to say the right thing to a respected, older couple. She pointed out that women were often forbidden from studying learned texts such as these and argued that women should be educated properly and encouraged to learn Latin, quoting Erasmus to back up her arguments. So far so good. She did, though, qualify what she was advocating by writing: 'I am not now arguing for an Equality of the two Sexes: I do not doubt God and Nature have thrown us [ie women] into an Inferior Rank.'[8] These words have inevitably damaged Mary's reputation among feminist critics ever since. But she was young and impressionable.

The next chapter in the courtship saga was that Kingston decided to settle on his two eldest daughters, Mary and Frances, some £10,000 each (about £70,000 today). Kingston had also been negotiating a marriage for Mary's only brother William. Now that William's wedding was going ahead, he was impatient to get everything financial resolved at the same time. Mary realised immediately that this changed things and gave her at least a token degree of power. 'A single woman may live very well on that money,' she wrote to Wortley. She was trying to weigh up, she wrote, whether she wanted to marry at all. She was not someone, she explained, who felt great passion. But she encouraged him to re-apply to her father for her hand in marriage. If he did so, she wrote, it would need to be on her father's terms: 'passive Obedience is a doctrine should always be received among wives and daughters.' Her translation of Epictetus was evidently still influencing her thinking. If her offer was not for him, she wished him well and hoped that his future wife would not be 'one of those ladies so very free of their expressions of tenderness, at best withering, generally false', which she was sure he would come to regret. Her flirtatiousness and her competitiveness with any other potential suitors gave the lie to the idea that she really intended to remain single.[9]

To her surprise Wortley did not respond but instead went silent. His time in Belgium was giving him some precious respite to ponder his future. Plus, his older friend Richard Steele was no longer forwarding Mary's various letters to him. Increasingly frantic, Mary wrote again and again, without receiving a reply. Finally, once Wortley had returned to England, he sat down and read all her letters to him in one session and then painstakingly responded to them, point by critical point. Inevitably Mary's enthusiasm cooled as she received his responses. 'I beg you will this once try to avoid being witty and write in a style of business,' he rebuked her.[10] Wortley would always operate 'in a style of business' but Mary's style was altogether different, emotionally open, often quick to say the wrong thing. They were not necessarily right for each other. Maybe, he suggested, they should arrange a rendezvous in London to see how things stood. Instead Mary and Frances travelled north as usual to Thoresby for the autumn and winter and letters to their friends began for the first time to codify their various potential suitors into 'hell', 'paradise', and 'limbo'.[11] Wortley certainly never signified 'hell' for Mary, but nor was he any longer her 'paradise'.

In February 1712, the two sisters travelled back south again to London, to join the social season there. Their youngest sister Evelyn married her own 'limbo', John Leveson-Gower, in a dynastic liaison which had been arranged by their infamous Aunt Cheyne. Meanwhile their brother's new wife Rachel gave birth to a son, also named Evelyn. Kingston was becoming impatient to fulfil his duties as a father and marry off his two remaining spinster daughters, so as to concentrate on securing a new wife for himself. At some point this spring, we do not know where or when, Mary had a brush with a man who felt like 'paradise' to her. A gossipy contemporary indicated this was Richard Lowther, second Viscount Lonsdale, but there is no firm source as to his identity. Whatever happened between them that spring, it went wrong and she wrote to her friend Philippa Mundy in April 1712 that she was 'perplexed and divided' because of him: 'The apparent impossibility of dear Paradise often makes me resolve to plunge to Hell and lose the Thought for ever.'[12]

Kingston, keen to marry her off as time ticked on, had in mind a new suitor for her, the Irish peer Clotworthy Skeffington. As soon as the two were formally introduced, though, Mary knew immediately that he was not for her, that he constituted 'hell'. Maybe his looks did not appeal. Wortley, after all, was undeniably handsome. Or perhaps it was immediately evident that their interests differed. Mary would have found the idea of being married to someone who failed to share her love of books a sort of hell. Skeffington had been in England for a few years now, canvassing the field for a possible bride. An heiress with the surname of Saunders looked as if she might suit but, like Wortley with Kingston, the marriage contract proved a sticking point. Of another potential future wife he wrote to his mother back in Ireland: 'I can't as yet find anything of the lady's temper but that she is inclined to be fat and is about 25 years of age.'[13] When he was introduced to the young Mary Pierrepont she did seem to be his liking. She was slight of build, after all. The courtship game, which Mary had so enjoyed a year or so before, suddenly seemed to be veering potentially disastrously off-course.

Then in June 1712, to her surprise, Wortley wrote to her again out of the blue to tell her he could not forget her and was still in love. Characteristically he expressed himself in the third person: 'I admire her more than I do any one living, and I am capable of Loving her to excess.'[14] He raised the idea of re-opening negotiations with her father. After all, his wealth and prospects were equal to if not greater than Skeffington's. Mary's 'paradise' was out of reach for her and negotiations with her 'hell' were gathering pace. Shrewdly she realised that her father would not want to go back over old ground with Wortley. The only way she and Wortley could now marry would be if she were to break totally with her family. She agreed to see Wortley again. The two met secretly, first at the home of his married friend, Richard Steele, and then at that of Mary's Italian teacher, Ludovico Casotti. But when they did so they fell back into the old familiar patterns of criticism on his part and spirited disagreements on hers. Wortley made it clear that his own business dealings make it a bad moment for him to think about marriage unless her father would reconsider his offer.

This time it was Mary's turn to feel overpowered emotionally by their courtship. Boldly she decided to write to her father, laying out the situation. Skeffington did not interest her, she wrote, and if he were the only choice available then she would rather never marry at all. Furious, Kingston summoned her to a meeting. He laid down the law. She had nothing to complain about, he told her. It was her duty to accept her father's choice of a husband for her. If she refused, then he would cut her off with only a tiny annual allowance. His tactic backfired, though. Rather than being cowed at this news, Mary saw it as a chink of hope. Perhaps, she reasoned, she really could live a single life in much reduced circumstances, instead of marrying a man she did not love. She toured her relatives announcing her intentions to remain single. Their response was simply to laugh at her. She should stop being a romantic, they told her. Hardly any woman in London loved her husband and yet many of them were extremely happy. Love was irrelevant.

Desperate, she wrote again to her father, choosing her words carefully this time. Her aversion to Skeffington was too great to be overcome, she wrote, and she would be unimaginably miserable if he forced a marriage. On the other hand, unhappy as she was, she realised she was in his hands and he must dispose of her as he thought fit. Inevitably her father ignored the subtext completely and simply took her letter as a licence to continue. From his point of view her happiness or unhappiness were immaterial. Faced with the threat of this ever-closing noose, marriage to Wortley suddenly looked like a better prospect, despite the fact her father had made it plain that he would never accept Wortley as her future husband. For his part, Wortley boiled with anger and confusion that he was no longer considered by her father a suitable official contender for her hand. How had things gone so wrong? He began fantasising about travelling abroad to the city of Naples, which he had visited on his grand tour. He wrote that he should perhaps set off again with his friend Addison and settle there to escape his woes. Mary misunderstood him and thought he was dreaming of travelling to Naples with her. The two of them could perhaps live a happy and peaceful life in Naples together, far from the rest of the world, she replied. She realised this would mean giving up on all the delights of society like dancing, flirtation and gossip, but on the other hand it would give her a way of escaping from her 'hell'. Wortley had struck a chord.

On Friday, 1 August 1712 Wortley changed the mood music again by for the first time, suggesting that they should elope. She replied to his letter the very same day: 'I cannot say enough to thank you for the Generosity of your proposal.'[15] This did perhaps present a way forward. Then, inevitably, he wavered. She promised she would give up her life of pleasure and sacrifice herself to him. He still remained unsure. Then she too began questioning the wisdom of this new plan to run away with a man whom she knew she did not love. How would they manage financially, she asked? Could she bring a companion with her? Their letters to each other grew increasingly conflicted, their few meetings muddled by the increasing drama of the course of action they were considering. Although it was imperative their plans remained secret she asked if she could consult with two male relatives, her brother William, and (probably) her uncle William Feilding, who had not condemned her, like everyone else in the family, when she talked about never marrying. Meanwhile, luckily, there were some minor errors in the paperwork in the proposed marriage contract with Clotworthy Skeffington and they were granted a reprieve of three weeks while it was sent back to Ireland for corrections. They began to ready themselves.

Maybe her sister Frances let slip something incriminating about the possible elopement. However it happened, her father got wind of the plan. On Monday, 11 August he came to the family home in Acton to tell Mary he was moving her again back to exile in West Dean. He had spent all of £400, he told her, buying her a trousseau for her wedding to Skeffington. It had to go ahead. Emboldened, Mary wrote to Wortley giving him the option of two scenarios for their elopement. Either they could meet that Sunday (17 August) under her garden wall in the house in Acton and set out together to Italy, or they could wait till she returned from West Dean and elope in the short period of time when she was back in London, before the wedding day itself. Wortley was delighted: 'I shall go to meet you with more joy than I should to take possession of Riches, Honour or Power,' he wrote.[16] Any misgivings on his part had been overcome.

The plan was on. They decided to make their escape from Acton and on Saturday, 16 August Wortley bought the marriage licence and booked the coach. An unidentified married friend offered the couple her home for their first night together. The same friend promised to stand with Mary on the balcony on the Sunday night in Acton watching for Wortley's coach to arrive. Nerves jangled. 'If I do it, Love me:' Mary wrote, 'if I dare not, do not hate me.'[17]

On the Sunday itself, with the elopement planned for that night, Kingston again arrived home unexpectedly. Mary had heard a rumour he was on his way the previous day and written a confused letter to Wortley about all their various plans. She was yet again summoned to her father's presence for a long meeting with him. He could tell from her demeanour that something was wrong and guessed that she and Wortley had been writing to each other. Mary, rattled, could not deny this and found herself agreeing to her father's wishes that the Skeffington wedding should go ahead as agreed. Meanwhile the plans to send her down to West Dean were to be accelerated. She would leave in the morning. Mary managed to smuggle a note to Wortley that evening despite 'the utmost difficulty [and da]nger,' and another at 5.00 am telling him that everyone at Acton would be too busy with the preparations for the journey to West Dean to notice her whereabouts.[18] If he could get to her within the next two hours they could elope: 'If this is impracticable, Adieu, I fear forever,' she wrote, melodramatically.[19]

Unsurprisingly, Wortley failed to make this impossibly tight deadline. Mary was dispatched by coach with her brother as her jailer, but without her maid. True to form, she rallied and immediately began making yet more plans, starting another letter to Wortley at the first inn they stopped at to change horses. If the project were still on, then she would write to him with every post and do everything she could. Sick with worry, at the next inn where they were staying overnight, she retired to bed early, not having yet sent him her letter, only the next morning to discover that Wortley had been lodging at the very same inn. Apparently, the innkeeper had suspected Wortley of being a highwayman: 'I hope some time of our Lives we may laugh together at this Adventure, tho' at this minute 'tis vexatious enough.'[20]

For his part, Wortley had returned to London to think things through. Skulking in inns and being mistaken for a highwayman were not how he had envisaged his life. He dined with his friend Richard Steele, whose house he and Mary had used as a secret rendezvous and who was also a member of the Kit-Cat Club. There is no record of what was said that night but the two must surely have weighed the pros and cons. Wortley was very much in love with Mary, he must have told his friend, but this did not blind him to her faults. Were they right for each other - he a man of business and she a sparky young woman eleven years his junior? But then again, he had, as Mary later wrote about him: 'at that time that sort of Passion for me, that would have made me invisible to all but himself, had it been in his Power'.[21] He could not deny the strength of his feelings. Two nights later Wortley's carriage drew up at the mound at West Dean. The time and place were finally right. Their long-awaited elopement was on.

As Edward Wortley Montagu checked his watch whilst he waited for his future bride in the darkness, he may well have recalled that only a few weeks beforehand he had written to her: 'If we should once be in a coach let us not say one word till we come before the parson, lest we should engage in fresh disputes.'[22] As it turned out, the elopement went relatively smoothly. In Mary's imagination it might have felt as if the two had been plotting to run away to some remote island, risking the 'possibility of being reduced to suffer all the Evils of poverty', but that did not happen.[23] No one at West Dean noticed her leaving the house and the coach rumbled away into the darkness undetected. Her family's response when they did eventually discover the elopement was simply to try to play the whole thing down. As Mary had predicted, her father never forgave her, but she and Wortley were certainly never poor.

The next day a lone priest in Salisbury took the couple through their wedding vows, dressed simply in the clothes they stood up in. Mary had had no choice but to leave behind the expensive trousseau her father had bought for her impending wedding to Clotworthy Skeffington. As there had been no time to post any banns, Wortley had applied for a special licence so they could be married 'at any convenient time and place'.[24] From here they travelled on to his bachelor lodgings in Catherine Street near Covent Garden, to start their married life together. Wortley may have had some sexual experience, but Mary was almost certainly a virgin. The whole arrangement all felt a bit botched and uncertain, but, as her sister Frances told a friend: 'She wri[tes] everybody word she's perfectly happy, and it seems has found paradise (as she terms it herself) when she expected but limbo.'[25]

Chapter 3

Early Married Life

'A proper matrimonial style'[1]

Catherine Street, where Mary and Wortley started their married life, must have felt very different from the grand Pierrepont house in St James' Park where Mary had spent much of her adolescence. Wortley was immediately immersed again in the political world and the family mining business. Mary was estranged from her family, but she hoped this would only be temporary. The notion that she was now a young married woman appealed to her enormously. Within a few weeks of the elopement she fell pregnant. Wortley was never to question the paternity of this baby, despite being explosively jealous of any other male interest in Mary at this stage of their marriage. Her role as wife and mother-to-be was confirmed.

Mary could wander through the fruit and vegetable markets of Covent Garden or watch the comings and goings at the theatres and playhouses, full of 'Opera Queens', fops, beauties and beaux hurrying home 'to put fresh Linnen on'.[2] As a married woman she now had the freedom to go wherever she chose, observing everything she saw, no longer under her father's control. Kingston remained implacable in his opposition to Mary and Wortley's elopement, leaving them exposed financially, their future uncertain. He received letters from them both, begging his forgiveness, but took characteristic offence that they sent their letters of apology by the standard penny post. They made attempts to bring other family members on side to argue their case, but one by one these came to nothing. Wortley was finally granted a much-delayed audience with his father-in law, with Mary sidelined whilst the two men in her life negotiated her fate. She wrote to Wortley beforehand, sarcastically asking him to convey 'My duty to Papa'. The two men arrived at some kind of truce, but relations remained frosty.[3]

Kingston did negotiate the kind of dynastic marriage he had had in mind for Mary for her favourite sister, but Frances' story demonstrated how this path could be just as fraught as Mary's elopement. She was married off to John Erskine, the sixth Earl of Mar, on 20 July 1714, a match which Mary instinctively mistrusted. Some fifteen years older than Frances, the Earl of Mar had been married before, with a teenage son by that marriage. His reasons for marrying again were quite simple. He needed status and wealth. Sister Frances brought with her the generous cash incentive of an immediate £8,000 (£1.1 million today) and a marriage settlement of £1,500 per year from then on (£213,000 today). Mar was in a precarious situation financially and Kingston was selling off his daughter. The marriage contract was long, solemn and forbidding, with the signatures of father-in-law and groom on every page and the initials of the bride herself discreetly beneath her future husband's. At least by choosing to elope Mary had avoided this kind of legal statement of the unpalatable truth, that marriage was above all a buying and selling of goods. The document carefully worked out what at the time must have looked like every eventuality for the couple's future life together. In fact, events gave the lie to this kind of legalistic planning.

Instead of being a Whig like the rest of the family, Frances' new husband was a member of the Tory party. At the time of the marriage he held a post at the court of Queen Anne, who favoured the Tories. Mar was Scottish and his sympathies were with the family of the exiled Catholic royal family, descendants of James II, living across the water in France. He was a Jacobite. As Thomas Burnet quipped about the marriage: 'there is a good Whig marr'd by taking a Scotch Jacobite for her Husband.'[4] From now on Mary always referred to Frances as Sister Mar. The following year, the day after Sister Mar gave birth to her only child, her husband would abandon both his wife and new baby daughter, to join the army fighting in support of James II's Catholic son, the Old Pretender, who had set sail from France for Scotland.

In the early months of their marriage, Wortley and Mary were often apart. She made various visits to friends and relatives whilst they decided where to set up home, and he went backwards and forwards from London, bent on finding a safe parliamentary seat for himself. Where her letters to him at this time were flirtatious, sparky, imaginative, his to her were business-like, formal and impatient with his impulsive young wife. The cracks were already beginning to show. She struggled to find a voice in these letters, a 'proper matrimonial style' as she put it. In the fairy tale *Princess Docile,* which Mary wrote many years later, the character of Prince Sombre was clearly based on the young Wortley:

> 'He had all the Qualities of an upright man, and no single quality of an amiable one…he was impervious to flattery, unshakeably firm, but so Jealous as to be perpetually mistrustful, true to his word, ungracious in his actions, tall and well-built but with a proud air and no charm.'[5]

To her unmarried friend, Philippa Mundy, Mary portrayed her marriage in these early months as a happy one, boasting 'it was certainly my good Genius that inspired me' to elope.[6] Philippa wrote to the newly-married Mary in January 1713, asking her advice on whether to marry the suitor her parents preferred or to hold out for the man she liked. Mary's reply sounded as if she and Wortley had discussed the dilemma and she was following his request that she 'avoid being witty and write in a style of business.' If it was simply that Philippa did not like the looks of her parents' suitor, Mary wrote back, then she was sure she would soon come round just as Mary herself had done. Wortley had been her 'limbo' and was now her 'paradise'. Philippa should also remember: 'tho' 'tis easy to be without superfluities, 'tis impossible to be without Necessaries.' Perhaps Philippa could manage without six horses but certainly not without a coach. Now she was married, Mary had dispensed with all her previous fantasies of idealised romantic poverty. Instead she acknowledged the financial incentives which were built into the marriage system.[7]

Without a proper marital home to call their own, the early months of Mary and Wortley's marriage were peripatetic. First stop in October 1712 was Wortley's family home, a few miles outside Sheffield. Sidney Wortley Montagu had left their ancestral house, Wortley Hall, to crumble into ruins, preferring instead to live at his gamekeeper's house, Wharncliffe Lodge. Mary's daughter later described it as 'a wretched hovel', but Mary herself always enthused about its situation, perched high on the cliffs looking down over an escarpment into the wooded Peak District below.[8] The company was not so much to her liking. Sidney, large and rough-looking, sporting a flapped hat, spent his time swearing at his servants from his great chair, while his brother,

Dean John Montagu of Durham, silver hair crowned by a cap of velvet, sat in silence, sighing and lifting his eyes to heaven at every expletive.

Next the young couple parted, Wortley to Durham with his uncle Dean John Montagu, probably to inspect the family collieries there, and Mary to Wallingwells Hall, in Nottinghamshire, where lived the White family with their five children. On her arrival the newly pregnant Mary went straight to bed, sick and exhausted from the carriage journey. She woke to the chaos of family life and fantasised in her letter to Wortley that they too would one day have a large family, 'and the noise of a Nursery may have more charms for us than the Music of an Opera.'[9] From there she travelled to Hinchingbrooke in Huntingdonshire to stay with Wortley's cousin, Lord Sandwich, head of the Montagu family, in the hope that he might help them financially and argue their case with her father. Left largely alone at Hinchingbrooke, Mary's letters to her new husband are a stream of consciousness: 'I see nothing, but I think of everything, and indulge my imagination, which is chiefly employed on you.'[10] For his part, he suggested she critique a play his 'bosom friend' Joseph Addison had been writing about the Roman stoic philosopher Cato. Mary set about her task enthusiastically once she was back in London in early 1713, but Addison only took up a few of her suggestions. Instead of her epilogue he used one written by a Kit-Cat Club friend, Dr Samuel Garth.

In May 1713, Mary gave birth to a son, christening him Edward after his father. Wortley was not present at the birth but perhaps Sister Mar gave her support. Edward would have been handed to a wet nurse, and Mary shut up in a darkened room for a month after her delivery. Towards the end of the month she could receive visitors, sharing the traditional drink of caudle, ale or wine thickened with egg yolks and sweetened with spices and honey. Wortley headed back up north on parliamentary business, only a week after she emerged. Mary's letter to him the day he left made it clear that they had quarrelled before he set off. She was quick to remind him that he was now a father with a son. It was the first of many such reminders. The other ominous piece of news in this letter was that her only brother William had contracted smallpox. Dr Garth, whose epilogue Addison had chosen over Mary's, attended him. Within a week the 19-year-old William was dead, leaving a widowed teenage wife and two small children, one of whom was now his grandfather's under-age heir. The whole experience sank Mary's spirits. She wrote to Wortley admitting: 'I should not be too much alone, which leads me into a Melancholy I can't help, though I know 'tis very prejudicial to my Health,' but there was no response from him.[11] He simply did not have the emotional vocabulary to help her at times like this.

Mary threw herself into the practicalities of finding their first home. It seemed likely that Wortley would be elected as a member of parliament for a northern seat and a rented house there might suit their finances. Leaving London in July 1713, she travelled north with her 2-month-old baby son Edward to her father-in-law's at Wharncliffe Lodge to look for the right house. She was anxious to get Wortley's agreement at every stage, but he was either disinterested or slow: 'I beg you will settle to your own mind,'[12] he wrote to her. Options emerged but fell through. One nearby property was only half-finished, at another the landlord wanted to reserve an apartment for himself and yet another was withdrawn from the market. Finally, Mary found the perfect house, just outside York: Middlethorpe Hall. It was large, modern and stylish with generous sash windows looking over the gardens, but it would still suit their budget. Visitors from York could be invited to call on them in the afternoon and not stay on for expensive dinners. Mr Barlow, the landlord, offered to throw in free beer and coals for them as part of their rental deal. All she wanted, she wrote to Wortley, was 'what will be most convenient to you.'[13] Wortley urged her to drive a hard bargain. He was concerned there were no iron bars on the windows of the house for security. He wondered whether they should wait until the results of the general election before committing. Their indecisive correspondence was agonising, both of them falling back into already-familiar patterns of behaviour. 'I am angry at your neglect of me,' she wrote to him.[14] Briefly it looked like another house might become available but despite Mary's best attempts at negotiation it fell through. Eventually there was no choice: Middlethorpe it was.

Wortley failed to win the seat of Aldborough in the general election that autumn. The young marrieds found themselves becalmed at Middlethorpe Hall with their new baby, their future uncertain. Wortley went backwards and forwards to London. For two years running he nominated Mary for the toast of another Whig-stronghold club, not the Kit-Cats this time but the Hanover Club. Mary ached with loneliness whenever Wortley was away and told him so in her letters. She quickly dismissed the social scene in York. Perhaps burying herself in the country had been a mistake. By January 1714 she was already urging Wortley to rent a house in London. She did not fall pregnant again.

Mary's first published work appeared anonymously in *The Spectator* on 28 July 1714. It was the first female contribution to the magazine. Its subject was marriage. It took the form of a spoof letter in which an elderly lady, president of the fictional Widows' Club, narrated the story of her life. She had been married six times but had survived all her husbands and was now considering a seventh. The letter was a pointed response to another spoof letter, published the month before, written by Wortley's friend Joseph Addison, editor of the *Spectator*. Addison wrote in the person of a male fortune hunter who had come across the Widows' Club and declared himself shocked at what he found. Traditionally widows' financial security had been protected under the 'dower' system where a widow was entitled to a third of her dead husband's property. As wealth was increasingly diversifying, land was becoming less important. Stocks and shares also played their part, as did new businesses such as Wortley's. The system was becoming more fluid. Potentially wealthy widows now had greater financial power. It was these changes which Addison was satirising.

Addison listed the members of his fictitious Widows' Club one by one. Mrs. Snapp, for instance, had been married four times to men from four different counties and Addison described her as being ambitious 'of extending her possessions through all the counties in England, on this side of the Trent'. She was on the make through marriage. Not only was Addison's fictional letter-writer threatened by the widows' economic power, he was also scared by their sexual rapaciousness. The widows met once a week to share stories and drink together, rather like the members of the Kit-Cat Club, and to 'deter the rest of their sex from marriage, and ingross the whole male world to themselves'.[15] Men should beware women.

In her response, Mary made a studied point about Addison's satire and responded with sharp wit. It was a feminist text, critiquing the position of women at the time, and demanded to be read as an equal response to Addison's. It was little wonder, wrote Mary, that Mrs President spent such a short time in mourning each of her husbands. She had first been married off at fourteen. Mary described each of the marriages in turn, analysing the shortcomings of the various husbands from philandering to foxhunting, from neurosis to financial misconduct. She would not waste time, she protested 'in grieving for an insolent, insignificant, negligent, extravagent, splenatick or covetous Husband.' Each of Mrs President's husbands have mistreated her: 'my first insulted me, my second was nothing to me, my third disgusted me, the fourth would have ruined me, the fifth tormented me and the sixth would have starved me.'[16] Where Addison portrayed women as sexually powerful, Mary catalogued the ways men can mistreat women emotionally. Where Addison satirised the financial power of widows, Mary showed men having the upper hand. Her widow trusted a husband who then defrauded her. Her only recourse, when another husband proved mean, was to put on a £2,000 diamond necklace (£285,000 today) to goad him into taking an opium overdose.

Her examples may have been comic, but Mary's underlying message was clear. As so often in her writing, the wit and playfulness masked the underlying seriousness of her criticism of the patriarchal system in which she found herself. It also allowed her to write in the primarily male domain of the *Spectator,* her sparkling style rendering her message palatable to readers of both sexes. Between Mrs President's various disastrous marriages, there was one constant suitor -The Honourable Edward Waitfort. He was an in-joke, a flattering portrait of Mary's husband and Addison's best friend. For anyone who knew that it was Mary who was writing this letter, she was sending them a message. Marrying her faithful if unexciting suitor had been the right thing to do.

On 1 August 1714 Queen Anne died, childless. Her heir, the future George I, Elector of Hanover, spoke no English and would have to travel from mainland Europe to England to take up his throne. Queen Anne's Catholic half-brother, who styled himself James III but was known as the Old Pretender, felt he had just as much of a claim to the throne as his distant, Protestant, German cousin. Civil war, which had taken place only a generation or so before, looked a distinct possibility again. Mary, who was alone at Middlethorpe Hall with her baby son when Queen Anne died, did not hear the news for several days. She watched in alarm as mobs in York yelled their support for the new King George and paraded a model Pretender through the streets, burning it on a bonfire. Middlethorpe Hall was on the road from York to Scotland, and soon the Jacobite troops began marching past Mary's front door on their way to raise an army against the new king.

The atmosphere felt incendiary. Some family friends, the three young Carlisle sisters at nearby Castle Howard, suggested Mary and young Edward go to stay with them there, 'which is the same thing as pensioning in a convent,' she assured the ever-jealous Wortley.[17] Mary stayed for three weeks. Politics began to settle. The country seemed to be reconciling itself to a continuation of the Protestant monarchy with a new German king. Parliament was dissolved and the government disbanded. New elections would need to be held within six months. Sister Mar's husband lost his governmental role as Secretary of State for Scotland, but she was at first optimistic about his future. There would be a large pension, she reassured her sister, and they would continue to live in London. Lord Mar was quick to swear allegiance to the new king: 'I must do the best I can for myself,' he wrote. Within a year, though, he would join the Jacobite troops in Scotland, abandoning his new wife and baby daughter.[18]

At the beginning of September 1714, Mary returned home from Castle Howard to Middlethorpe. Young Edward's health concerned her. His joints were worryingly swollen. She ensured he was taken to a nearby well to be dunked in its cold water. She had heard this would be good for him. She herself was suffering from bad toothache, a weakness which was to recur throughout her life. Her coachman John gave in his notice. He had heard (wrongly) that the Wortley Montagus were intending to stay in Yorkshire, and he was missing London. Mary could not persuade him to stay on, but she wrote to Wortley that she had had a new, 'very quiet sober Country Coachman' recommended to her.[19] Wortley remained in London, intent on finding the right parliamentary seat, and Mary turned campaign manager from Middlethorpe. She had an impressive knowledge of the political scene, having grown up with the Pierrepont family interest in Whig politics. Her letters expressed her frustration when Wortley delayed too long in declaring he wished to contest the parliamentary seat of Aldborough for a second time, and again when it became evident that he was not in the running for the seat of York. When Wortley's father Sidney took the plum seat of Huntingdon for himself, she nagged Wortley to go for a pocket Cornish borough. Instead Wortley settled on the City of Westminster. Once the elections took place the following year, he won the seat. Their future finally began to feel more settled.

George I immediately started handing out government posts. A role in government for Wortley would ensure that the young marrieds were properly rehabilitated back into London society. Wortley's distant cousin,

Lord Halifax, was quickly made the First Lord of the Treasury and Wortley was soon offered a junior commissioner role there, alongside his young fellow-Whig, Robert Walpole. He hesitated, though. He had been involved in a bill seeking to prevent members of parliament from also holding government posts at the same time, and he felt this would look hypocritical on his part. Mary disagreed and argued her case strongly: ''Tis a sort of Duty to be rich, that it may be in one's power to do good,' she lectured him, quoting Demosthenes: 'No modest Man ever did or ever will make his Fortune.'[20] On 13 October he finally accepted the role. His decision was not the result of Mary's passionate persuasion but because her wealthy uncle, Gervase Pierrepont, from whom the couple were hoping for a legacy in due course, had advised him it would be for the best.

Mary was not in London for George I's coronation when it took place in London in October 1714 and parliament was prorogued as planned. She continued to campaign-manage Wortley's election campaign from Middlethorpe Hall but was increasingly frustrated at being sidelined. The new Princess of Wales, Caroline of Ansbach, was beginning to choose her Ladies of the Bedchamber. In the past Mary would have been eligible for one of these posts but her marrying a commoner without a title had put her out of the running for an official role at court.

By November, Mary and Wortley had been apart for five whole months. She had had enough. She wrote to him venting her anger. He appeared totally disinterested in their child, she complained. When she had fallen ill with a fever and her face swelled up, he had shown no concern. The replacement coachman had not worked out and had overturned their coach in a ditch, potentially threatening both her life and that of his son. She was short of money, lonely and melancholy. Her main complaint, though, was the tone of his letters. He was never anything more than business-like with her: 'I think you use me very unkindly,' she vented. If he wrote her any more cold and unfeeling letters, she would simply return them. Things needed to change.[21] Her anguished plea for once seemed to have an effect. Wortley took note. He began searching for a house to rent in London's Duke Street near her old neighbourhood of St James' Park.

Nevertheless, Mary's anxieties continued. She had heard that the past tenants of the new rental house in Duke Street had died of smallpox there and was concerned the bedding might still be infected. She was right to be concerned. Smallpox was potentially fatal, and her brother had recently died from it. She was proud that young Edward was in much better health now and boasted of her maternal skills to Wortley, but she was also unsure whether to bring him to London with her. She wanted him to get to know his father, but his new nurse would not leave Yorkshire. As always, Wortley wanted Mary to be the one to make the decisions when it came to things domestic. She dithered. The weather worsened. It looked as though the current tenants were manoeuvring to stay on in the new London house and she scolded Wortley that they had no right to do so. How was he doing sorting the bed linen? Christmas came and went at Middlethorpe Hall without Wortley. Eventually on 5 January 1715 she made her decision. Leaving young Edward in Yorkshire, she set out to be reunited with Wortley. The role of playing the absentee dutiful wife left behind in the shires, scrimping and saving, was not for her. She would never have to play it again.

Chapter 4

Smallpox

'False was his Oath! my Beauty is no more'[1]

In London again, reunited with Wortley in the new house in Duke Street, Mary slipped into a social routine: Mondays in the drawing room, Tuesdays visiting other ladies of similar rank, Wednesdays at the opera, Thursdays at the theatre, Fridays making visits again. At some point young Edward was brought down from Yorkshire with his nurse, who was always on hand to take care of him. The royal court was the centre of social life in London for someone of Mary's social status. She set about playing her part there. Under the new Hanoverian King George I the court was dull, rigid and formal. Mary probably wrote at least a first draft of her perceptive *Account of the Court of George I* at this time, confidently and eloquently analysing the life there. The new king she described as 'an honest blockhead', with little interest in the throne he had acquired.[2] Back in Hanover he had swiftly divorced his wife when she dared to have an affair. Her name was never mentioned in his hearing again. The German mistresses he brought with him were ugly and dull. Undeterred, Mary set about using her considerable charms to improve the Wortley Montagus' fortunes at court. Since the King refused to speak English, she began to learn German. One of her friends, the Scottish Lady Loudoun, drily noted that it was unlikely to make a difference, given the monarch's preference for larger ladies.

George I's son, the Prince of Wales, the future King George II, and his ambitious, forceful wife Caroline of Ansbach, occupied a separate set of state rooms from King George I within St. James' Palace. George I mistrusted his son's family and they him. Mary wrote that Princess Caroline had 'a Low Cunning' and a tendency to cheat. Caroline was brighter than her husband and did her best to dominate him, Mary explained.[3] The princess was always quick to put down any potential rivals for the Prince of Wales' attention, including Mary herself. Inevitably Mary failed in her attempts to flourish at either court. A contemporary wrote that Mary's beauty 'was only one of her various powers to charm.'[4] But it was her intellect that set her apart and her intellect needed nourishing.

The Irish artist Charles Jervas lived just across the park from the house in Duke Street. Next door to Jervas lived Mary's friend Dolly Walpole, who had been hurriedly married off to Lord Townshend. Mary would spend her mornings with Dolly at Jervas' studio, watching as Joseph Addison sat for his portrait. All the most prominent writers, artists and thinkers of the day passed through Jervas' studio as he painted. Soon Mary had an entirely new group of stimulating friends. The playwright William Congreve, whom she had first come across as a child at the Kit-Cat Club, was now aged 45 and enjoying the fruits of his labour, writing poetry and enthusing about Whig politics. John Gay, a grammar-school boy from Devon and closer in age to Mary, was beginning to make his way as a poet. He was always dependent on the patronage of others, anxious to make ends meet. Gay would go on to have great success with *The Beggars' Opera,* taking popular folk ballads of the time and weaving them into something perceptive and original. Dr John Arbuthnot, Scottish by birth and aged 45 at this point, was the polymath of the group. He was the royal physician and a fellow of the Royal Society. He was also passionate about mathematics and the author of a series of satirical pamphlets featuring his comic creation, the character John Bull. Genial and amiable, it was said of Arbuthnot that the only fault any enemy could find with him was the slight waddle in his gait. Lastly and most importantly was the celebrated poet Alexander Pope. He and Mary very quickly became the greatest of friends.

The two met properly for the first time in April 1715, at Jervas' studio, where Pope would stay whenever he was in London. Just a year older than her, Pope had suffered as a child from tuberculosis of the bone, known as Pott's Disease, and this had stunted his growth. He was only 1.2m in height. George I may have discounted Mary's looks because she was little and slender but for Pope this was a definite advantage. Emotionally scarred by this early illness, Pope used his wit and intelligence as protection from the scorn of other people. Like Mary, being clever was a vital part of his identity. Pope was very different from his new aristocratic friend. He was born of middle-class elderly Catholic parents and was a

Tory rather than a Whig. But there was an immediate spark between the two. Mary's social status gave her confidence with him. He was an incorrigible snob. He was already famous, whereas she had only so far had one piece published. Yet publication was not something she sought. For someone of her class and gender it was considered more trouble than it was worth. She could write for pleasure not for profit. This gave her greater freedom than she would have had as a writer for hire.

Pope was working on his version of Homer's *The Iliad*. Mary began showing him poems and essays she had written. Previously she had written either for her sister Frances, or at the request of Wortley to be published anonymously in *The Spectator*. Now she began writing for a whole new set of friends and admirers. Her literary friends circulated copies of their work amongst themselves and to trusted allies, relying on them not to let anything fall into the wrong hands. Very little of Mary's writing from these months remains, although there exists one short poem, *Let us Live my Lesbia and Love*, a free adaptation she made of an epigram by Catullus. She almost certainly wrote it at this period. Here she was following in the footsteps of famous authors such as Sir Thomas Campion and Sir Walter Raleigh, trying out free adaptation and translation. Pope's reversioning of *The Iliad* served as inspiration. The poem may have been intended for another woman. It fizzes with sexuality as Mary urges the recipient to 'Renew again the Amorous play/ And kiss my ravish'd Soul away.'[5] She was the only woman in the set who turned her hand to writing. As such she did not shrink from expressing her emotions.

Another valued friend she made at this time, who was not a member of her London literary set, was the Abbé Antonio Conti. He arrived in London from Paris on 22 April 1715 to view the eclipse of the sun and to meet with celebrated scientists. Born in Venice, Conti had initially entered the priesthood. In time he realised he no longer believed in the concept of the Trinity. He could not therefore continue to take confession. By the time he met Mary he styled himself Abbé not Padré to signify his distance from the Catholic church. He and Mary would remain friends for the rest of their lives. As a young woman in her mid-twenties, forging a friendship with an internationally established figure like Conti, twelve years her senior, must have felt a significant honour. It demonstrated her social and intellectual confidence. Like Conti, by now Mary had little time for established religion. Pope had written a *Universal Prayer*, a sort of deist manifesto, praising a god 'whose temple is all space', and she owned a copy.[6] She too was instinctively a libertarian. Now she also began to meet radical churchmen who debated the very existence of a god.

In 1715 the eminent portrait painter, Sir Godfrey Kneller, was commissioned to paint Mary's portrait. He had painted her when she was still Lady Mary Pierrepont but now here she was as a married woman, carving her own role in London society. An assured beauty with her dark hair swept back, her favourite pearl drops in her ears and wearing a simple white silk dress, she gazed thoughtfully into the middle distance. She exuded serenity and confidence, with a smile playing on her red lips. She looked as if she had just discussed with Kneller her thoughts on the book she was holding. There was gossip that Lord Stair was her first 'gallant' at this time but there is no firm evidence that she was unfaithful to Wortley, just that she was stretching her wings socially.[7] Wortley was increasingly involved in his own new career at the Treasury, so her time was her own. She could pursue platonic friendships with this new group of clever individuals.

In the autumn of 1713 John Gay first had the idea of writing a contemporary version of Virgil's pastoral eclogues and proposed collaborating with Pope and Mary on the project. Their satirical *Town Eclogues* took Virgil's shepherds and shepherdesses and substituted them with London's rakes and court beauties. It consisted of a poem for every day of the week. Mary, Pope and Gay tried out their different versions of the various poems on each other. They worked as equals, suggesting new lines, giving notes, revelling in their love of language and the expression of their shared ideas. The poem *Roxana*, which Mary had written earlier in the year, was chosen as Monday's poem. It tells the story of a young female aristocrat who would have preferred to spend her time modestly but is forced instead to sacrifice her desires for the worldly ones at court: 'Ah cruel Princesse! for thy sake I've lost/ That Reputation which so dear had cost.' Although the princess is not named, she is clearly Caroline of Ansbach. Despite Roxana's sacrifice she is overlooked as a lady-in-waiting and the Princess instead chooses Coquettilla: 'Let the Nice Hind now suckle dirty Pigs/ Let the Proud Peahen hatch the Cuckow's Eggs.' Coquettilla and Roxana represent two of Mary's contemporaries, the Duchess of Shrewsbury, who had been given a post at court, and the Duchess of Roxburgh, who had not. Mary's group of friends enjoyed the joke when the poem was circulated.[8]

In December 1715 disaster struck. Mary contracted smallpox. As so often, Wortley was far away in the north. She would have to face her illness alone. She sent away young Edward, now two and a half years old, as soon as she realised what was happening. The memory of her brother's death only a couple of years earlier still haunted her. She knew the previous tenants at Duke Street had died from the disease, but it was impossible to know how she herself had caught it. The first sign of illness was a high fever. Her head and body ached. She began vomiting copiously, her throat parched. At this stage, realising what was happening, she made sure she was shut up in the house in Duke Street. The shutters were drawn, and straw was spread on the cobbles outside to muffle the traffic.

The disease was at its most virulent for the next four days. Mary developed a rash of small red spots on her tongue and the roof of her mouth, making it hard to breathe or even to speak. As the spots changed into sores, her entire skin became swollen and red, her face by now unrecognisable. The breaking sores gave off a thick, yellow, foul-smelling pus. On the fifth day she knew she was past the worst and likely to survive. Her fever started to decline. The bumpy sores gradually became pustules, round and firm to the touch like dried peas under the skin. Slowly they started to form into scabs, leaving the infamous pock marks which would scar her for life. Before her illness Pope had written that her eyes were the envy of 'other Beauties'. Now she had lost all her eyelashes to the pox, she was left with the 'Wortley stare', fierce and uncompromising.

The best doctors in London attended her: Samuel Garth who had been at her dying brother's bedside, along with Richard Mead and John Woodward, all three part of the Whig establishment. Sir Hans Sloane, the first medical practitioner to be made a knight, and who would later play a part in Mary's smallpox inoculation campaign, also visited her to observe the progress of the disease. There was little they could do. Garth bled her and purged her in an attempt to encourage diarrhea, which was seen as a sign of recovery. As she lay in solitary confinement through the Christmas period, the word went out that she was going to die. When it became evident that she would survive, speculation focused on how badly she would now be scarred. As one wit put it: 'she was very full and yet not pitted [pitied].'[9] She may not have been pitied, but she must have reflected that her life had now changed irrevocably. With her looks altered, her career at court was likely to be very different, her influence with any male monarch much reduced. As she wrote in two separate poems, she knew very well that 'Monarchs and Beauties rule with equal sway'.[10]

For the rest of the winter, while she recuperated, Mary wrote the final poem of the *Town Eclogues*, her own work this time, not a collaboration, a therapeutic means of expressing her feelings: its title, *The Small Pox*. The tradition was that an eclogue cycle ended in a lament on death but instead Mary's lament was for her own beauty and the power she had lost. The heroine Flavia turns away from the new face she sees in the mirror: 'Ah Faithless Glass, my wonted bloom restore/Alas, I rave! that bloom is now no more.' She looks back on her past charmed life, 'When Opera Tickets pour'd before my Feet.' Now though, 'Beauty's fled, and Lovers are no more.' Mary was writing shrewdly and starkly about the currency of beauty in the society in which she lived. She was the only early English feminist to write about beauty and its loss in this way. Samuel Garth, one of the doctors who attends Flavia in the poem just as he had attended Mary, with his red cloak and 'Superior frown', promises her: 'You shall again be well, again be fair.' Flavia, though, knows the truth: 'False was his Oath! my Beauty is no more.'[11]

By mid-January, Mary had begun to recover. When she finally felt well enough to push back the shutters and looked out of her bedroom window, she saw a London transformed. Around her a severe frost covered the whole city, the light bright and sharp as it reflected the white surroundings. The frozen Thames was alive with ice fairs. The blinding light was acutely painful to Mary's eyes, which were still inflamed by the smallpox, and this sensitivity to light was to be another lasting legacy of her disease. Her new friends, Pope, Gay, Jervas and Kneller, doubtless came to visit her as she recuperated. Wortley, too, returned to Duke Street. His wife was still alive but altered forever. He was reported to be inconsolable at the change in their fortunes now she had lost her looks. There was something else, though, that increased his mood of despair.

While she lay perilously unwell, Mary's first *Town Eclogue: Monday. Roxana or the Drawing Room*, had fallen into the hands of Princess Caroline. Somehow someone had shown it about at court. As her contemporary the Scottish aristocrat Lady Loudoun wrote:

'I have not yet seen it, but I'm told it is very pretty and not a little wicked. I'm promised it in a day or two. The Princess has seen it. Poor Lady Mary will not know how to come to Court again.'[12]

The poem had been written as an ironic joke about two different potential ladies-in-waiting vying for an official role in Princess Caroline's bedchamber, but Caroline herself failed point blank to see the humour. She might have forgiven Mary the loss of her looks - she herself had suffered from smallpox - but this new mistake looked likely to seal Mary's fate at court. But it was this frisson of scandal that increased the poem's cachet elsewhere. People suddenly wanted to read it.

In February 1716, the *Eclogues* fell into the hands of the infamous publisher, Edmund Curll, 'The Unspeakable Curll', as he had been nicknamed. He knew a best-seller with its potential for scandal when he saw one. In March, he published three of the *Eclogues* in a slim volume called *Court Poems* and promoted the volume in all the newspapers. Officially, Mary was not named as the author but everyone who mattered knew exactly who had written that first poem. They were keen to buy the volume and read it. Mary emerged from her sick bed no longer as simply the witty young friend of Pope and Gay, passing her time making up and sharing verses with them, but as a writer famous in her own right, the controversial 'It Girl' of her day. Wortley, always proud, must have been furious. He would have wanted to avoid publication in salacious pamphlets at all costs.

Curll claimed the poems had been found in a note book lying in Westminster Hall and that they were written by three people: by a 'Lady of Quality', not naming Mary but leaving those who knew her in little doubt; by John Gay; and by a 'translator of Homer', in other words by Alexander Pope. John Gay had indeed written one of the three poems and his being named here did him the most damage. He had hoped for some kind of court employment. Unlike Mary he needed the income. But this was clearly now out of the question. Pope and Curll had history and Pope was a powerful enemy. Pope made some kind of threat to Curll even before publication but once the *Court Poems* were on sale, he decided to take revenge in his own style. He could have taken Curll to court for defamation, but the case might have been difficult to win. Instead he chose an altogether rougher justice.

He arranged for Curll to meet the printer Bernard Lintot in a London tavern for a drink and then appeared himself, as if by chance. There he argued violently with Curll about the poems and secretly added a strong emetic to Curll's drink. Pope had shown what he would do to someone who crossed him.

Whilst she was recovering, Mary completed the sequence of *Town Eclogues* poems, drawing on the twilight world she had got to know when she started her marriage in Catherine Street. In Tuesday's poem, the erotic and Hogarthian *St James' Coffee House,* two gentlemen about town compare their various conquests in a world of opera evenings and games of dice. Sexual favours are objects of exchange here and prostitution is only a step away, a world where Pope's revenge on Curll would have been nothing out of the ordinary. Wednesday's poem, *The Tête a Tête,* portrays the married Dacinda trying to hold off the attentions of her male admirer. When her husband returns, she encourages her lover to slip down the back stairs. Mary and Pope probably collaborated on this poem. He described her as crying out to him: 'No, Pope, no touching! For then, whatever is good for anything will pass for yours, and the rest for mine.'[13] In both the poem and in Pope's description of their writing process there was sexual tension, with something altogether more passionate and sinister bubbling just beneath the surface.

Meanwhile Wortley's career at the treasury had floundered. Robert Walpole had taken over from Wortley's cousin Halifax and he wanted Wortley's job for one of his acolytes. Walpole proposed to Wortley a compensation package of £3,000 a year for life (£460,000 today), but the money never materialised and Wortley would forever afterwards feel aggrieved about it. With his wife disgraced and his own career at the treasury at an end, on 7 April 1716, Wortley was offered a post which was to change both their lives forever: ambassador to the Turkish Ottoman Empire. Postings such as this usually lasted about five years. Ambassadors had to sign an agreement that they would stay for the entire period. Here was a chance for Wortley to create a whole new career for himself, away from the treasury and from Walpole's supporters. At the same time Mary could accompany him, giving her an honourable exit from the literary circle which Wortley increasingly viewed as unsavoury. At first Wortley refused the posting on financial grounds but when he was offered generous compensation at the end of his stint as ambassador, he agreed.

Both threw themselves into the preparations. Diplomatic wives normally stayed at home while their husbands travelled without them, but there was no question of that. Mary was looking forward to the adventure and undeterred by the risks they might face. She arranged for a young girl she knew to travel down from Yorkshire as a nurse for young Edward. She set about appointing English servants to travel with them. She bought twenty suits of livery for their Turkish servants once they arrived. She hired their own private surgeon to travel with them: Dr Charles Maitland. She was determined to persuade her unmarried friend Sarah Chiswell to accompany them, but Sarah's family were too fearful of the dangers for her to accept. Mary was made of sterner stuff.

The political situation in mainland Europe was looking increasingly unstable. Turkey had been at war with Venice since 1714 and George I's government was keen to prevent the Austrian Habsburg Empire from entering the war on Venice's side. Wortley made plans to travel out to Turkey by way of Vienna and take with him a letter from George I to the Austrian Emperor. This he reckoned would help both the British cause and his own in his new role. He was presented with his credentials as ambassador on 2 July 1716. Meanwhile Mary had to say her goodbyes to her literary friends and most significantly to Pope. He passionately pleaded with her to give him some of her 'last Moments', as if she were not simply going travelling but dying. The prospect of five years' absence with all the dangers that accompanied it must have felt like a kind of death. Their intense friendship was developing for Pope into something stronger: 'indeed I find I begin to behave myself worse to you than to any other Woman, as I value you more.'[14] He travelled up to town from his house in Chiswick for a last goodbye, and as a parting gift presented Mary with five of their *Town Eclogues* bound in an album of the finest red Turkey leather.

Finally, they were ready. Their luggage had been sent on to Turkey ahead of them, but they were nevertheless accompanied by twenty servants. To the amusement of her friends, Mary decided to wear a large black wig for the journey. Perhaps, having suffered the ravages of smallpox, she felt more confident wearing it. As she grew older there were to be many gossipy comments on the eccentricities of her wardrobe. The coach left London on 1 August 1716 and the next day they boarded a boat at Gravesend bound for Holland. The journey would be neither comfortable nor easy - not least with a 3-year-old - but the experience would change their lives and the lives of countless others forever.

Whereas they set off expecting Wortley's career to flourish now he was His Majesty's Britannic Ambassador, in fact it was to be his black-wigged wife who seized the moment and whose trip was to have the greater impact. Many years later she described her feelings on setting off to her friend Joseph Spence:

> "'twas a sort of dying to her friends and country. But
> 'twas travelling; 'twas going farther than most other people
> go; 'twas wandering; 'twas all whimsical and charming;
> and so she set out with all the pleasure imaginable.'[15]

Chapter 5

Traversing Europe

'when our Wives cheat us, nobody knows it'[1]

For the first time in her life Mary crossed the English Channel. Their 'yatcht' was becalmed for two days. When the wind started blowing hard again, Mary was relieved not to suffer from seasickness. But the captain started panicking. The party put in at Helver Sluyse and travelled on in hired 'Voitures' so as to reach their first stop, the city of Rotterdam, all the faster. Mary was charmed by the cleanliness of the place, devoid of beggars and 'Fellows and Wenches that chose to be nasty and lazy'.[2] She described to Sister Mar, back in London, the way women in Rotterdam sorted their own hairstyles, rather than relying on their maids. From here the travelling party changed their plans and headed north to The Hague. Perhaps news of the Battle of Petrovardin in Eastern Europe had already reached them. The Austrians had now entered the war between Venice and Turkey on the side of the Venetians. Prince Eugene, who headed the Austrian army, had defeated the Turks there. The victory would impact on Wortley in his new role as British ambassador to Turkey.

Mary was already enjoying the life of the traveller, observing the passing countryside from their coach. If they travelled 'post' they would stop at coaching inns to exchange their sweating horses for fresh ones. If not, then they had to go more slowly so as to avoid tiring the horses, which were needed to pull them all day. Mary travelled with her own makeshift sleeping bag, a feather-bed portable mattress with a cover. She wore a riding habit, something seen as subversively unfeminine at the time, but which gave her a bit of physical freedom. The trip to the Hague was particularly easy, with rows of trees and canals to please the eye and well-maintained roads. She wrote cheerful, chatty letters to her friends Jane Smith, who had asked Mary to send her some lace, and Sarah Chiswell, whom Mary was still regretting having left behind.

Nijmegen, she reported to Sarah, reminded her of Sarah's hometown of Nottingham. She was highly critical of a Calvinist church service there. She was sure that Sarah's brother-in-law, the rector at the family seat of Holme Pierrepont, would 'excuse a digression in favour of the Church of England.'[3]

They were heading for Vienna, where Wortley had letters from George I to deliver to the Emperor. *En route* they stopped in Cologne. Despite having had very little sleep the night before, Mary was determined to see the sights while she was there, 'that is to say the churches, for there is nothing else worth seeing.' She was struck by the opulence of the Jesuit church with its relics of the martyrdom of St Ursula. Her traveller's observations were strongly anti-Catholic: 'I could not help murmuring in my heart at the profusion of pearls, Diamonds and Rubys bestowed on the adornment of rotten teeth, dirty rags etc..'[4] Being Anglican was itself an article of faith. Although she was not a believer, Mary was being politically correct for the time. The rejection of the Catholicism which had caused such bloodshed in her grandparents' day was something she accepted without question. Several of her friends in England, notably Alexander Pope, were of course themselves Catholics.

Next the travelling party stopped at Regensburg for about a week, as Mary had caught a cold. Here they were entertained royally by Madame von Wrisberg, wife of the Hanoverian envoy. Mary professed herself irritated by the constant petty disputes among the people she met at Regensburg, most of which seemed to centre on the use of the title 'excellency'. Attempting to make light of the situation, she suggested that they should all be called 'excellency', but her joke fell flat. Again, she visited Catholic churches stuffed full of relics. She began to question whether the emeralds and rubies she was being shown were really precious jewels or (more probably she suspected) made of glass. Good Anglican that she was, she 'was very much scandalised' at a large silver image of the trinity.[5]

They travelled down the Danube in a houseboat rowed by twelve men to the city of Vienna, where they would stay for two whole months. Mary was relieved that her young son had some physical freedom here after the long journey in their carriage. She wrote to Sister Mar that Vienna was less impressive than she had imagined. She was struck by the height of the buildings, all crammed together, each one five or six storeys high, with families only occupying a floor or two, so that 'the Ministers of state are divided but by a Partition from that of a Tailor or a shoe-maker,' an arrangement which would not have suited Mary herself.[6] She and Wortley were immediately welcomed into Austrian society and they found themselves dining nightly at dignitaries' houses.

Wortley was received the day after their arrival by the Austrian Emperor Charles VI, whose son Prince Eugene had just been victorious against the Turks. Lady Mary had to wait before she could be presented to the empress. The right dress must be made for her. She wrote to Sister Mar to describe in detail the elaborate outfit she wore: 'the dress very inconvenient, but which certainly shows the neck and shape to great advantage.' Most striking of all was the head-dress, a structure which was built around something called a *bourlé* which reminded Mary of the rolls of fabric milkmaids in England wore on their heads to carry their pails. Wads of gauze were built up to create a tower about three foot high. This was then covered with the wearer's hair, augmented by false tresses. The whole headpiece was then decorated with diamonds, pearls and precious jewels. Mary found herself complying with what she termed 'these Absurd Fashions'.[7]

When Mary finally got to meet the empress herself, she found Elisabeth-Christine of Brunswick-Wolfenbüttel charming and beautiful. But the court she presided over was dull and overly formal. Doubtless Mary was reminded of her own feelings back in London at the court of King George. She also liked the emperor's pious mother, whom she met the next day. She admired the way older women were treated with great respect here. On marriage, women were given total financial independence from their husbands. Mary's own finances had been destabilised by her marriage, but she did not point out the contrast in her letters home. She was careful not to pass judgement. Another social convention in Vienna unnerved her. Every married woman took a 'galant' or lover: 'it is the established custom for every Lady to have 2 Husbands, one that bears the Name and another that performs the Dutys.'[8] When a young count approached her to offer his services, Mary was unsettled by the encounter. She was careful to explain that her heart did not engage very easily. She wrote home that: 'Galantry and good breeding are as different in different climates as Morality and Religion.'[9]

Mary described to Alexander Pope her two trips to the theatre in Vienna. She attended the first night of an opera by Johann Joseph Fux, performed in the garden of the Favorita Palace. She noted with admiration the ambition of the design and the elaborate and speedy changes of scenery. When it started to rain, the audience dispersed, and she felt as if she were being squeezed to death by the crowd hurrying to get past her. She also went to the playhouse to see a German farce. She had learned some German to please George I but she took a translator with her nevertheless. 'I never laughed so much in my Life,' she told Pope. But she disliked the vulgar moment in the play when two of the characters pulled their breeches down in front of the audience.[10]

Pope found the increasing physical distance from Mary freed him up to express himself far more openly about his feelings towards her. Confessing his 'Love', he wrote that she had 'ruined me for all the Conversation of one Sex, and almost all the Friendship of the other.'[11] Above all he longed to be taken seriously by her. His wit, he wrote, was really 'the natural Overflowing and Warmth of (my) Heart, as it is improved and awakened by an Esteem for you.' The further away she travelled, the less inhibited he became. Soon it was impossible to ignore the eroticism in his writing. The distance removed what he termed 'punctilious Restrictions and Decorums.' He and Mary were, he said, like a couple who behave modestly when around other people, but who once by themselves 'can untie garters or take off Shifts without scruple.' Always aware of his own physical limitations he imagined a place where women 'best like the Ugliest fellows…and look upon Deformities as the Signatures of divine Favour.'[12]

Lady Mary's attitude to all this was at best ambivalent. She was disparaging in letters home about the court dwarves which were a feature of life in Vienna. That said, she respected Pope intellectually and was careful to copy his letters into her journal, along with those written to her by William Congreve. Her literary friendships were important to her even at this distance. While Pope's letters to her survive, her replies to him at the time have been destroyed or lost. Later, back in London, she would edit all her *Embassy Letters*, with the help of Mary Astell. Together they prepared all the letters to have them ready for publication on Lady Mary's death. That way she could avoid scandal during her lifetime but find recognition posthumously. As a result, the letters we have today which Mary wrote to Pope were all rewritten by her once she was back in London. They were clearly influenced by Mary Astell, who acted as Lady Mary's editor. Astell herself never married and was wary of her younger *protegée's* relationships with men. It may well be that the letters Mary wrote to Pope during her trip were more flirtatious and emotionally open, matching his.

The little party now had to divert in a north-westerly direction towards Hanover, rather than south-east to Turkey, so Wortley could meet with King George I. The English king was visiting the principality where he had grown up and where he was still elector. They travelled by way of Prague, Dresden and Leipzig. The journey was uncomfortable and dangerous. Sometimes it felt better to keep going all night, wrapped in furs, rather than stop and rest in what Mary described as stinking hovels. At one point, Mary awoke in the carriage as it was trundling through the night, with Wortley sleeping by her side, to find the horses were galloping unchecked while the postillions who rode them slept in their saddles. When she shook Wortley awake, he admitted that he had crossed the Alps on five separate occasions as a young man on his grand tour but had never before seen a road as dangerous as this. Mary, of course, delighted in the drama.

They arrived in Hanover in November 1716 and found George I in residence. He provided them with an apartment at court and seemed delighted at the presence of Lady Mary. In a letter to Princess Caroline (probably rewritten at a later date like many of her *Embassy Letters*) Mary was careful to praise Caroline's eldest son, Prince Frederick Lewis, who was also at the court in Hanover. His fair hair was just like his mother's, she wrote. After Caroline's having taken umbrage at Mary's *Town Eclogues,* there seemed to have been some kind of rapprochement between the two. Here in Hanover, Mary and Wortley were wined and dined. A flurry of snow meant that Mary did not get to see the gardens of Herrenhausen Palace in all their beauty but she nevertheless marvelled at the hot-housed orange trees and revelled in eating a pineapple for the first time in her life. She wrote to her older friend Lady Bristol that she admired the way the Hanoverians used stoves to heat their greenhouses, something she had never seen in England. The people she met encouraged her to remain in Hanover rather than travelling on with Wortley to Turkey, but she was adamant she would continue. The adventure was proving far too exciting to call a halt to it now.

First the party had to return to Vienna, Wortley with dispatches from George I to the Austrian emperor, Mary with a letter to the empress from her mother, the Duchess of Blankenberg. Again, Mary was taken by the elegance and style of the empress, who was now pregnant.

She had lost a son just before Mary's first visit. Mary was categoric in her letter home that this had been caused by the empress weaning her son at the wrong time of year. As a young mother herself, she felt herself an expert on these matters. She and Wortley were again invited to all the right social occasions. As one acquaintance put it: 'they all own she is a witty woman, if not a well-dressed one.'[13] For someone so interested in clothing, Mary was already gaining a reputation for being eccentrically dressed. Like the Hanoverians, the Viennese also advised against Mary's continuing on the trip to Turkey. Prince Eugene himself - he had returned to Vienna from his military success in Petrovardin while they were in Hanover - suggested she delay and travel by boat once the Danube was no longer frozen. Again, Mary was determined to continue. She wrote to Sister Mar from Vienna melodramatically: 'Adieu, Dear Sister. …If I survive my Journey you shall hear from me again.'[14] Her own death did not concern her unduly, she wrote, but she feared leaving her son Edward without a mother. To Pope she was more cheerful and comic about the journey into the unknown: 'How my Adventures will conclude I leave entirely to Providence.'[15]

The wheels of Mary and Wortley's coach had runners fitted to them, so they could slide over the snow. Next the party arrived in the city of Raab, where they were treated well. The local bishop visited them, with presents of winter fruit, Hungarian wines and a young hind. From there they travelled on to the city of Buda, across plains which had been ravaged by war. Now they were in the midst of the Hungarian territory, ownership of which was disputed between the Austrians and the Turks. The Hungarian king's palace had been destroyed in the recent war, but the governor lived in the castle and he and his wife received them there. On they went, over plains where the country people, dressed only in sheepskins, came out to see them and give them presents of game. Mary noted with pride that Wortley was always scrupulous about paying for what they were given. The poverty struck her forcibly. They crossed the Danube. Wortley wrote to the local ruler, the *bassa* - a replacement as his predecessor had been assassinated - asking for safe passage to Belgrade. On an excursion to the Serbian town of Bocowar, Mary admired the beauty of the women in their scarlet velvet gowns, lined with sables.

The political situation was unstable here and their presence potentially threatening to the inhabitants. They drove across the battlefield of Petrovardin, where Prince Eugene had defeated the Turks only a few months earlier. The contrast between the dead bodies strewn on the ground and the memory of their recent encounter with the urbane Prince Eugene must have been striking. Mary was shocked at the corpses lying in the snow. She had never seen anything like this before. She wrote a letter full of righteous indignation about the futility of war to Pope, referencing the philosopher Hobbs, who argued that by nature man pursues war rather than peace. As a woman she queried man's love of war. Pope's physical condition meant he could never join the armed forces. This freed her up to write openly to him about her reaction. What shocked her most, she confessed, was 'the rage with which they contest for a small spot of Ground, when such vast parts of fruitful Earth lie quite uninhabited.'[16] The distance she and Wortley had travelled over the past few months could only have served to emphasise that fact.

They heard from the *bassa* that he could now give them safe passage through this dangerous territory. So, a couple of nights later they set out with a private army of about two hundred soldiers or *janizaries* to protect them. When they got to the agreed meeting place at Beska, a village midway between Petrovardin and Belgrade, they were met with another army of at least three hundred soldiers. They feared the two armies might be tempted to fight each other, with disastrous consequences. Nevertheless Wortley, Mary and their enormous retinue of both armies struggled on, through deep snow, to arrive in Belgrade on 5 February 1717. Here they learned the bloody story of the assassination of the *bassa's* predecessor, who had been killed by his own troops, hacked to pieces with their scimitars. Nervous at being somewhere where tensions were so high, Mary and Wortley hoped to press on after a single night. Instead they learned that the *bassa's* orders were to detain them in Belgrade until he received word from the sultan. This might mean a delay of up to a month.

Nevertheless, Mary and Wortley had a stroke of good fortune here. They were billeted with a man named Achmet-Beg, who was well-born (his title a bit like a German count's as Mary explained it) scholarly, educated and friendly towards them. They dined every evening with him, sitting on cushions and eating individual dishes, each one highly spiced. As the weather outside was still very cold, they huddled round Achmet-Beg's stove, the windows of the room frozen even on the inside. Achmet-Beg and Mary formed an immediate, strong bond, keenly discussing a huge variety of topics in their shared language of Italian.

Mary noted with interest that he drank wine freely, despite being a Muslim. He explained to her that Mohammed's law was designed for the common people, not for those who knew how to drink in moderation. They discussed the Koran, which he assured her she would like very much if she were able to read it. Writing to Abbé Conti, she analysed Achmet-Beg's faith as deism, very like that of the liberal Anglican priests she knew back in London. She and Achmet-Beg laughed together about the foolishness of worshipping images or adoring the Virgin Mary. He explained that after death Muslims believed women went to a different heaven from the one designed for men. The idea appealed to Mary.

Their favourite subject was the relative condition of women in their two cultures. The western view was that Islamic women were imprisoned. Achmet-Beg disagreed. 'Only, says he, we have the advantage that when our Wives cheat us, nobody knows it.'[17] That irony struck a chord with Mary. Achmet-Beg himself had his own harem in the house where they were staying, but Mary decided to ignore this fact. She was charmed by him, after all, and delighted to find someone educated and eloquent she could talk with freely. Here was an intellectual friendship like the ones she had enjoyed so much back in London. His arguments made her challenge her own assumptions about the west's superiority to the east. She enjoyed the mental stimulation. They discussed poetry too. He was hugely impressed that she knew the *Persian Tales*. When she explained she had read them in translation he was all the more delighted. For his part he had begun to learn the English alphabet.

After three weeks Wortley received official permission to continue their journey. It was time for them to move on again. They were still accompanied by their entourage of five hundred *janizaries,* who carried all their tents and provisions. The land they travelled through was exceptionally poor, but the soldiers simply looted whatever they could find from its inhabitants. Lady Mary was in tears every day at their cruelty. Wortley had been assured the area was free from bubonic plague. When that advice turned out to be false, he hid the truth from her. Dr Maitland was left behind to care for those in their party who had fallen victim to the plague. He would rejoin them once they were settled in Turkey and Mary would learn about the plague at that point.

Next they arrived in the city of Sophia (today the capital of Bulgaria) in the heart of the Balkans. Mary and Wortley visited the ruined sixth-century church together, which gave Sophia its name. The next morning Mary went by herself incognito to visit Sophia's famous bath house. The city of Sophia was renowned for its fresh-water springs and Achmet-Beg had perhaps suggested she make the trip to see the Turkish bath or *hammam* there. Her account of her visit in her *Embassy Letters* would rightly become celebrated once it was published. She hired a heavy, un-sprung Turkish coach or *araba*. It was enclosed by a wooden lattice, painted and gilded with pictures of baskets and bunches of flowers, so no one could see inside. The un-sprung coach rattled uncomfortably, but she had experienced far worse during her trip.

The building housing the *hammam* was beehive-shaped with a five-domed roof, lit by skylights. A lady porter stood guarding the door, waiting to be given her tip. Mary duly obliged. The first room she entered was spacious, with a marble floor, two levels of stone seating round the walls, and channels for the flowing spring water. The heat was overpowering. A sulphurous steam poured in from the two rooms beyond, the cold water regulating the temperature in the first, but the heat unchecked in the second. The thick, camlet riding habit Mary was wearing suddenly felt unbearably restrictive. The rooms were crowded with about two hundred women, all completely naked. To her surprise they were not fazed by the sight of this young English woman in her unsuitable western outfit, nor did they indulge in 'satyric whispers', as Mary was sure women in London would have done. Instead they treated her with the utmost civility. 'Uzelle per uzelle', they called out, which Mary understood meant 'charming, very charming'. As she put it, there was 'not the least wanton smile or immodest Gesture among 'em'.[18]

The atmosphere was egalitarian and consensual, the women relaxed in their nudity and seemingly unaware of the power of their unscarred beauty. None of them bore the tell-tale marks of smallpox, nor the red stripes which western women's tightly laced clothing left on their skin. The male travellers Aaron Hill and Jean Dumont, who had both travelled here relatively recently, had had very different experiences from Mary's. Hill was refused entry to the *hammam*. Dumont did manage to get inside but on seeing him the women covered their 'Distinguishing Parts'. They gave Mary an uninhibited welcome.[19] Mary was a Christian and these women were Muslim but at this moment they seemed to her anything but oppressed; they were her equals.

Mary wrote that she had often thought that if it were fashionable for everyone to go around naked, the body as a whole would have been the measure of beauty, rather than just the human face. The exquisite proportions of these unclothed, unscarred female bodies struck her powerfully and erotically. She marvelled at their shining white skin and their glossy long dark hair, either hanging naturally over their shoulders or braided and held in place with ribbons or pearls. She likened the women to the goddesses drawn by the Renaissance artists Titian and Guido Reni or to the three Graces from Greek mythology. She was reminded of Milton's description of Eve before The Fall as having no 'guiltie shame, dishonest shame' in her nakedness but instead standing proud. She joked that she wished her friend the society portrait painter Charles Jervas were with her now. Observing these beautiful women would surely have improved his artistic technique.

Seeing the women mingling and talking amongst themselves, drinking coffee and sherbet, Mary found herself likening the scene to a London coffee house. Not that she would have ever stepped foot inside a real coffee house herself. As an aristocratic woman, to enter a coffee house would have meant risking social condemnation. Here in the Turkish bath 'all the news of the Town is told, Scandal invented, etc.,' the women staying talking for four to five hours at a time, like men gossiping in a London coffee house.[20] As someone who was passionately interested in the issues of the day, Mary must have longed to have the freedom men enjoyed back in London. The inference was clear: these women had more agency than she did.

The most important Turkish lady then beckoned Mary over to sit by her, gesturing that she should take off her clothes. A crowd gathered round, all entreating her to get undressed. Mary struggled to communicate why this was so difficult. Eventually she resorted to opening up her skirt and showing them her hooped petticoat with its whalebone stays. She registered the looks of surprise and shock on their faces. As she put it: 'they believed I was so locked up in that machine that it was not in my power to open it, which contrivance they attributed to my Husband.'[21] Again, Mary found herself questioning the received wisdom in the west, that women in the east were imprisoned by their culture. It was she who appeared to be locked up to please her husband, not them.

As they left Sophia and travelled on to Adrianople (today the Turkish city of Edirne) the spring days lengthened, and the weather warmed. Suddenly they were in an idyllic world of gardens and fruit trees, camels and mosques. The Turkish empire was a powerful one and the lives of the people the carriage passed reflected this. The sultan was at Adrianople with his army for the spring. Wortley settled into the embassy there, meeting the sultan for the first time and getting to know his staff. His aim was to negotiate a peace between the Austrians and the Turks, while the French ambassador negotiated separately for peace between the Turks and the Venetians.

The French ambassador Jean-Louis d'Usson, the Marquis de Bonnac and his wife Madeleine-Francoise, soon became friends with the Wortley Montagus. They were about the same age and the two wives took to seeing the sights together. Having been on the road for six months, Mary enjoyed settling into their new home. The sultan had specifically set aside lodgings for them. The building was made of wood and designed with separate living quarters for men and women, joined by a narrow passage. Rather than containing furniture, each room had a built-in platform covered in carpet, which was decorated with cushions to lounge on. This was a feature Mary liked very much. She ordered herself a Turkish costume - voluminous trousers with a caftan to go over the top and a veil - and wore it to go exploring. The artist Jean-Baptiste Vanmour, who had been based in Turkey for many years, soon painted her portrait dressed in Turkish clothing. A few weeks after they arrived in Adrianople, Mary realised she was pregnant. As she jested to a friend in a letter home: 'Idleness is the mother of vices (as you know) and having nothing better to do, I have produced a daughter.'[22] A daughter who would alter the course of medical science in the west.

Chapter 6

Turkey

'entirely harmless by the invention of engrafting'[1]

Mary soon settled into her new life in Turkey, first in Adrianople and then in the Constantinople suburb of Pera. She threw herself into exploring the sites and soaking up the culture. As she had always had an aptitude for languages, she started learning Turkish. But she did not forget England. The letters she wrote and received were still extremely important to her. Wortley was often away, and she was left alone with her two children and a household to run. It was during one of these absences that she decided to have Edward inoculated. Far too soon, their time in Turkey came to an end. Shifting political alliances both here and in England led to Wortley's being recalled. Mary was forced to hide her sadness at leaving this fascinating city behind.

As always, it was women's lives which interested Mary. Turkey was no exception. She was honoured to be the first European woman invited to dine alone with the grand vizier's wife and then with Fatima, wife of the sultan's *kayha* or steward. Fatima was the younger of the two, but she was already a mother of grown-up daughters. She treated her guest to a performance of Turkish belly dancing. Mary was struck by the paradox that the clothing the Turkish women wore gave them greater freedom than was enjoyed by women in the west. Her overall impression was that Turkish women were well looked after by their husbands and 'are the only Women in the world that lead a life of uninterrupted pleasure.'[2] The emphasis, she realised, was placed firmly on the need to produce children. If a woman died unmarried or childless this was looked on as something shameful. The ironic contrast of this with the veneration given to virgin saints by the Catholic church was not lost on her.

Occasionally Mary saw a darker underside to female life here. When she arrived in Adrianople, she had just missed the wedding of the sultan's oldest daughter, Princess Fatma. Although Fatma was only a 13-year-old, this was her second marriage. Her first husband had been killed a few months before at Petrovardin. A woman of noble birth could not stay unmarried, even if she were pre-pubescent. Mary wrote that Fatma's first marriage was a love-match and this second, to a man three times her age, was out of duty: 'He is a Man of merit and the declared Favourite of the Sultan, which they call Mosayp, but that is not enough to make him pleasing in the Eyes of a Girl of 13.'[3] There is no historical evidence to support Mary's view. Arranged marriages were the norm here, but Mary's empathy with the young Fatma is understandable. Another time, Mary came across a naked, blood-soaked, female corpse just lying in the street, wrapped in a sheet. She could make out two knife wounds, one in the woman's side and the other in her breast. This was a cruel punishment for some indiscretion. Mary was acutely aware that the victim's case was never brought to justice.

Mary wanted to make sure that she sent back letters to her friends and relatives with the ship that was due to sail from Turkey on 1 April 1718. These would go on to form the basis of the *Embassy Letters*, which she put together once she was back in London. To Sister Mar she wrote at length about the Turkish clothing she had started to wear, and the fashion for accentuating women's eyes using kohl; to Conti and Pope she wrote giving detailed descriptions of Turkish culture; and to her friend Anne Thistlethwayte she wrote about how her riding side-saddle caused 'as much wonder as the ship of Columbus was in America'.[4] To her father and her friend Sarah Chiswell she described the Turkish practice of engraftment against the smallpox. Her letter to her father does not survive but the one to Sarah Chiswell has provided an invaluable description of the process. In it Mary detailed the shallow cuts to arms and legs, the use of a walnut shell to convey the diseased matter and the mild form of inoculated smallpox that the volunteers suffered - as well as suggesting she would 'war with' the medical establishment about it if ever she returned. She also began studying the Turkish language, boasting to Pope of her 'Oriental learning' and writing poetry inspired by her new life.[5]

Mary and the French ambassador's wife, Madame de Bonnac, toured the sights of Adrianople together. As Madame de Bonnac would never venture out without a full escort, the two elaborate retinues of coaches and servants drew vast crowds wherever they went. Monsieur de Bonnac admired the spirit and intelligence of his wife's new friend but was also nervous of her forceful personality; he was adamant that she was not to teach his wife Latin. Meanwhile both husbands threw themselves into the negotiations for peace between the Turks and the Austrians after the bloodshed at Petrovardin. The sultan himself soon left Adrianople to join his army, which were camped outside the city. Mary went with various other diplomatic wives in Turkish coaches or *arabas* to inspect the troops. The sultan's decision to lead his army back into active service against the Austrians was not good news for Wortley. He had hoped things could be resolved diplomatically. But this now looked unlikely. The Wortley Montagus and the de Bonnacs decided to move from Adrianople to the capital of Constantinople (Istanbul today). At least diplomacy could continue there.

They soon settled into life in the diverse and prosperous Constantinople suburb of Pera where the embassy was based, across the Golden Horn from the main sites of the city. Looking over the water at the domed palaces and mosques, Mary was reminded of a wooden cabinet with china ornaments all proudly displayed on its shelves. The ambassador and his family availed themselves of a splendid seventeenth century palace, the official diplomatic residence. Pera was a cultural melting pot, with a dozen or so different languages distinguishable in the street-cries Mary heard every day. 'My Grooms are Arabs,' she wrote about this diversity, 'my footmen French, English and Germans; my Nurse an Armenian; my Housemaids Russians; half a dozen other servants Greeks; my steward an Italian; my Janizarys Turks.'[6] This was her kind of place. She was keen to go exploring. Madame de Bonnac never once ventured across the Bosphorus, but Mary soon set off again, disguised in Turkish clothing, to explore the sites across the water.

The searing summer heat meant that only a few weeks later, in order to escape the plague, the family decamped yet again to a village close to the Black Sea, ten miles outside Constantinople. The house here was situated in a grove of fruit trees. Mary was charmed by the life in this rural retreat. She occupied her time studying the Turkish language, writing, hunting partridges, doing needlework and listening to music. Various letters to friends she wrote during this interlude put them right about false assumptions they had made about Turkish life. It would be impossible to send one of her friends a Greek slave as jokingly requested, she wrote, as all the Greeks were the sultan's subjects, not his slaves.

Nor would she send her any Balm of Mecca. When Mary had tried the cream on herself her face had swelled up for three whole days.

Her letters home mostly made her life that summer sound idyllic but she wrote to Pope in a different vein: 'I am Sometimes very weary of this Singing and dancing and Sunshine, and wish for the Smoke and Impertinencies in which You toil.'[7] Back in London Pope wrote prolifically, inspired by his longing for her. His narrative poem *Eloisa and Abelard* described an impossible love which still remained strong despite the many obstacles in its path. It was full of images of eyes, like Mary's own. Pope sent out to Turkey a copy of the latest volume of his recent poems and a letter dropping heavy hints that the tragic end of *Eloisa* described his own feelings. Mary received both the book and the explicit letter once she had returned to Constantinople. She carefully and deliberately wrote the word 'mine' in her copy of the poems. But at the same time, she dispatched a letter to William Congreve in London asking why he allowed Pope to go on making these 'Lampoons.'

Wortley sent a set of terms to end the fighting, which he believed the Turks would accept, to the Austrian emperor in Vienna and the government in London. He was unaware that Sir Robert Sutton, his predecessor as ambassador in Turkey, and Abraham Stanyan, the newly appointed ambassador to Austria, were set on undermining him. They could see that the Austrians were likely to dominate. Stanyan also mistrusted Mary's role. As he saw it, she had interfered in affairs of state and made matters worse. She had been impressed by the sultan, he wrote to a friend, and was guilty of over-influencing her husband. On 16 August 1717 the Austrians under Prince Eugene began besieging Belgrade, the city where the Wortley Montagus had lodged with Achmet-Beg only six months earlier. The Turks surrendered the city after just a week. Nothing more was ever heard of Achmet-Beg. These new events made Wortley's peace terms look all the more unwise.

At same time, back in England there was a change of government. Wortley's best friend Joseph Addison now became the Secretary of State for the Southern Department (foreign secretary in today's terminology). Addison decided to ask Stanyan and Sutton to take over the Austrian-Turkish negotiations from Vienna and to recall his old friend Wortley to London. He sent Wortley a private letter, explaining the reasoning behind his decision. He offered Wortley what he ambiguously termed a place for life, back in London. The news that his friend was to return home would take several months to reach Turkey.

Unaware of his impending recall, on 10 September 1717, Wortley set off yet again, leaving his family behind in Pera. The sultan had set up camp near Philippopolis and Wortley pursued him there to continue the negotiations. Rumours that he had been given notice abounded in the ports, where sailors talked to merchants, but as yet there was no official word. When it did come, Wortley's ego would be profoundly wounded. He had been required to spend large sums of his own money in the post and he would never feel that he was given the right amount of compensation for his 'extraordinaries'. For someone as punctilious over money as Wortley, this would prove to be a painful blow.

While she was heavily pregnant with her daughter - also to be called Mary - Lady Mary spent her time sitting writing poetry and letters home, with her feet resting on a low table positioned over a stove, covered by a Turkish carpet, a contraption known as a *tendour*. Despite its being a fire risk, Mary loved the arrangement. She could sit and write in early January 1718 with the windows wide open and the sun shining. Her poem *Verses Written in the Chiosk of the British Palace* praises the beautiful views from where she sat and the fertility of nature compared to cold England: 'Gardens on Gardens, Domes on Domes arise/And endless Beauties tire the wandering Eyes.'[8] Virtue and pleasure did not necessarily need to be seen as opposites, she argued. They could coexist. Virtuous mother that she was, she had found real contentment.

There would only ever be two children from the Wortley Montagus' marriage. This does not necessarily mean it had already gone stale. Mary may well have had miscarriages. Or she perhaps practised simple birth control. For this second birth Mary was attended by their faithful surgeon Dr Maitland and by the well-known physician Dr Timoni, whom Wortley had engaged in Constantinople. Unlike in England, the custom here in Turkey was not to wait an entire month before leaving the darkened birthing room. This delighted Mary. Just three weeks after the birth of her baby daughter she set off again across the Bosphorus. In Wortley's absence she had young Mary christened by their chaplain, Mr Crosse. The de Bonnacs stood as godparents.

In March 1718, still without Wortley, Mary decided to inoculate their young son against the smallpox. It may well be that she had learned more about the process from Dr Timoni. Maitland was with her for the experiment and later wrote about it in his *Account of Inoculating the Smallpox*. He did not mention Timoni's being with them for Edward's inoculation, but he did write that Mr Crosse the chaplain warned Mary against it. Young Edward's inoculation was not the groundbreaking event that the inoculation of young Mary would be three years later, back in London. After all, Sir Robert Sutton's children had already been inoculated. But it was still a bold move. Mary wisely waited five days before informing her husband. Ten days later she wrote again, irritated at his apparent disinterest in the welfare of their son: 'I cannot forbear telling you so, though you do not so much as ask after him.'[9] As when they were separated in the early years of their marriage, Wortley seemed happy to leave everything domestic to Mary whenever he was away.

For her part, Mary expected to have a key role in Wortley's career, even though they were apart. She wrote him several letters full of news and advice. Relations with her father back in England continued to be strained, and so she suggested Wortley write to his father-in-law dating the letter as if their baby daughter had only just been born. Kingston would approve of that gesture, she felt sure. She also wrote several anxious letters asking Wortley's advice about the repayment of a loan she had received from her uncle Feilding, which had arrived from London in gold pieces. She was trying to weigh up whether it would be better to convert the gold pieces into pounds or instead to avoid duty by using them to purchase things in Turkey. She always prided herself on being financially astute.

Mary's Turkish lessons were progressing well. When she visited the *kayha*'s wife Fatima again, this time in Constantinople, they could now converse in Turkish. This had made her forget all her English, she jested. She was also able to tour the vizier's palace but was disappointed not to be allowed into the sultan's seraglio. Harems interested her. Increasingly she saw that they provided a valuable separate space for women and a secure unit for family life. She noted to herself: 'Women not locked up.'[10] She also visited the famous church-turned-mosque of Saint Sophia. Years later she told her friend Joseph Spence that she went to see it with a Greek friend, both disguised as men. Her friend was moved to tears by the sight of a Christian stronghold now under Muslim control. At this Mary grew nervous their disguise might be discovered. She herself was critical of Islam and thought all the priests scoundrels, she wrote to Abbé Conti, who was himself a defrocked priest.

In Paris Abbé Conti showed his friend Nicolas-Francois Rémond the letter Mary had written him about her experiences in Constantinople. Contemporary diarists described Rémond as: 'ridiculous, unattractive and pretentious, extremely clever and unscrupulous in ingratiating himself with people to further his fortune'.[11] Mary's lively writing and astute comments struck a chord with the impressionable Rémond. He sent her a fan-letter from Paris. He doubted he would ever meet her, he wrote, and yet he felt he completely understood her spirit. Mary failed to read the warning signs. Flattered, she wrote back. He replied immediately in an amorous frenzy.

In late spring Wortley returned to his wife and young family and his official recall became public. The couple began making their preparations for the journey home. Both regretted their departure. Wortley wrote an essay on fame as a way of working through his feelings. 'Almost all wise men of old praise a private life and advise the contempt of fame,' he wrote, though it was hard to accept this.[12] Mary had found her time living abroad immensely stimulating. The thought of the long journey they would have to undertake to return to London only made her anxious. Characteristically, she concealed these feelings.

Wortley hesitated over their means of transport. Should they return on board the man-of-war Addison was sending out for them or would it be better to travel overland? The *Preston*, captained by Robert Johnson, arrived in Constantinople on 19 June 1718 and moored in the Golden Horn near Seragalio Point. Perhaps returning by boat would be best. On 4 July the ambassador and his family went aboard to a five-gun salute which startled the children. The next day they set sail. Both Mary and Wortley looked back over the Bosphorus at the towers and domes of Constantinople. Neither would ever return to Turkey. The lives of the women she had met there had had a huge effect on Mary's thinking. She had also begun the experiment with inoculation which was to become her greatest legacy. For his part, Wortley's opportunity for a glittering career had been thwarted, partly but not entirely due to his own actions. He would never hold a significant public office with real agency such as this again. It was hard to swallow his bitter disappointment.

The voyage westwards through the Aegean on board the *Preston* proved magical. First, they sailed through the Hellespont. Mary was in raptures at seeing the classical texts she had pored over at Thoresby brought to life before her eyes. Anchoring at Troy, she and Wortley visited the ruins together, Mary with her copy of Homer in her hand, her imagination stirred at the account of the Trojan wars. They came across a stone slab with a Greek inscription commemorating a peace treaty of 279 BC. This was a living piece of history, theirs for the taking. Like many visitors to sites such as these at the time, they decided to take it home with them as a souvenir. Back in London Wortley would often show it proudly to anyone who visited.

They moored overnight near Troy and the next day Mary got up at 2.00 am to visit the city again by herself. The opportunity was too good to miss. She hired a donkey and toured the ancient walls as the sun rose. Next their ship skirted mainland Greece. She longed to land there but it was too dangerous to go ashore. In her imagination, 'after drinking a dish of tea with Sapho, I might have gone the same evening to visit the temple of Homer in Chios.'[13] The large island of Crete loomed on the horizon, where she could just make out the archaeological site at Knossos. They sailed past the foot of Italy and could see the flames of Mount Etna erupting on Sicily. They put in at Cape Passero on the southern-most tip of Sicily to mend their sails. Their next mooring point was the bay of Carthage in modern-day Tunisia. Here it was Ramadan. The British consul took them in his carriage to see the Carthaginian ruins by moonlight. The extreme heat the next day made Mary half-blind. She was not as keen on the inhabitants - dark-skinned and sporting ornamental tattoos - as she had been on the Turks. She sat by the ruins resting and the local people came to stare at this strange, white, female visitor. She stared right back at them.

Heading north, skirting Sardinia and Elba, they passed the Italian port of Leghorn (modern-day Livorno) but continued on to Genoa, arriving on 15 August 1718. Mary was delighted with the city. She went to visit the famous mansions designed by Palladio, two of which had been models for Thoresby. She wrote to Sister Mar describing the tradition in Genoa known as *tetis beys* where every married woman had her own young unmarried male follower, whose role was to attend to her every wish.[14] Whereas customs such as this had made her nervous on her trip out, now she found much to admire in the respect shown to Genoese women.

Wortley was keen to get back to England. The journey so far had been slow. They had only covered a third of the distance. After ten days of compulsory plague quarantine, the couple decided they would travel back home overland instead, leaving the children and their Armenian nurse to continue by sea. Their voyage would take six months and involve several encounters with hostile Spanish ships. Twenty-eight of the crew would be sent to hospital once the ship did finally arrive back in England in January 1719. Miraculously, the children were safe, but no thanks were due to their parents. For us this feels woefully un-maternal of Mary, but we are judging her by today's standards.

The Wortley Montagus stayed on once their children had departed, as guests of the consul in Genoa. Then they travelled to Turin, which proved a disappointment after Genoa. Mary did not think much of the famous Turin Shroud - 'the holy Handkerchief' as she described it to her sister.[15] She was granted an audience with the queen, who spoke good English and was proud of the fact she was the grand-daughter of Charles I. Next they crossed the Alps, via the pass of Mont Cenis, carried by porters on little seats strapped onto poles. This was Mary's first experience of a high mountain range. She admired the dramatic scenery and marvelled at the snow, but she immediately succumbed to a bout of 'flu, brought on by the extreme cold on the mountain pass.

The couple spent a week holed up in a 'sorry inn' in Lyons, while Mary recovered from her high fever. As she put it, she thought that 'all my Journeys were ended here.'[16] She could find nothing on her first visit to France to inspire her. The trip onwards from Lyons towards Paris did not alleviate her sense of misery. Recent political events had brought about great poverty in the French countryside and Mary and Wortley encountered beggars wherever they stopped. It was not until they reached Fontainebleau that she saw what she described as 'French Magnificence'.[17]

They arrived in Paris on 18 September 1718. Again, Mary found the French capital underwhelming. The women, she felt, used far too much make-up. She nevertheless enjoyed an outing to see Racine's play *Bajazet*, particularly as it was set in the Ottoman empire. She now counted herself an expert on all things Turkish. She made sure to visit the family of Madame de Bonnac and was delighted to see her old friend Abbé Conti again, having written to him extensively throughout her trip. More awkward was her first encounter in the flesh with Conti's friend, Nicolas-Francois Rémond, who had sent her a fan-letter back in Turkey. He was small, ugly and proud of his intellect, a bit like Pope. Embarrassingly, he suggested that from now on he wear a ring as a token of their eternal friendship.

Then completely by chance she bumped into Sister Mar. The two sisters fell into each other's arms, both marvelling at their enormous good fortune. The whole serendipity of events reminded them of the Scudéry romances they had read together as teenagers. Sister Mar was on her way out to Italy to meet up with her husband. The sisters had two precious weeks together visiting the sights. While Sister Mar sat for her portrait twice a day, Mary used the free time to explore on her own. But all too soon it was time to set off again.

The weather was stormy for their passage across the Channel. Mary was amused to share her cabin with an Englishwoman who prayed melodramatically while the storm raged outside but then, the instant it stopped, turned to ask for help rearranging her headdress. They landed at Dover on 30 September 1718 and arrived back in London a few days later. Wortley had an official audience with the king at Hampton Court. Addison had advised his friend when he wrote to him in Constantinople that 'you would find your ease and advantage more in being nearer his person.'[18] But Addison was probably only trying to be kind. Like his wife, Wortley was not a natural courtier. For a long time, Wortley would attempt to reclaim some of the expenses he had shelled out in Turkey. When this failed, he turned his attention to making money from the coal mines his family owned in the north east of England.

As the Wortley Montagus left Paris and headed towards England, they were drawing ever nearer to one significant problem: the situation with Alexander Pope. A letter from Pope awaited Mary when she landed in Dover, expressing his longing to see her 'Oriental Self'. Mary had taken Pope's translation of the *Iliad* with her to Constantinople and had written to him that she found reading it in situ illuminated several passages which previously she had not 'entirely comprehend(ed) the Beauty of.'[19] In another letter she sent him her own translation of some love poems. They had been written by the Sultan's favourite to his beautiful *fiancée,* describing his frustration that he could not visit her until their marriage ceremony had taken place. Little wonder, then, that Pope had misinterpreted Mary's feelings for him.

Pope had been so excited about the news of Mary's return that he had even offered to travel to Italy to accompany her home. Even this was only a literary conceit on his part. He would never be well enough to travel abroad. Alongside the letter awaiting her in Dover, Pope also sent Mary a poem he had written about a recent tragedy when two young lovers, who lived at the village of Stanton Harcourt in Oxfordshire, had taken their own lives in a double suicide-pact. He had sent his poem to other people as well, but by sending it to Mary he was signalling that his feelings for her were as powerful and as potentially destructive as those of the lovers. Nervous, Mary dealt with this in the only way she knew how. She wrote her own poem in response to his - light, satirical, cynical - and sent it back. If the two lovers had lived, she wrote, their future marriage might not have been as picture-perfect as he had imagined it:

> 'For had they seen the next year's sun,
> A beaten wife and cuckold swain
> Had jointly curs'd the marriage chain;
> Now they are happy in their doom,
> For P. has wrote upon their tomb.'[20]

Her poem not only questioned what Pope took to be the moral of the story but also gently poked fun at the very idea of his writing an epitaph to the two dead lovers. Significantly, the metaphor she now used for marriage was a chain. But it was clear she did not see herself and Pope as being star-crossed lovers. Pope understood her meaning. Once she arrived in London, he was careful not to hurry to see her. When they did eventually meet again, and whenever he was then in her presence after that, mutual friends noticed that Pope would resort to ghastly puns.

Wortley and Mary's return to England was tinged with regret. The glamour and excitement of their Turkish adventure would never be repeated. For Mary life there had opened her eyes to new cultures and a different way of being. The experience was unforgettable. She wrote to her friend Abbé Conti back in Paris, as soon as they landed at Dover. In her letter she imagined an English squire and praised him for preferring his home-made beer to foreign wines. She admitted to Conti she hoped that: 'since I must be contented with our scanty allowance of Daylight, ...I may forget the enlivening Sun of Constantinople.'[21] Forget she never would.

Chapter 7

Campaigning against Smallpox
'abused and deluded by the Knavery and Ignorance of Physicians'[1]

Three years elapsed back in London before Lady Mary decided to take action and have her only daughter inoculated. Smallpox epidemics in England had become increasingly frequent and severe in the early years of the eighteenth century. There was an outbreak in 1710, a second in 1714 when Mary lost her only brother, a third in 1716 when she herself narrowly escaped with her own life and then yet another in 1719. During the epidemic of 1719 the Wortley Montagus had returned from Turkey and were settling into London life. Mary probably felt it best to keep her un-inoculated daughter safely indoors and ignore the fact she knew of a better way of protecting her - better but controversial. In London that year 3229 people were recorded as having died from the disease. Mary would find it hard to remain silent for long.

The year 1721 began with unseasonably warm weather. Roses and violets were already coming into bloom in early January. Soon rumours began spreading of yet another serious outbreak of the smallpox. As Dr Maitland wrote in his account of events, that year the smallpox seemed 'to go forth like a destroying Angel.'[2] Alone in Twickenham with her two children, Mary received news of the deaths of friends and relatives. Doctors seemed inclined to do very little, maybe because they feared dangerous contagion from sick patients. At the same time a power struggle was taking place within the medical profession itself as the College of Physicians sought to limit the powers of unlicensed competitors. They began fining humble apothecaries for even attempting anything bordering on the medical. It was time for Mary to put into action her threat that she would 'war with 'em' once she was back in England.

In March, Mary wrote to Dr Maitland to ask for his help. Both understood the likely consequences of their actions. As Mary put it:

'what an arduous, what a fearful and, we may add, what a thankless enterprise it was.'[3] She told her family that nearly every day for the rest of her life she would regret having put the process in motion. Nevertheless, knowing what they had seen with their own eyes in Turkey, Mary and Maitland decided to act. Mary held her three-year old daughter still, while Maitland made the shallow wounds with his surgeon's lancet and inoculated her against the deadly disease. Mary was particularly wary of the physicians Maitland had insisted must come to inspect the patient, once the spots began to show. After all, she had already predicted that the establishment would set themselves against the whole process.

Several of Mary's influential friends, or 'Persons of distinction' as Mary's grand-daughter Lady Louisa would later describe them, came to inspect the little girl as well. Nothing in the accounts of the time mentioned that young Mary would still have been infectious at this stage. Presumably the 'Persons of distinction' had already had the disease, as none of them fell ill. Mary had already deduced this important scientific point, which was why she had moved to protect young Mary's Armenian nurse back in Constantinople. This same Armenian nurse had accompanied young Mary and Edward on the ship back from Genoa to London while their parents travelled home overland. The fact we know nothing more of the Armenian nurse's fate once she arrived in England indicates that she soon was no longer part of the household in Twickenham. Maybe, her immune system lowered, she had fallen prey to any one of the diseases rife in England, perhaps even to smallpox itself.

Medical historians have often played down Mary's role, and she sought to keep her contribution anonymous. Certainly, Dr Maitland helped her with the engraftment and he and Dr Keith would go on to receive public acclaim, but it was Mary who initiated things, Mary who bravely volunteered her own daughter for inoculation and Mary who accurately analysed the risks and rewards of doing so. Mother and daughter would go on to spend their time crossing the country in Mary's carriage to administer inoculations to friends and relatives, at times facing enormous prejudice against their actions, with people jeering at their carriage as it went past. Although Mary resolved to keep silent about this vital work, she was a formidable campaigner. She began working behind the scenes to ensure that word of their scientific breakthrough was spread far and wide.

The next inoculation experiment has a theatricality which ties it to Mary, even though there is no clear evidence that it was at her instigation. The three physicians who had come to observe little Mary's progress at Twickenham had been 'deputed by the government.'[4] These physicians made the case to the crown for what became known as the Newgate experiment. Six prisoners from Newgate gaol were to be offered inoculation against the smallpox. It was agreed that if they survived, they would be given their freedom. On 14 June 1721, only a couple of months after young Mary's inoculation at Twickenham, the secretary of state, Lord Townshend (the man to whom Mary's flighty friend Dolly had been hurriedly married off in the past) wrote a letter to the Attorney General, Sir Robert Raymond, and the Solicitor General, Sir Philip Yorke, checking whether it would be legal for the king to grant a pardon to criminals in this way. On 17 June the secretary of state and the attorney general wrote back giving their permission. At the end of July, the newspapers started reporting that preparations were being made. Several Newgate prisoners were removed to better quarters. That month a Frenchman visiting England wrote home describing the plan for the Newgate experiment. He mentioned that Lady Mary had had her daughter engrafted and that the Townshends were following suit. He even claimed - exaggerating for effect - that all the fathers and mothers in England were doing the same thing.

The instigating force behind the Newgate experiment was Princess Caroline of Ansbach. Writing many years after the events, the royal physician Sir Hans Sloane confirmed that it was Princess Caroline's idea to experiment on the Newgate prisoners. Back in 1716, when Mary was suffering from smallpox, Sir Hans Sloane had visited Mary's sickbed. She had satirised him in her *Town Eclogues* as being totally ineffectual in dealing with the disease at that point. She could not count on him as an ally. Sloane wrote what was seen as the definitive account of how smallpox inoculation came to be introduced to the west. In it he acknowledged that the Wortley Montagus had written home from Turkey describing the process of inoculation. He related how they returned with their healthy, inoculated son. His emphasis was very much on Wortley rather than Mary, however. Significantly he omitted to mention Mary's all-important experiment with her daughter at Twickenham.

There is no firm evidence that Princess Caroline heard about little Mary's inoculation at Twickenham, that it was Lady Mary who told her about it and that the two decided together to take the experiments further with the Newgate prisoners. Yet Lady Mary seems the most likely person to have enlisted Princess Caroline's support. Voltaire, who visited later, wrote that: 'at least ten thousand children of good family thus owe their lives to the Queen and Lady Wortley Montagu,' but his linking the two women does not prove the chain of events.[5] Voltaire's main reason for writing was to condemn French women, among them Madame de Bonnac, who he argued had lacked Mary's courage. He praised Mary as being 'one of the most intelligent women in England, and with a powerful intellect into the bargain'.[6] For her part, Mary always told her family that Princess Caroline 'was her firm support and stood by her without quaking,' implying that the driving force was Mary herself with Caroline in a supporting role.[7] Whatever the dynamic, the two remained firm allies throughout, a powerful, non-professional two-woman pressure group with an unrivalled list of contacts between them.

Initially, the ever-cautious Maitland declined to be involved with the experiment to inoculate the prisoners at Newgate. Then he changed his mind. On 9 August 1721 Sir Hans Sloane and Dr John George Steigentahl supervised the inoculation of the six Newgate convicts, three of each gender, which Dr Maitland performed. They were watched over by twenty-five surgeons, physicians and apothecaries, including members of both the prestigious College of Physicians and the even more prestigious Royal Society. The incisions made by the surgeon's lancet were smaller than usual and a few days after adding the smallpox matter to their cuts Maitland feared the experiment might not have worked. He even set about procuring some fresh smallpox matter just in case. He need not have feared. The next day the spots appeared. One of the convicts had already had smallpox and so he had no reaction but the other five followed the inoculation pattern of mild illness and then complete recovery. All five who had suffered inoculated smallpox were pardoned.

Maitland felt a huge sense of relief and a burst of confidence as a result. His friend Isaac Massey, an apothecary at Christ's Hospital, described their meeting by chance at Child's Coffee House in St Paul's Churchyard soon after the Newgate experiment. The exuberant Maitland was clear, wrote Massey, that the prisoners he had inoculated against the smallpox would never again fall prey to the disease. Massey suggested that they should wait for a decade or so to see what happened, since 'then he w(ould) have fewer adversaries in this matter.'[8] There were already a host of adversaries lining up over the subject of whether or not the Newgate experiment had been a success. Opinion fell largely along party political lines. The Whigs felt confident that it proved conclusively that inoculation worked. The Tories were more circumspect. They were opposed in principle to the idea that the state had handed control over six human lives to the Royal Society.

The motivation for Princess Caroline's involvement had been her oldest daughter, Princess Anne, who had suffered a dangerous attack of smallpox in the outbreak of 1721. There were two younger princesses - Princess Amelia and Princess Caroline - and their mother feared for their health. Following the success of the Newgate experiment, Caroline decided to go ahead and have her two younger daughters inoculated. Dr Maitland was to carry out the inoculations again, this time supervised by Claude Amayand, the king's surgeon. On 17 April 1722, exactly a year after little Mary's inoculation, Amayand cut open the wounds and Maitland applied the smallpox matter. The process was a success and Amayand then went on to have his own children inoculated. Maitland and Mary must have felt that they were winning the battle for acceptance of the new process.

Sir Hans Sloane reported that next Princess Caroline initiated yet another scheme. All the orphan children in Westminster were to be offered free inoculation. The plan was controversial and there were delays while its merits were debated. Eventually only six children were treated. This was also the first instance of using smallpox matter which had been taken from someone suffering from inoculated smallpox rather than natural smallpox. Again, the experiment was successful. Advertisements appeared in the London newspapers inviting people to come and inspect the six inoculated Westminster orphans.

Printed accounts began to appear, both for and against smallpox inoculation, which Mary must have pored over. A Dr Walter Harris had given an address to the College of Physicians in April 1721, in which he made a passing reference to the practice being common in Constantinople. In August his address was published, along with an appendix giving more detail about the practicalities. Then on 19 August 1721 *The Weekly Journal* reprinted Dr Timoni's paper to the Royal Society of 1714, *De peste Constantinopoli grassante*. In general, though, the newspapers were sceptical. They were wary of the powers conferred on the Royal Society for the Newgate experiment and resented the idea of freedom being granted to the Newgate prisoners. They also opposed the concept of deliberately causing someone healthy to become unwell. Rumours started circulating that rather than contracting smallpox the prisoners had in truth been given chicken pox or even swine pox. The newspapers also began questioning whether inoculated smallpox really would give the patient ongoing immunity. To prove them wrong Sloane and Steigentahl paid for a 19-year-old woman, one of the Newgate prisoners who had been inoculated and was now healthy again, to travel to Maitland's practice in Hertford and to lie for several days in the same bed as someone who was suffering from natural smallpox. Dr Maitland oversaw this and, as he had predicted, the young woman prisoner remained perfectly healthy.

The only definitive account of events written at the time was Dr Maitland's. He had wanted to see the results of the Westminster orphan experiment before publishing but when it got delayed and scaled down he decided to go ahead and publish anyway, at his own expense. *Mr Maitland's Account of Inoculating the Smallpox* appeared on 13 February 1722. Maitland was understandably cautious about what his involvement would do to his own professional reputation, but perhaps publishing was better than remaining silent and enduring continued slanders from the press. Diplomatically, he dedicated his account to the Prince and Princess of Wales. He made it clear that 'the process is certain, the Prognostic infallible.' His carefully chosen words praised Lady Mary anonymously, describing her only as 'the Ambassador's ingenious lady'. He gave an account of their experiments on both her children and spelled out that 'the Practice is most plain, rational and easy, intended only to prevent the malignant Infection and to preserve Life.' He thanked 'divine Providence' for the discovery and stressed that 'my Design is only to advise everyone that attempts it to be cautious.' Rather than calming things, Maitland's account only poured oil on troubled waters. A fierce pamphlet war ensued.[9]

Although Maitland was to carry out twelve more inoculations in 1722, increasingly the process was seen as controversial. The royal family were portrayed as foreign and therefore not be trusted, and anti-Turkish feeling also ran high. The fifth and youngest son of Lord Sutherland, William Spencer, still only a toddler, died of 'Convulsion Fits', having been inoculated by none other than Claude Amayand, the royal surgeon.

As *Applebees Journal* put it, inoculation had proved 'an unhappy Experiment to this young Nobleman'.[10] It is unlikely that the smallpox inoculation killed him, since he lived for nearly three weeks after having recovered from inoculated smallpox. But his death certificate, which was signed by surgeons, not by more eminent physicians, was a hostage to adverse publicity. To make matters worse, soon afterwards there was a second high-profile death. Lord Bathurst, a friend both of Mary's and Pope's, had his six children inoculated successfully that year, but his young servant then died. His children would have been infectious during their treatment and the servant probably caught natural smallpox from them. Regardless of the truth of the matter, these deaths were a gift for the newspapers. Circulation soared as everyone scoured the printed arguments, both for and more generally against.

Princess Caroline remained firmly in favour of the new discovery throughout. Her eldest son, Prince Frederick Lewis, was not in London with the rest of the royal family, but was still living in Hanover, where Mary had met him on her journey out to Turkey. Again, the evidence is sketchy, but it seems likely that it was Lady Mary who suggested to Princess Caroline that she should have her son inoculated as well. Now she was back in London, Mary was busy editing her correspondence into her *Embassy Letters*. She was careful to include a flattering reference to the prince, knowing that this would please Princess Caroline. Maitland travelled out to Hanover in 1724 to perform the prince's inoculation. Whilst he was there, he engrafted ten other people as well. He made sure he wrote a daily account of his experiences to Sir Hans Sloane back in London. For his part, Sloane still vacillated about the process. Although he had had his own grandchildren inoculated, he was wary of shouldering the responsibility for the royal experiments. He had taken the precaution of asking advice of King George I, Prince Frederick Lewis's grandfather, before Maitland's departure. King George estimated that only one in a thousand patients was likely to die from inoculation, so he agreed to it. Only then had Sloane given his assent for Maitland to proceed.

Among the medical establishment Dr William Wagstaffe was the most powerful and outspoken opponent. He predicted that posterity would find it hard to believe that a practice performed by a 'few ignorant Women' should 'upon a slender Experience, so far obtain in one of the Politest Nations in the World, as to be received into the Royal Palace.' Although he referenced 'some *sanguine* Traveller from Turkey' he mentioned neither Mary nor Maitland by name.[11] He saw the process as a folk practice, unreliable and dangerous, and was anxious to protect the College of the Physicians from 'private people', apothecaries and surgeons. His arguments demonstrate what Lady Mary and Princess Caroline were up against.

Mary's old friend from her days at Charles Jervas's studio, Dr John Arbuthnot, was the most eminent member of the medical profession who was in favour of inoculation. He was also the highest profile member of the Tory party to advocate the new process. Like Maitland and Dr Keith, he was a Scot. In 1722 he published a powerful argument in favour of Maitland's experiment on little Mary. He also proposed the use of mathematical analysis to rebut the arguments that William Wagstaffe was putting forward. In 1727 Arbuthnot gave an oration to the College of Physicians in which he outlined the tasks facing the medical profession. He put subduing smallpox at number one. His speech was published anonymously.

In an attempt to get to the truth of the matter, James Jurin, the secretary to the Royal Society, began compiling the facts and figures. He wrote that by February 1723, 182 inoculations had been carried out by a total of fifteen operators. In the two previous years Maitland alone had inoculated eighty-five people in London. Jurin's figures show that the inoculations were mainly carried out by surgeons under the supervision of physicians. His analysis was helpful in proving that once people had recovered from inoculated smallpox, they were no longer infectious. Jurin also attempted to analyse the deaths which had occurred and to compile figures which showed how many had died from natural and how many from inoculated smallpox. He proved that inoculated smallpox was far safer, and that, once inoculated, they had 'all to a Person done well.'[12]

Another powerful set of voices against inoculation was that of the clergy, 'the zeal of reverend railers', as Mary's contemporary Aaron Hill described them.[13] The churchmen argued that what was happening amounted to tampering with God's natural order. On 8 July 1722 the Reverend Edmund Massey (Isaac Massey's nephew) preached a widely reported sermon where he described smallpox as a judgement on the sins of the sufferer and therefore as something with which man should not interfere. Maitland, he said, was sinfully boastful and was only pushing the process of inoculation for his own benefit. In response, the gentle, timid Maitland published a second edition of his account and Massey issued a further vindication. Massey did not direct his anger at Mary, because her role in the inoculation process was still relatively unknown. But she would not be able to keep quiet for long. In 1725 William Clinch wrote a pamphlet railing against her directly. 'The common people were taught to hoot at her as an unnatural mother, who had risked the lives of her own children,' as Lady Louisa put it.[14] No wonder she was regretting her actions.

Mary occupied a unique position. She was always convinced that the Turkish method of engrafting, using only a tiny quantity of smallpox matter, was best. She was the only person to say that a doctor was not necessary and that there was no need for purging or sweating either before or after treatment. In fact, she warned against 'miserable gashes' and the unnecessary weakening of patients.[15] She grasped that it was in doctors' interests to medicalise the process and opposed this. Mary's exact whereabouts at the time are hard to track but the first wave of parents who had their children inoculated all tended to be aristocratic and to have had a personal acquaintance with her. She was probably responsible for their various inoculations. The upper classes also wanted to ensure that their servants were free of smallpox, so Mary probably inoculated them as well. The Fielding family, the children of her cousin the playwright Henry Fielding, were all inoculated, for instance, probably by Mary herself. Later in life several of these inoculated children, such as Wilhelmina Tichborne, were to become her friends as adults.

She was wary to guard her reputation throughout, having learned her lesson from the scandal when her *Town Eclogues* were published. Any action she took was unofficial and came about through her social networking skills. She wrote very little about her experiences in her letters of the time. She admitted to Sister Mar that she had run away to her house in Twickenham to get some well-earned rest from all the requests for inoculation, and she wrote to tell her that their nephew had died of the smallpox, un-inoculated. In March 1725, Mary's estranged father had his grandson and heir inoculated, along with his eldest daughter by his second marriage. Mary had written to him about engraftment when she was living in Turkey. She must have felt vindicated.

Eventually Mary could no longer resist writing something for publication about her experiences, albeit anonymously. *A Plain Account of the Inoculating of Smallpox by a Turkey Merchant* appeared in *The Flying Post* in September 1722, written in a straightforward, assertive prose style very different from Mary's poetry and letters. She was determined to tell the truth about the medical profession's involvement. She had explained to her editor at *The Flying Post* about 'the private satisfaction of having done good to mankind'. She only desired to put the record straight. Nevertheless, the editor was careful to soften her tone in what he published, particularly when it came to her writing about doctors. Where she talked in her early draft of 'the murders that have been committed,' he changed the reference for publication to 'misfortunes that have happened.' Where she wrote 'I am not of the College,' he changed the anonymous Turkey merchant's words to 'I am not a Physician.' He was careful to take out the sarcastic reference she had included that she hoped the members of the college would still receive their two guineas a day. Where she wrote ''tis in the power...of doctors to kill by prescriptions,' he changed her words to 'kill by Errors in prescription.' Two weeks later the Reverend Edmund Massey attacked this 'Sham Turkey merchant's letter', regardless. [16]

As for Dr Maitland, he returned to Scotland in 1726 to stay with relatives in Aberdeenshire. When an inoculation he performed there went wrong, he stopped inoculating patients in Scotland altogether. The process itself would go on to be banned there. Jurin's statistics have Maitland inoculating ten more patients later in 1726. Maitland seems to have made one final trip to England, where he inoculated two people in London and six in Durham, and then in 1727 another four in London and one in Durham (Jurin's statistics were not unfailingly accurate). Maitland and Lady Mary never met again. Maitland died in 1748 in relative obscurity and was buried in Scotland alongside his parents. He described himself on his headstone as a *chirugeon*, still just a humble surgeon.

It was not until the end of the century, after Lady Mary's death, that Edward Jenner took the fight against smallpox to the next stage. In 1798 the medicalisation of the process he himself had had to undergo when he was inoculated motivated him to devise something easier and safer. Like Mary before him, he felt that doctors were not helping matters. The medicalisation of inoculation had only increased in the years since 1721. Jenner noted that milkmaids hardly ever suffered from the smallpox and he realised that inoculation from the pustules of cows who were suffering from cowpox - vaccination- rather than from human smallpox pustules - would work just as well. The process of vaccination as opposed to inoculation could then be used in the fight against many other diseases, rather than simply against smallpox.

In the meantime, in 1755 the College of Physicians publicly endorsed inoculation against the smallpox for the first time, but by then Mary was living far away in mainland Europe. In 1745 the first smallpox hospital had been set up in two houses just south of Pentonville Road in London. Later it was moved to Battle Bridge, the site of present-day Kings Cross Station. Mary's fellow-traveller Aaron Hill wrote a pamphlet praising the contribution of 'this Ornament of her Sex, and Country'. He described the Muses begging Apollo to bestow the art of inoculation on Mary as a gift, as if she were simply a passive recipient rather than the instigator of the campaign. The Muses, like old women and spinsters, were envious of Mary's beauty, wrote Hill.[17] By the 1750s Sir Hans Sloane had finally clarified to his readers that it was Mary not Wortley, as he had first implied, who was responsible for introducing inoculation. When Mary was an old woman the writer and politician James Burges praised her for 'conferring health and life to thousands, by bringing into her own country a practice, of which ages to come will enjoy the benefit.'[18]

In 1767, five years after Mary's death, a poem called *The Triumph of Inoculation, a Dream* appeared anonymously. It described a fictional landscape devastated by smallpox and Lady Mary leading through it the allegorical figure Variola, who brought health to all who came across her. The author claimed that he had sent Lady Mary the poem and she approved it, although nothing in Mary's existing papers confirms this. In 1789 Henrietta Inge, Mary's great niece and a descendant of Sister Gower, had a monument erected to her aunt in Lichfield Cathedral: 'To perpetuate the Memory of such Benevolence/And to express her Gratitude/For the benefit She herself has received/From this alleviating art.'[19] The monument still stands today. Mary herself would probably have been most pleased by Oliver Goldsmith's play *She Stoops to Conquer* of 1773 where the character of Mrs Hardcastle remarks: 'I vow, since inoculation began, there is no such thing to be seen as a plain woman.'[20] Smallpox represented potential death but for Mary it also represented a loss of beauty. It may have made her plain, but it made her bold.

Chapter 8

Friends and More-Than Friends

'I have a burning desire to see your Soul stark naked'[1]

Mary and Wortley were catapulted back into London life. Wortley immediately resumed his career as the member of parliament for Westminster and threw himself back into the family mining business. Mary's role was less circumscribed. Although her relationship with Pope had been shaken, she maintained her literary friendships. Her reputation as one of the cleverest women of her generation was enhanced by her compiling and circulating a collection of the letters she had written during their Turkish trip. Her circle was artistic and bohemian, but she also kept close ties to government and court. Friends and acquaintances included poets, politicians and peers of the realm, ranging from an elderly feminist bluestocking to a celebrated Italian castrato. As soon as Mary and Wortley returned, they needed to find somewhere to live. They decided on renting a house in Covent Garden and in time they added a second home, just outside London in the village of Twickenham. For the next twenty-one years, from 1718 to 1739, this would be the shape of Mary's life.

The rental on the new house in Covent Garden piazza was £125 per year (about £20,000 today). Covent Garden was the area of London where Mary's parents had been lodging when she was born, and it was also close to the rooms in Catherine Street where she and Wortley had started their married life. It remained a marginal district, packed with theatres and taverns and where residents always needed to be mindful of pickpockets. Their friend James Craggs was a neighbour, as was Mary's Uncle Feilding. Having already shown her enthusiasm and flair for interior design in Pera and at Middlethorpe Hall, Mary set to work. The fashions she had come across on her travels clearly influenced her ideas for her new home.

With Sister Mar abroad, Mary's relations with her own family remained poor. Her other sister, Sister Gower, remained as semi-detached as ever. Mary's father would be a distant figure for the rest of his life. In a family anecdote, her daughter, little Mary, was playing as a child in her mother's dressing room when a forbidding male figure, 'still handsome', burst in. This was Kingston, the grandfather whom little Mary had never met. He had 'the authoritative air of a person entitled to admittance at all times', and little Mary's mother, Lady Mary, taken by surprise, fell to her knees in front of him, 'with her hair about her ears'.[2] It would be the only time they ever met in private. Kingston's second wife, Isabella, had given birth to a daughter by the time the Wortley Montagus returned from Turkey. A second would follow. There would be no further male heir. On Kingston's death, the dukedom would pass to Mary's nephew, the son of her brother William, who had died of smallpox. Mary at least found some familial support from Lady Denbigh, her dead mother's stepmother. Lady Denbigh pronounced that she would very much like to see Mary's children. They only visited once though. Lady Denbigh died at the end of the year, aged 96.

The political situation in England on the Wortley Montagus' return was clouded by the recent rift between King George I and his son's family, the Waleses. Mary soon found herself attending social occasions hosted by both sides, but she was still not a natural courtier. Politically, she remained a friend and supporter of Sir Robert Walpole, who was in opposition at this point but whose star continued to shine. She found herself agreeing with Walpole's analysis that George, the Prince of Wales, and his wife, Princess Caroline of Ansbach, represented the future. Soon Mary took Walpole's advice and stopped frequenting George I's *soirées*. Instead, in the summer of 1720, when she received word from Princess Caroline that the royal couple would be spending the summer in Richmond and hoped to see Lady Mary there, she gratefully accepted the invitation.

Wortley's friendship with Addison never recovered from his being recalled from Turkey. With his friend occupying the key role of secretary of state in the new government and Walpole out of office, Wortley must have hoped for another proper public position, but nothing concrete was forthcoming. Addison died the year after they arrived back, and his death brought Walpole to power. From then on Wortley's political ambitions were in effect at an end. In 1722 Wortley would give up representing

Westminster and become member of parliament for Huntingdon, a seat controlled by his cousin, the Earl of Sandwich. In 1734 he swapped seats again and began representing Peterborough. In time he would become almost totally inactive in the Commons, but he held onto the role for the rest of his life for the social status it gave him.

Wortley was increasingly involved in the family coal mining business. He and Mary had pinned their hopes on Wortley inheriting a title from his cousin, Lord Hinchingbrooke, but soon after their return Lady Hinchingbrooke gave birth to a baby son. Wortley would travel north from London to reach the family coal mines, staying either with his uncle Dean John Montagu at Durham or with his father at Wharncliffe Lodge. The journey, which he routinely did on horseback, would normally take nine days. Sidney, Wortley's father, was a hard taskmaster. The mining industry was tough and uncompromising, physically harsh for the miners themselves but also for the mine-owners. Industrial relations, price wars, fatal accidents and the threat of potential take-overs from other owners now occupied Wortley's every waking hour. Mary rarely if ever went north with her husband, but they corresponded while he was away as they had done in the early years of their marriage.

Mary preferred to cultivate her own role as one of the cleverest women of her generation. She continued to be celebrated for her intellect and her learning. The ubiquitous Edmund Curll published an anthology of contemporary authors' work, but he headed Mary's poem which he had included, as 'By a Lady', rather than naming her. He was well aware of the social stigma for a woman of Mary's class of being published commercially. Thomas Burnet circulated a poem which he claimed had come to him from Parnassus, 'made upon a Lady that is famous for Reading.' In it the poet praised Mary's beauty and wit but also gave a warning that if men disliked Eve for tasting one apple of the tree of knowledge, there would inevitably be much more anger for someone who had tasted the whole tree. When the poem was attributed to Pope, he did not deny it.[3]

Mary was the proud owner of many books, including poetry, drama and prose. She could read English and French and owned books written in both languages. Since her teenage years exploring the library at Thoresby, she had always had a special interest in work written by women. She also collected works by her many literary friends, Pope and Congreve among them. Her own reputation as a writer continued to grow.

Encouraged by her older friend and mentor, Mary Astell, she began collecting her correspondence from the time in Turkey, editing her writing to form her *Embassy Letters*. These and much of the poetry she wrote she made sure were circulated among her friends. One of the letters she had written from Turkey to Abbé Conti appeared in print in an unauthorised version. At least by editing and circulating her *Embassy Letters* herself, she kept editorial control.

Mary continued to develop her friendships with other writers. When Voltaire visited England in May 1726, he sought out Lady Mary, just as he visited Pope and Gay. Voltaire had been writing an essay in English on Milton and he showed it to Mary. After reading a few pages she told him she could not believe he could have written it. The English was too good to be by him but too bad for an established English writer to have been the author. She made sure to buy two copies of Voltaire's epic poem *Henriade* for her growing book collection. She also became a literary patron to younger writers, notably to her cousin, Henry Fielding. With her help, Fielding had his first play accepted at Drury Lane Theatre. His second play *The Modern Husband* was about difficulties within marriage. Mary helped him by having some creative input into the creation of one of the characters, Lady Charlotte Gaywit. In thanks, the following year he dedicated his anonymous adaptation of one of Moliere's comedies to her.

Mary was also known as a great wit. She had unparalleled powers of perception and was often bold enough to say the unsayable. She was visited one day by a lady wearing a pair of diamond earrings. Everybody knew the earrings had been given in exchange for securing a place for someone at court. As Mary rationalised it to a friend, 'How would you have people know where wine is to be sold, unless there is a sign hung out?'[4] Another time she wrote to Sister Mar about a woman named Jane Lowther who had been told a man 'dyed' to see her and waited in vain to receive him. Several ballads circulated about such an unattractive woman desperate for a man and Mary wrote a poem in the person of Jane Lowther, poking gentle fun at her situation: 'I'm now abandoned, though I once was Fair.'[5]

In March 1719, Pope began renting a house in Twickenham, just outside London. He had been planning the move for some time. The river setting and the proximity to the city made it a perfect retreat from the dirt and grime of the capital. Mary and Wortley soon visited Pope there and during their stay they decided to find a house of their own. Negotiations began to rent a property named Savile House from Sir Godfrey Kneller, the portrait painter, who himself owned a grand estate in Twickenham. Savile House had been built in Queen Anne's reign in the flat outskirts of the village, not far from the Thames, a short walk from Pope's villa. A door through a brick wall at the bottom of the garden led towards Pope's house and the river. Wortley initially put up obstacles when it came to negotiating terms on Savile House. He wanted a short lease, he explained. But Kneller stood his ground and Wortley capitulated in favour of a long one. Mary may well have forced his hand. The couple would go on to buy Savile House from Kneller in 1722 and would live between their two homes, one in London and one in Twickenham, for the next twenty years.

With the more leisured life that Twickenham offered, an all-consuming craze for gardening developed among its inhabitants. Pope began creating his famous garden the autumn after he moved in, delighted by his 'enchanted bowers'.[6] In time he would also build a grotto there, decorated with shells, mirrors and pebbles. The Prince and Princess of Wales enjoyed their garden at Richmond, where they were now spending every summer. Mary too became a passionate enthusiast. She wrote to her sister in France that she was forever riding past all the nursery gardens which bordered the road between London and Twickenham, presumably dreaming up planting schemes. As yet there was no bridge to cross the Thames between London and Twickenham but there was a ferry which operated in the summer months. In Twickenham Mary found herself very contented with all things domestic. Her older friend, Mary Astell, praised her skills in drawing, singing, cutting paper patterns and sewing. She gave equal weight, as Mary Astell put it, to 'the Pen and Needle'.[7] Lady Mary also loved riding in Richmond Park whenever she was in Twickenham and often went hunting there with the royal staghounds.

Mary's friendship with Pope continued, facilitated by their proximity in Twickenham. In 1720 Gay wrote a celebration in verse of Pope's having completed his translation of *The Iliad*. He described a troop of Pope's lady admirers and Mary as being one with particularly distinctive eyes. In response Pope wrote his poem *To Mr Gay* in which he described the melancholy he felt at being alone: 'Joy lives not here; to happier seats it flies/And only dwell where Wortley casts her eyes.'[8] He likened himself to a deer struck down by an arrow, bleeding to death drop by drop.

At one level this was simply a literary joke between two friends but at another it employed humour to express Pope's true feelings. Mary and Pope would still often read poetry together. He showed their mutual friend Lord Bathurst (who had been involved in the inoculation battle when his servant had died) his beautiful manuscript of their *Town Eclogues*. He wrote again to Lord Bathurst in the summer of 1721 recounting that he and Mary had walked around his garden together. By the following spring, however, Mary wrote to Sister Mar that she only saw Pope very infrequently.

In early 1720 Pope commissioned Sir Godfrey Kneller to paint Mary's portrait wearing westernised Turkish dress. Kneller, who was 74 at this stage and no longer painting full time, probably agreed as a favour to Pope. Mary must have chosen to wear clothing she owned herself, inspired by what she had seen worn in Turkey. The painting started a fashion in London to dress *en turque* and for decorative items with a Turkish theme. Mary was portrayed without her pock marks and with her eyebrows and eyelashes still extant. Kneller had hoped he could have one sitting with her and then work from memory, but he realised he needed to return to get the likeness of her face correctly. It was Pope who asked permission for this second sitting on his behalf. It was worth it. Mary's face in the painting is particularly beautifully drawn. The picture would hang in Pope's Twickenham house in the 'best room fronting the Thames', until Pope's death.[9]

Although Mary wrote to Sister Mar that she saw Pope 'very seldom',[10] a mutual acquaintance reported that the two were so close that it was the 'talk of the whole town'.[11] In April 1722, Mary wrote to Sister Mar about Pope's grotto in his garden in Twickenham which he had 'furnished with Looking Glass.' 'They tell me it has a very good effect,' she wrote, implying that she had not seen it for herself, contradicting Pope's account of her visit.[12] In the same letter, though, she enclosed the poem Pope had written in answer to Gay's when he praised her eyes and described himself as a wounded deer. Their friendship remained as enigmatic as ever.

In her settled life back in England Lady Mary had time to cultivate several more deep and lasting friendships. She would have known of Mary Astell before the Turkish trip and had read Astell's work when she was a teenager, but now something altogether closer developed between the two women. Mary Astell was twenty-three years older than her young friend, a mother figure for her. The two lived very differently. Mary Astell never married, kept no carriage and lived simply in the relatively undesirable neighbourhood of Chelsea. Her income was a mere £85 to £90 a year (about £14,000 today) whereas Mary's pin money alone, had she done what her father wanted and married the suitor he had in mind for her, would have been £500 a year (approximately £75,000 today). The original bluestocking, Mary Astell believed that women should create societies of their own, away from men. She was critical of Mary's various flirtatious relationships, but she made it clear when it came to writing that she saw Lady Mary as her anointed successor. On four separate occasions she used the image of laying laurels at her young *protegée*'s feet. Lady Mary's *Embassy Letters* were her idea. She was involved in the editing and rewriting that went on and she even contributed a Foreword.

Besides her friendship with Mary Astell, Lady Mary continued her close relationship with her childhood friend and cousin, Henrietta (now Lady Harley, later Lady Oxford). Another friendship which grew stronger on her return was that with Griselda Murray. As Lady Louisa described her, Griselda was 'very pretty, very agreeable, and very generally admired'.[13] She and Lady Mary would have known each other before the Turkish trip but when Mary returned, Griselda was separated from her husband, childless, and living back with her parents. Scottish by birth, Griselda's family were descended from Covenanters and part of the Whig elite in Scotland. They had narrowly escaped prosecution after the first Jacobite Rebellion. It was Griselda's mother, Lady Grizell, who had written so critically of Lady Mary's relationship with Pope. Griselda often invited Mary to dine at her parents' house. The differences of opinion politically did not prevent the friendship growing.

At the time Griselda was having an affair with the Reverend Gilbert Burnet, the son of the Bishop of Salisbury whom Mary had sought to impress while exiled at West Dean. In October 1721, the newspapers reported a shocking incident. Arthur Gray, the footman at Griselda's parents' house, entered Griselda's bedroom and reportedly attempted to rape her, armed with pistols and a drawn sword. The family decided to go to the press, perhaps motivated by their insecure social position as Covenanters. When the case came to court, Arthur Gray's defence was that he suspected the Reverend Burnet was with Griselda that evening and that he had wanted to protect Griselda's virtue. But the court did not believe him and on 9 December he was sentenced to be hanged. At the last minute, Griselda's family intervened and a couple of weeks later he was instead deported to America. Mary would use Griselda's rape as the inspiration for at least one, probably two poems.

Lady Mary could have chosen as friends a conventional group of aristocratic young marrieds just like herself, but she was attracted to something rather different. The friendships she cultivated on her return, with Griselda and with others, tended to be with social outsiders. Another such friend was Claude-Charlotte, Countess of Stafford. Some twenty years older than Mary, Claude-Charlotte was French by birth. Mary said that her friend 'knew me better than anybody else in the world.'[14] The two met in 1720 when Nicolas-Francois Rémond introduced them during one of his visits to England. Claude-Charlotte inspired in Lady Mary a love for all things French and a pride in being European. Witty but not beautiful, Claude-Charlotte had met and married the much older 10th Earl of Stafford while he was living in France, but their marriage went wrong. When he died in 1719, she decided to come to England with her lover of the time, Lord Peterborough. Gossip had it that they would marry but in 1722 he secretly took as his wife the alto singer Anastasia Robinson, who had been lodging with Lady Mary in Twickenham. The friendship between Mary and Claude-Charlotte survived this heartache and they remained the greatest of friends until Claude-Charlotte's death in 1739.

Another friend, Maria Skerrett, was also an unusual choice as a close friend. Maria was the daughter of a London merchant of Irish origins, very different from Mary's own family. The two were introduced by Claude-Charlotte in 1720 when Maria was 18 and Mary 31. The age difference, too, made it an imbalanced friendship. The young woman immediately reminded Mary of Sister Mar at that age. By September 1721, Mary had moved 'my little thread satin Beauty' into her home in Twickenham, as a companion rather than a friend. They spent their time reading and walking together.[15] The two singers, Anastasia Robinson (who would marry Lord Peterborough) and the Italian castrato Senesino, were lodging with Mary in Twickenham at the same time. Maria had a beautiful voice, so Mary started holding musical supper parties at which all three would sing. When Pope loaned her the use of his harpsichord, they began using the gallery in his house for impromptu concerts.

Ironically given what was to take place, the thing Mary initially found most appealing about Maria Skerrett was her unworldliness. She wrote: 'I remember my contracting an intimacy with a girl in a village as the most distant thing on earth from power and politics. Fortune tosses her up (in a double sense).'[16] What fortune tossed up for Maria was a meeting with the prime minister, Sir Robert Walpole, almost certainly through Lady Mary. Twenty-six years older than Maria, Walpole was at the peak of his success at the time and hugely preoccupied with building his vast country estate of Houghton Hall in Norfolk. He was unhappily married to Catherine Walpole, overweight and spoke with a Norfolk accent. Mary wrote a poem *A Man in Love* about the intensity of Walpole's feelings for Maria, causing him to shun all other pleasures. In another poem, *The Lover - a Ballad* she imagined herself in Maria's shoes, chastely scorning other lovers and holding out for an impossibly perfect man, while meeting with Walpole over 'Champagne and a Chicken' for a few happy hours. Maria probably sent the second to Sir Robert.[17] Both poems hint at the key role Mary played as Maria's confidante.

Maria became Walpole's mistress towards the end of 1724. He would remain faithful to her for the rest of her life. He set her up in a house in Richmond Park, not far from Mary, who could visit whenever she was riding there. He began pressurising Princess Caroline to have Maria received at court. In 1725 Maria gave birth to their first daughter, but little evidence remains of their relationship and both parties were careful to burn their correspondence. In August 1737, Catherine Walpole died and Walpole immediately proposed to Maria. They were married in March 1738. Apparently, the night before the wedding Walpole insisted that Maria destroy a whole trunk full of Lady Mary's letters. To Walpole's despair, Maria died in childbirth only three months after the wedding. He suffered a severe depression at her loss.

Another new friend of Lady Mary's at the time was Philip, Duke of Wharton. An unstable character, Wharton rented James Craggs' former house in Twickenham from 1722, after Craggs died from smallpox in the outbreak of 1721. Wharton soon began organising masked balls. Mary enjoyed these enormously, despite the scandal they attracted. 'We wild Girls always make your prudent Wives and mothers,' she defended herself to Sister Mar.[18] Wharton and Mary became literary sparring partners, initially causing Pope great pangs of jealousy. Pope noted that Wharton's undoing was his need of praise from 'Women and Fools'.[19]

Mary wrote at least two poems for the duke, one about male infidelity and the other comparing Elizabeth I with Mary Queen of Scots. Wharton was a Jacobite, hence Mary's linking him to the Catholic, Scottish queen. Elizabeth I triumphs in the poem. Mary repeated the phrase she had used in her poem *Saturday* in the *Town Eclogues:* 'Monarchs and Beauties rule in equal sway,' but here she sided with Elizabeth's power over Mary Queen of Scots' beauty.[20] Wharton and Lady Mary had a tempestuous friendship. There were frequent quarrels and frequent *rapprochements*.

The final significant friendship of Lady Mary's which began to flourish at this time and which would last for the rest of their lives - always a platonic one - was with the courtier John (later Lord) Hervey, 'amphibious thing' as Pope called him.[21] Good-looking, aristocratic, eloquent, charming and witty, Hervey was superbly placed to shine both at court and in political life. Hervey's mother, Lady Bristol, was already a friend of Lady Mary's. Lady Bristol doted on her oldest son but disliked her daughter-in-law, Molly Lepell. Lady Mary remained cordial to both parties, but she found a twin soul in Hervey rather than in his wife or mother. In summer 1720 Mary wrote that the newly-weds Hervey and Molly were constant visitors at her house in Twickenham, 'perpetually cooing' in her rooms.[22]

Hervey was also bisexual, something Mary never openly acknowledged. Like most of the society in which she lived, Mary regarded homosexuality as something which existed, but which was not to be talked about. Hervey was unusual in that he was very open about his long love affair with Stephen Fox, known as Ste, and dropped broad hints about it to Mary. Very few of his letters even acknowledge Molly his wife or their many children, but they are full of protestations of his love for Ste. When Hervey eventually broke with Ste he confided in Mary about his feelings, how life for him was now merely 'buying mellow apples and mealy potatoes at a guinea a piece instead of a penny a dozen.'[23] As Mary put it: 'this world consisted of men and women and Herveys.' In turn he described her as 'one of the most agreeable things (the world) contains.'[24]

As well as his relationship with Stephen Fox, Hervey kept a mistress, Anne Vane. In the summer of 1732 Prince Frederick Lewis, George II's oldest son, whom Maitland had travelled out to Hanover to inoculate, also started an affair with Anne. Although Hervey had officially finished his own relationship with Anne, he reacted badly to this news.

In support of her friend, Mary wrote a bawdy ballad about the situation. She portrayed the prince as a puppy playing with a cracked bottle (a not wholly sisterly description of another woman) while Hervey stood innocently by, getting bitten when he attempted to untie the bottle. Mary and Hervey also agreed politically, whereas Mary and Wortley increasingly disagreed. Walpole was now dominating the political scene and both Hervey and Mary supported him strongly. Wortley did not. In 1733 when Walpole introduced his unpopular Excise Bill, Hervey spoke in its defence in parliament while Wortley spoke against it.

By 1724, Mary was 35 years old. She wrote to Sister Mar that she disliked 'the damn'd damn'd quality of growing older and older every day', and that her 'present joys are made imperfect by fears of the future.'[25] She had quarrelled with Wharton, and although their rows were fairly frequent this seemed more of a rupture than usual. She was frustrated by Sister Mar's failure to respond to her letters, not having yet grasped the reason for this silence. She and Griselda Murray had also recently fallen out very publicly. She found the quarrels between Lady Bristol and Molly Lepell, Hervey's wife, hard to bear. And there was a tiny hint of a spurned love interest. She mentioned in a letter to Sister Mar that she met Lord Irwin at a masked ball and that he was both witty and 'Diabolical', and someone 'who 'tis impossible to love and impossible not to be entertained with.'[26] Arthur Ingram, Viscount Irwin, was the same age as Mary and would never marry. Another letter to Sister Mar dropped heavy hints that her sex life with Wortley was non-existent. The world, she wrote to Sister Mar, was like as a Dutch cheese and the people in it merely mites. If a great rat came along and ate up half of it, she would be relatively relaxed.

The following year, Wortley's father died. Wortley's immediate response was that the family should move to Yorkshire. Mary disagreed. She refused to live at Wharncliffe Lodge, or at Wortley Hall, the grand house in the village itself, which Wortley's father, Sidney, had always let out. She would only move to the house Sidney had built for his mistress at nearby St Ellen's Well. For understandable reasons this was unacceptable to Wortley. Perhaps this was a ploy on Mary's part to squash any talk of moving north. Instead in 1731 Wortley and Mary gave up their house in Covent Garden Piazza and moved to Cavendish Square, where they became neighbours of Mary's old friend Henrietta, Lady Oxford.

The twenty years living between London and Twickenham were peopled for Mary with these many friends. Some were lost. Claude-Charlotte and Maria Skerrett both died within a few months of each other. Her friendship with Pope was lost for other reasons, as was the one with Griselda Murray. The relationship with Hervey weathered two crises but survived them both. Mary's mentor Mary Astell died of breast cancer in 1731. She fought the disease with enormous courage. When she was given the diagnosis, she agreed to have one of her breasts removed to try to stop the cancer spreading. The operation without anaesthetic must have been unbearably painful. She only lived two months more. As she lay dying, she summoned Lady Mary to her bedside and confessed that she knew her days were numbered. If God permitted such things, Mary Astell told her, then she promised she would appear to Lady Mary as a ghost, such were the ties that bound them. Sadly, Mary Astell's ghost never did haunt Lady Mary.

Chapter 9

The South Sea Bubble Crisis

'I thought I had managed prodigious well'[1]

Mary had acquired a second over-enthusiastic, unwanted admirer, different from Pope but just as difficult to manage. This was Nicolas-Francois Rémond, the Frenchman she had met in Paris, who now sent her increasingly passionate letters. The highly educated, manipulative Rémond was well-known for his social snobbery, for his love of all things English and for his habit of extracting money from his friends. 'Think of me sometimes and be assured that no woman has ever been loved as much as I love you,' he wrote to her in 1719.[2] In December he wrote again, ruminating on the difference between the French verb *aimer* and the English 'to love'. The relationship with Rémond was destined to cause her lasting damage.

That spring Rémond wrote Mary three more letters. He spelled out that he longed to spend his life by her side. For the first time he mentioned that she had given him some financial advice 'to guarantee my little tottering fortune'.[3] Both sides of the channel were fascinated by all things financial that year. Get-rich-quick schemes abounded, and people loved to gamble on the lotteries which the governments ran as a way of making money. As a clever woman, Mary prided herself on her understanding of the financial markets and had begun helping her friends to make a gain by speculating for them. 'Out of a high point of Generosity (for which I wish myself hanged)', as Mary later put it, she decided that a way of defusing the situation with Rémond might be to talk money with him rather than affairs of the heart.[4] By March 1720, he was already writing about his stocks. He expressed himself astonished at her long silence and claimed that if he were as indiscreet as their mutual friend Abbé Conti he would be thinking of making money by publishing the letters she had written to him. That way, he claimed, he could profit as much as he had done by investing in Mississippi stock. Already, the whiff of blackmail hung in the air.

The Mississippi stock to which Rémond referred was a French scheme created by a Scot named John Law, a 'deity' as Rémond described him when it came to investments. A colourful character, Law had killed his opponent in a duel as a young man in London and been forced into exile, roaming Europe and making a fortune at the gambling tables through putting his mathematical skills to good use. He began to formulate a theory that gold and silver coins should be superseded by paper money and he tried unsuccessfully to encourage several European rulers to adopt it. Finally, he was able to persuade the French regent, the Duke of Orléans, that the way to pay off the French national debt was to print paper money and issue stock. Next Law saw that he could massage the government's debt via a trading entity, the Mississippi Company, promising untold riches to its investors from across the Atlantic. He started issuing shares. Rumours swarmed that there were huge sums to be made in states such as Louisiana and the company's share price exploded. Rémond and many other French and foreign investors had speculated in Law's Mississippi Company. By the end of 1719 shares were selling for thirty times their original value.

Inspired by what was happening in their rival France, the English began a scheme of their own. While John Law led the charge in France, John Blunt was his equivalent on this side of the channel. A Baptist by birth, the fat, pompous, self-made Blunt was also charming and energetic, with an uncanny ability to make money. In May 1711, he formed the English equivalent of the Mississippi Company, which he named the South Sea Company, with its motto 'From Cadiz to the Dawn'. In France there was at least a theoretical chance that there were gains to be made in the Mississippi. That was quickly not the case for the English in the south seas. The government signed the Treaty of Utrecht less than two years after Blunt set up the South Sea Company and ceded all trading rights in the area to Spain and Portugal. Undeterred, Blunt transformed his South Sea Company into a vehicle whereby investors could buy into the national debt instead. He created the Sword Blade Bank as the engine-room for the whole process and opened a smart new building, South Sea House, in the city of London.

In November 1719 George I lectured parliament on the need to sort out the country's finances. At £31 million pounds (about £4.5 billion today) government debt was too high, he told them. Blunt came up with an offer to solve this problem. He would pay the government for the privilege of buying the entire national debt, he said. He would then issue shares to lay off this debt, in a sort of futures exchange where investors' money would be redeemed twenty-five years later. He had a further wheeze, too. If his investors were short of cash, they need not necessarily lay out any in order to buy into the scheme. Instead they could be granted rights in the stock and then sell once the market had risen. At that point they would pay back their South Sea Company loans and pocket the profit - providing, that is, the market kept rising. If the government were to adopt Blunt's scheme, in one stroke the South Sea Company would become larger than the entire Bank of England. Blunt needed support from members of parliament to pass the legislation which would permit the South Sea Company to start issuing shares, but understandably they hesitated.

Blunt's tactic to get parliament to approve his scheme was simple. He set about bribing its members. He handed out up to £1 million worth of stock to oil the political wheels (£146 million today). By January 1720, Robert Walpole had acquired £18,000 worth of shares in the South Sea Company (£2.5 million today) and sold them for £24,383 (£3.6 million today). Yet, as the bill to issue shares in the national debt made its way through parliament, Walpole began to get cold feet. In March, he put forward a motion to try to limit the South Sea Company's powers. At the beginning of April, the shares were standing at £325 (£47,000 today). When the South Sea Bill duly went before parliament it was passed by a majority of ninety-six. South Sea stock then rose steeply. On 7 April 1720, the bill was given royal assent. At this point Sir Isaac Newton sold his entire £7,000 holding (£1.1 million today) and doubled his money. Meanwhile in France, Mississippi stock was already starting to fall.

On 14 April 1720, Blunt offered £2 million worth of new stock (£2.8 billion today) at the market price of £300 (£44,000 today), in what was called the 'First Money Subscription'. If subscribers were short of cash, they were only required to pay for twenty per cent in advance. The rest could be paid back over two months, by which time it looked likely that the market would have risen. Blunt also secretly expanded the issue by another £2.25 million (£3.3 billion today). Then on 30 April 1720, he promoted the 'Second Money Subscription', offering a further

£1 million in stock (£1.4 billion today). By early May all this activity had caused the share price to shoot up dramatically. It now stood at £500 (£73,000 today) and was continuing to rise. That month Rémond arrived in London, partly to satisfy his curiosity about the South Sea Company and partly to see Lady Mary. During his first fortnight in London, Rémond was disappointed to catch a glimpse of her only once, at a supper party. She spent the evening chattering excitedly with her friends, caught up in the South Sea Company bonanza. He did not get a chance to speak to her at all and wrote to a friend complaining about the situation. He had hoped to seek her advice on how he could get accepted onto the list of investors for the South Sea Company. He needed to get to Lady Mary.

Blunt knew he had to have another share launch to keep the whole scheme buoyant. On 15 June 1720 he announced the 'Third Money Subscription', pitched extremely high at £1,000 (£146,800 today) and again with superbly generous purchase terms. Few could resist. Even the sceptical Walpole bought more shares, as did the king. London society was morphing before everyone's eyes as fortunes were made overnight and conspicuous consumption abounded. As the *Original Weekly Journal* put it: 'The City ladies buy South Sea jewels, hire South Sea maids, and take new country South Sea Houses.'[5] One of those bribed by the South Sea Company was Mary's friend, James Craggs. He raised nearly £750,000 in subscriptions (£110 million today) and laid them off with friends. He then set about purchasing for himself an entire terrace of houses in Whitehall, so he could demolish them and build a smart new home.

Mary provided her services as an intermediary so James Craggs could lay off some of his investments. Her plan was to help her friends and relatives invest in the scheme and benefit from it. The market had not yet been regulated, so women could speculate on the same terms as men. Mary's friend Mary Astell wrote 'we hear no more of Lady Mary Wortley's Wit but of her Bargains.'[6] Mary Astell mistrusted the whole situation. Lady Mary wrote to her Sister Gower's mother-in-law in June 1720, confirming that she had arranged to have £5,000 of stock set aside for Lady Catherine (£734,000 today), providing only that the older lady pay £500 immediately (£73,000 today). This was probably one of several transactions of this sort Mary arranged. She may well have bought some stock for herself and she perhaps also used her influence to get Rémond onto the list of subscribers. However he managed it, Rémond was able to buy £2,000 worth of stock in this issue (£294,000 today), when it was already proving difficult to source.

In July, Rémond wrote Mary another of his over-familiar letters. He pressed her for financial input: 'you who are the advisor of the most enlightened people.' Should he sell for a modest profit immediately or should he hold on in the hope of a larger one? He longed to discuss all this, but it was difficult to talk to her, he complained. While he was waiting, he would try to find some more cash, to prevent his being struck off the list. 'I beg you for an interview because I don't understand anything about all this,' he admitted, 'and I am more inclined to have faith in you than in anyone.'[7] Mary continued to escape his clutches. Then by chance he was walking in the park in London when he bumped into Sister Mar, who was on her way to church. She was in London trying to defuse the increased tension between her father and her husband over the Mar estates, which had been frozen while the Mars were in exile. Rémond knew nothing of this, and it did not interest him. Delighted to see her, he would not let this golden opportunity slip from his grasp. He waited at her house until she returned. He had found a means of getting to Lady Mary.

Mary was cornered. She had no option but to give Rémond the financial guidance he was seeking. He should sell early, she told him, and claim his profit. As it turned out, this was very sensible advice. He did as she suggested and made a total of £840 (£123,000 today), an approximate forty per cent profit on his initial investment. To her enormous relief he headed back to France in early August, with many 'tears and grimaces'. Only once he was back in France did he learn the full extent of the disaster that the Mississippi scheme now represented there. The share price had catapulted, the economy had faltered and there were bankruptcies wherever Rémond looked. Before he left England, though, he had made Mary promise to reinvest his £840 for him. He had very little money to his name, he told her, and this was a relatively small sum, but all he wanted in the world was to buy a little estate and retire. If that was the case, then he would be foolish to risk it all on the South Sea Company again, Mary advised. He refused to listen. He would rather have double or quit. She was to reinvest it for him.[8]

Everyone knew there would be another subscription very soon. On 18 July 1720, Mary had written to James Craggs, begging him to have her name entered on the next list of subscribers. He wrote back formally ten days later. He would add her name, but he could not guarantee that the directors would take it up, he explained. Even before the subscription opened, the stock had risen to £900 (£132,000 today). On 22 August, Pope wrote to Mary pressing her to invest. He had learned the previous night that there would be a certain gain in a matter of weeks, he reported, adding: 'I can be as sure of this, as the nature of any such thing will allow.'[9] Even though Walpole had opposed the South Sea Bill, he also still decided to invest in this fourth subscription. Luckily for him, by chance his banker delayed and failed to get him onto the list. This would mean that Walpole could argue forever afterwards that he was relatively untarnished by the debacle that followed. By the time John Blunt offered this final subscription he already knew that the stock was at much too high a price. There was not enough cash in circulation in the economy to support it. The price would inevitably soon start to fall. Nevertheless, on 24 August 1720, Blunt opened the 'Fourth Money Subscription', and it was immediately sold out. Mary must have counted herself lucky to be admitted to the list. As promised, she reinvested Rémond's £840 two or three days before the subscription closed. Sister Mar went with her to pay Rémond's funds in at the broker's office. As Pope put it: 'the scent of money was in the air like the breath of spring.'[10]

Mary thought she had done well when she sold out Rémond's holding the very next day, still for a small profit, to the goldsmiths Cox and Cleeve. When she went to collect the money, though, she was alarmed to find they had absconded. Against her wishes, Mary still had ownership of Rémond's stock. And now the price was beginning to fall. As soon as the subscription was announced, it dropped to £820 (£120,000 today). A week later it was £700 (£103,000 today). Then it slumped to £400 (£59,000 today). Mary wrote to Rémond immediately explaining what had happened and asking what he would like done with the remaining assets. We have her account of events from the letter she wrote to Sister Mar the following spring when the South Sea Bubble had well and truly burst, justifying all her actions. He wrote back. If she ever came to France, he would treat her better than she had treated him. Choosing a metaphor to match the times, he proclaimed he would 'love you without exacting any return'.[11] If only.

People in Paris were beginning to mistrust the supposed success of the South Sea Company. From across the Channel, Rémond did not know the true state of the falling share price, of course. This made him wonder 'whether Mr Montagu could be persuaded to realise straight away'. With an uncanny ability to find the weak spot, he wrote as if Mary were acting with Wortley's full knowledge. In fact, nothing could be farther from the truth. Wortley, who was in London or in Newcastle while Mary was in Twickenham, knew nothing of what she had been doing. The Frenchman signed off airily: 'you both have common sense and judgement. I don't think you err through recklessness. Only receive this little hint as a proof of my attachment.'[12]

The South Sea stock continued to fall. On 1 September, John Blunt suggested to the directors that they raise yet another subscription. For the first time they resisted. By 10 September, the stock price, which in June had been as high as £1050 (£154,000 today) fell to £180 (£26,000 today). The bubble had burst. On 24 September, John Blunt's Sword Blade Bank, the engine of the whole South Sea enterprise, closed its doors for the last time. The stock was now worth nothing. Entire fortunes had been lost overnight. Those who had been encouraged to borrow now had nothing with which to make their repayments. Beyond the personal tragedies, which were everywhere, the country itself was bankrupt. Distraught at what it had unleashed, the government tried to hide the truth from George I, who was safely in his beloved Hanover, enjoying his summer break. They delayed the autumn recall of parliament, stalling for time. When George finally arrived back on November 10, he found the country in meltdown. Parliament, including Wortley, who was MP for Huntingdon at the time, finally met again on 8 December 1720. The king needed their support. For their part, they were determined to flex their muscles and punish the guilty. They decided the first thing to do was to hold an enquiry into how and why this had happened.

In January 1721, the House of Commons held a secret ballot to elect the Committee of Secrecy. All thirteen members were independent-minded figures, known for calling a spade a spade, men whom the commons felt they could trust to get to the truth. Wortley was one of them. On January 14 the committee began their hearings, determined to get to the truth. They based themselves in South Sea House itself and sat for fourteen hours a day, six days a week, taking evidence. The hearings would last until June 1721 and the committee produced seven reports during this period. What made the committee's work so important and so delicate was that, although parliament had set up the Committee of Secrecy, parliament itself was also implicated. After all, parliament had voted through the South Sea Bill. More than 450 MPs held South Sea stock. Four MPs were even directors of the South Sea Company. Blunt and his fellow directors, including those who were MPs, were all arrested. Blunt came before the Committee of Secrecy to answer their questions on 27 January.

While Wortley was hard at work hearing evidence on the enormous scale of the fraud which had been perpetrated, Mary was struggling with her own South Sea problems. She still had Rémond's now-worthless stock. Since he had stressed that the sums involved were relatively small, she decided to do nothing until she heard from Rémond himself. In January 1721, just as Wortley was appointed to the Secrecy Committee, Rémond wrote to her, accusing her of tricking him. He was sure she had not invested his money but had kept it untouched. Unless she returned his entire £840 in cash then he had decided he would ensure Wortley knew what was going on and make good his previous threat of publishing all her letters to him. Mary panicked. She knew she did not have any money to return. Plus, any published letters from her advising Rémond to invest could compromise Wortley's position as well as her own.

On 16 February 1721, the committee published its first report into the full scale of the fraud. It was evident that stock had been sold by John Blunt and by Robert Knight, his cashier at the Sword Blade Bank, even before the South Sea Bill had become law. When one of the committee queried their methods Knight had told them: 'it was a transaction of a private nature, and that a great part of it was disposed of to persons of distinction.'[13] In other words, the entire establishment, including many members of parliament, had been given preferential treatment. The committee found themselves having to tread a delicate line between on the one hand finding and punishing the perpetrators and on the other protecting their friends and colleagues. Having given evidence, Robert Knight then fled the country, taking with him his Green Book, the ledger which was the only definitive account of who owed what to whom. Wortley's cousin Lord Hinchingbrooke appeared to give the game away when he said that Blunt should be allowed to keep £10,000 of his own wealth (£1.47 million today), because the Committee of Secrecy had promised him some kind of favour in return for his being open with them. Clearly there had been some kind of plea bargain.

All the more reason for Mary to keep her own situation hidden from Wortley. Writing to Sister Mar in March, she recounted her whole monstrous story. The scales had fallen from her eyes about Rémond, she wrote. Mary did have in her possession a handwritten note from Rémond specifying his instructions to her to invest the money, but she was sufficiently fearful of Rémond's potential to do her damage that even this did not feel adequate ammunition in her defence. She was understandably nervous that Wortley would never forgive her if he discovered what she had been doing. She had witnesses as well, she explained. 'Nothing can be clearer than my integrity in this business,' she wrote, her anxiety showing in her emphasis. It was of paramount importance that Sister Mar try everything she could to make 'the wretch' realise that Mary was speaking the truth when she said the money had all gone. Sister Mar must get hold of all Mary's letters to 'this Mad Man' as soon as she could.[14] Rather than replying to Mary herself, Sister Mar should send anything she obtained to the house of a mutual friend.

Rémond's threats continued throughout the spring of 1721, while Mary existed at a fever-pitch of anxiety and Wortley sat on the Secrecy Committee. Mary now wrote to Rémond begging him to appoint a lawyer to go through her own accounts in detail and see if there were any discrepancies. Rémond decided simply to ignore this offer. He instead demanded £2,000 from her for his lost stock (£294,000 today). For her part Mary valued it at £500 at most (£73,000 today). Even that would be a difficult sum for her to come by, particularly without Wortley finding out what had happened. In June, Rémond upped the stakes even further by sending a letter to Wortley himself, via a mutual friend. Luckily the friend - maybe Claude-Charlotte - saw fit to hand the letter straight to Lady Mary rather than passing it on to Wortley. In May, Claude-Charlotte showed Mary the reply she had received from a letter she herself had written to Rémond several months earlier, asking him to stop harassing her friend. It was evident Rémond had no intention of doing any such thing. Claude-Charlotte wrote back contemptuously, cutting off all communication with 'so despicable a wretch'. Mary became increasingly paranoid that Rémond might simply turn up in London and confront Wortley directly, while she herself was still in Twickenham.[15]

In June 1721, Mary wrote again to her sister: 'For God's sake do something to set my Mind at ease from this business.'[16] Until the crisis was over, she wrote, she was totally obsessed by the nightmare in which she found herself. It felt as if her house were on fire. Mary was someone who normally relished the latest gossip and yet at this moment she was incapable of hearing any news other than her own, she confessed. Appealing to Wortley would not help Rémond's cause. His presence in London would not obtain a farthing more from her than she had already offered. The £500 was fair and she had right on her side. The only explanation she could think of for Rémond's motives was that: 'Fear is his predominant passion.' It was Mary's own fear which seeped through her letters. She complained of 'an Anguish of Mind that visibly decays my body every day'.[17]

Next Mary tried another tack. Perhaps professionals could resolve this seemingly intractable problem. She had already had her broker give a sworn statement before 'a Lawyer of Reputation and Merit', Isaac Delpeche, an eminent notary to the Bank of England, and Rémond's lawyers were free to question her over every part of it. Nevertheless, threatening letters continued to arrive. Mary was as much capable of giving Rémond the £2,000 he asked for as she would be to send him a million, she wrote. She was beginning to think that Rémond was ashamed of all the lies he had told about her. For her part she was prepared to send him the £500 he had initially requested but only on condition he agreed never to contact her again. All she asked for in return was a signed deposition from him, giving up any claim he had over her. Surely this was a reasonable request to protect herself? After that he would be free to tell as many lies about her as he wanted over 'this execrable affair'.[18]

He never sent her the quitclaim she asked for. By September, Mary had consulted Delpeche and he had advised her that it would not be safe to deposit Rémond's £500 with anyone except by express order of Rémond himself. She received no word on this and professed herself sick of the whole situation. In fact, she was beginning to think that, rather than continue like this, she would be prepared to let him keep all her letters after all. Again, she begged Sister Mar to talk to him. Instead in December, Rémond sent her yet another letter continuing to demand his £2,000 and again threatening blackmail. He would ensure all her letters to him were made public, he wrote. The argument had become circular. Even though at some level he must have known she was not to blame, his tactic was to continue behaving as if she were and aggressively trying to extract whatever he could from her.

Some time that autumn, Mary finally confessed all to Wortley. Either Mary gave him the letters or Rémond somehow succeeded in making sure he read them. Exactly what Mary had dreaded for so long now took place. She had to defend herself to her husband. She kept Rémond's letters among her papers and in later years her daughter decided not to destroy them. She must have felt her mother was vindicated. We can only guess if Wortley agreed. The Secrecy Committee had concluded its seven reports and Walpole had ensured his own rise, phoenix-like, from the ashes to lead a new, post-South Sea government. Wortley must have suspected that Walpole had been instrumental in neutralising events. The Secrecy Committee was compromised. They could never get to the whole truth. Even John Blunt only ever suffered a fine of a mere £1,000 (£147,000 today) and retired to Bath to live out the rest of his life there. This turn of events only confirmed Wortley's dislike of Walpole and made him all the more determined to turn his back on politics and concentrate on building up his own personal fortune.

It is difficult with hindsight to judge whether Mary was justified in feeling such terror at Rémond's threats. We do not know what went on between husband and wife when she finally confessed all, but logic would suggest that Wortley was furious at the news. This was a far more personal transgression than the *Town Eclogues* scandal. He must have asked himself whether there was any truth in Rémond's blackmail threats. On the face of it, when it came to the investment of Rémond's money, Mary had not acted improperly. She could argue the logic of every step she took. And yet she felt deeply ashamed and had attempted to keep her actions secret even from her friends. With the whole country reeling from the after-effects of the South Sea Bubble, what she had done made her look foolish and elitist. By contrast the strict Wortley was always ultra-careful with money. This inevitably tainted her in his eyes. Worse of course was that Wortley himself had spent much of the previous year delving into exactly what went wrong over the whole affair. Now to find his wife was implicated must have left a sour taste. A man who prided himself on his principles, Wortley would never forgive Walpole, while Mary by contrast remained a strong supporter of the new prime minister. In this as in many other things, the couple's paths increasingly diverged. When Mary then went on to fall out with Alexander Pope, Pope would also use her part in the South Sea Bubble against her. From Mary's point of view, this was a chapter in her life best kept firmly closed.

Chapter 10

Feminist Writing

'Too, too severely Laws of Honour bind/The Weak Submissive Sex of Woman-Kind'[1]

The women around her and how they lived their lives interested Mary as a writer. She wrote poems, essays and letters about women's lives, focusing on loveless marriages, sexual scandals and extra-marital affairs. Often her writing was simply a creative means of working out her own feelings about how women were being treated. She was critical, sometimes angry, at the ways that men behaved towards women, particularly when the courts passed judgements in favour of men, or when society condemned women for their actions. Her instinct was always to champion the victim, and the victims were nearly always female. Much of this writing was meant only for Mary herself and her close friends. She and Mary Astell often sat together, each writing a poem on the same feminist subject, but some of her writing was more widely circulated and helped enhance Lady Mary's reputation as a writer. She never wrote directly about her own marriage.

At some time before 1732, Mary wrote a confidently argued essay in French entitled *Sur la Maxime de Mr de Rochefoûcault,* in praise of marriage. She argued in favour of the institution, that 'it is married love only which can be delightful to a good mind.'[2] It was to become the piece of writing for which she was most renowned during her lifetime. In the previous century the French essayist, Monsieur de la Rochefoûcault, had written a long piece and Mary was responding to him. Marriage might be a convenient institution, Rochefoûcault argued, but marriages were 'never delightful'. Mary respectfully disagreed. Lasting happiness could only be found if husband and wife became friends, she explained to her readers. A long marriage was 'a life infinitely…more elegant and more pleasurable, than the best conducted and most happy gallantry.' Passion was dangerous and dark, something best avoided. She advised couples against weaponising their words against each other and counselled them to look out for each other's interests. She described Adam and Eve as being governed by passion alone. That was insufficient, she argued, for a lasting relationship. Marriage was for life. Couples were 'united by eternal ties.'[3]

The fame of Mary's essay during her lifetime says much about her readers. They wanted something which eloquently supported the institution of marriage. Mary made sure to take a copy with her when she travelled to Europe ten years or so later and gave it to friends there so they could read and admire it. Mary Astell's ghost may never have haunted Lady Mary as she had wished, but her spirit pervaded Lady Mary's Rochefoûcault essay. Mary Astell's preference was that men and women lived separately, but if not then she approved of her *protegée's* emphasis on marriage as a lifelong bond of mutual respect. Lady Mary's definition of men and women as having distinctively different, complementary roles feels very much something she would have written to please Mary Astell. Since she wrote her response to Rochefoûcault in French, Lady Mary may also have been writing for her friend, Claude-Charlotte. Perhaps the two friends had discussed marriage, particularly since Claude-Charlotte's experience had been a bad one.

Mary ended her essay with a discussion about men and women in Turkey. Whereas in England society tended to condemn women for being unfaithful, Mary explained that in Turkey it was men rather than women who got the blame in these circumstances. Remembering the various discussions she had had when she dined with the *kayha's* wife, Mary wrote frankly about the problems of western women appearing to be sexually available. It was a bad idea, she believed, for a woman: 'to shew her neck in full day; to dress for balls and shows, to attract admirers, and to listen to the idle flattery of a thousand and thousand fops.' The freedoms enjoyed in the west meant that too much temptation was put in the way of seducers. This was the view of her Turkish hostesses and Mary agreed with it. She concluded that it was not surprising that happy marriages were relatively rare in libertarian England, where women could entertain men easily and where wine flowed freely.[4]

Wortley also wrote his own response to the Rochefoûcault essay. In the spring of 1729, he was staying by himself at the spa town of Tunbridge Wells. While he was there, he amused himself by composing a series of *Maxims after Monsieur de la Rochefoûcault*. His maxims were in English, unlike Mary's. Wortley's maxims were far more in tune with Rochefoûcault's. They come across as the work of someone who also saw marriage as convenient rather than delightful. For instance, Wortley's Maxim Number Eleven stated that 'when we think we have the desired security we are apt to lose the Passion.' His Maxim Number Thirty observed, perhaps thinking of his trip back from Turkey with Mary, that: 'the world is like a ship in which a man finds his own cabin too little and seldom agrees to the end of a long voyage with the person lodged next to him.'[5]

The fact that Mary's essay - as the person lodged in the cabin next to Wortley - argued for marriage more strongly than Wortley's does not necessarily mean that she was more in love with the institution than he was. She may well have been writing her piece as a literary exercise, to please her readers, rather than as an expression of her true feelings. These kinds of responses to pieces of writing were fashionable exercises at the time. By contrast Wortley's maxims appear to come from the heart, the straightforward arguments of a straightforward man. With Mary, as so often, it is more difficult to read between the lines. She probably read Wortley's maxims, observed his cynicism about marriage, and decided to write something more nuanced in response, which turned out so well that she then circulated it. Taken together, the two pieces of writing offer a fascinating glimpse into the tensions that existed between these two middle-aged people - he 51 years old by now, she 40.

Griselda Murray's mother, Lady Grizell, was critical of Mary's treatment of Wortley, gossiping that she was 'using Mr Wortley like a dog.'[6] Mary might have written graciously about the secret of a long and happy marriage but she did not seem to be living according to her own rules, according to Lady Grizell's letter. Another contemporary, Mrs Verney, also gossiped about the couple, around the time Mary wrote her essay. Mrs Verney implied that the Wortley Montagus' marriage was an unhappy one and the distance between them was not purely geographical. There is no evidence that either Mary or Wortley were unfaithful or that their relationship was now celibate. Mrs Verney even hinted in one of her letters that Mary - nearly 40 by now - had fallen pregnant. If this were true, then Mary must have miscarried. Or maybe Mrs Verney simply got the facts wrong.

Sometimes Lady Mary and her older mentor, Mary Astell, would challenge each other to write separate poems on a particular feminist subject which interested them. They both wrote competing pieces, twelve lines of rhyming couplets long, about the case of a young woman by the name of Eleanor Bowes. The 14-year-old had married a man much older than herself. She then died almost immediately afterwards, rumour had it at the hands of her violent husband. Where Mary Astell's poem was a straightforward description of a tainted marriage, Lady Mary's *Written ex tempere on the Death of Mrs Bowes,* was a far more powerful piece, shot through with Mary's characteristic irony. She praised Eleanor for escaping from earthly life while her marriage was still new, before the inevitable jealousies, neglect, infidelities and coldness set in: 'You had not yet the fatal Change deplored/ The tender Lover for th'imperious Lord.'[7] The poem has its own particular tone of controlled rage at the fate awaiting women within the constraints of marriage. It painted a very different picture of long marriage from the one in Mary's Rochefoûcault essay. Mary kept her criticism of marriage general in the poem, rather than attacking Mr Bowes in particular. Eleanor Bowes' husband owned a colliery near Wortley's, so this perhaps explains why.

Another poem of Mary's, *An Elegy on Mrs Thompson,* mourned the passing of Arabella Thompson whose husband had rejected her when she was unfaithful to him. He then pimped her out to his own brother-in-law and she died, probably giving birth to this man's child. Mary honoured Arabella in verse and pointed out that human scandal does not survive the grave. Where most of society condemned Arabella's actions, Mary supported her. Her poem was roundly criticised as a result. Later Arabella Thompson's husband, although he had remarried in the meantime, started making advances to Mary herself. When Lady Mary told Mary Astell about him, the two friends decided to respond by each writing him a poem of rejection. Mary Astell, who was dying at the time, used hers to praise the close friendship she and Lady Mary had enjoyed. Lady Mary argued in hers that his remarrying should surely be enough for Mr Thompson. Why did he need to destroy things by also seeking to seduce her?

Even without Mary Astell to spur her on, Lady Mary continued to write about the way men treated women. Like Arabella Thompson, Mary Yonge had had an affair. Furious, her husband dragged both his wife and her lover through the courts. The lover was forced to pay £1,500 plus costs for the privilege of adultery (£230,000 today) and Mary Yonge was shamed and divorced. Her husband took control of almost all her fortune. He then promptly remarried someone younger.

The young Mary Pierrepont. (© *National Trust for Scotland, Falkland Palace*)

The statue of Mary's grandfather at West Dean, with the splint on his broken leg. Borbach Chantry, West Dean, Wiltshire. (*Photo, author's own*)

Right: Mary's father, Evelyn
Pierrepont, first Duke of Kingston.
(© *Robert Brackenbury, Holme Pierrepont*)

Below: Thoresby Hall, Mary's family
home, where she lived as a teenager.
(© *Government Art Collection*)

Godfrey Kneller's portrait of the newly-married Lady Mary. (© *Christies & The Prince's Foundation, Dumfries House*)

Right: Mary's husband, Edward Wortley Montagu. (© *The Master and Fellows of Trinity College, Cambridge*)

Below: Wharncliffe Lodge, Wortley, Yorkshire, where Wortley's father lived. Her daughter described it as a 'wretched hovel', but Mary herself loved its wonderful views.

Jean-Baptiste Vanmour's portrait of Mary in Turkish dress, holding young Edward's hand. (@ *National Portrait Gallery*)

The French artist Jean-Auguste-Dominique Ingres was inspired by Mary's visit to a *hammam* for his *Le Bain Turc,* painted in 1863. (*Musée du Louvre*)

LETTERS

Of the RIGHT HONOURABLE

Lady M--y W---y M----e:

Written, during her TRAVELS in

EUROPE, ASIA AND AFRICA,

T O

Perfons of Diftinction, Men of Letters, &c.
in different PARTS of EUROPE.

WHICH CONTAIN,

Among other CURIOUS Relations,

ACCOUNTS of the POLICY and MANNERS
of the T U R K S ;

Drawn from Sources that have been inacceffible to
other Travellers.

IN THREE VOLUMES.

V O L. I.

L O N D O N:

Printed for T. BECKET and P. A. DE
HONDT, in the Strand. MDCCLXIII.

The title page to Mary's *Embassy Letters*. (*Private Collection/Bridgeman Images*)

Mary in a turban, with no eye-lashes, still wearing her favourite pearl earrings. (© *Hugh Matheson*)

Alexander Pope, Mary's great friend-turned-enemy. Portrait by their mutual friend, Charles Jervas. (*Bodleian Library, Oxford*)

Above: Pope kept this Kneller portrait in 'the best room' of his Twickenham house until his death. (© *The Bute Collection at Mount Stuart*)

Left: Lady Mary's childhood friend and distant cousin, Henrietta Cavendish Holles, later Lady Oxford. (*The Portland Collection, Harley Gallery, Welbeck Estate, Nottinghamshire/Bridgeman Images*)

Pope's friend Jonathan Richardson painted this portrait of Mary just before the infamous quarrel. (*Private Collection/Bridgeman Images*)

Lady Mary's only son Edward, demonstrating his love of all things Eastern. (*Granger/Bridgeman Images*)

Above: Mary's niece and nephew,
Evelyn later 2nd Duke of Kingston
and his sister Lady Frances Pierrepont
(who eloped with Phil Meadows) along
with the two daughters by Kingston's
second marriage. (© *Hugh Matheson*)

Right: Francesco Algarotti, Lady
Mary's great love. (*Rijksmuseum,
Netherlands*)

LADY MARY WORTLEY MONTAGUE

The older Lady Mary, commissioned from Francesco Carlo Rusca by Henrietta, Lady Oxford, just before Mary left London in pursuit of Algarotti. (© *Government Art Collection*)

Right: Horace Walpole,
Mary's fierce critic,
by Rosalba Carriera.
(*Getty Images UK*)

Below: Mary's plans
for the garden she
created at Gottolengo.
(© *Harrowby Manuscripts*)

The memorial in Lichfield Cathedral, commemorating Mary's pioneering work on inoculation.

Again, the system was weighted in favour of the man. In *Epistle from Mrs Y(onge) to her Husband,* Lady Mary wrote a poem as if she were Mary Yonge: 'For Wives ill used no remedy remains/ To daily Racks condemned and to eternal Chains.'[8] Double standards ruled. In another brief satirical essay Mary assumed the role of a dead man waiting in the afterworld for his wife, who was still alive. He admitted that during the marriage: 'I utterly forgot you when you were but some few inches from me.' He was relaxed, he explained, that she had so quickly found another man as a lover. He knew she has always disliked 'that odious rusty black, which is half worn out' and far preferred 'pink colour'd Riband'.[9]

Sometimes Mary would loan her services to friends who needed her eloquence to express their feelings. In 1733 a lady of the queen's bedchamber, Lady Catherine Dashwood, received a love poem from a suitor named James Hammond, who was both younger than her and penniless. Mary helped her write a response in *The Answer to the foregoing Elegy.* In it she put herself in Catherine's shoes. Catherine confidently and eloquently argued the case for rejecting Hammond's advances. They could never marry, she explained. She described how other young women pursued 'a shameless Path' and encouraged lovers they did not love. Catherine would do the opposite, 'And though I like the Lover quit the Love.'[10] Mary gave another woman a voice, arguing from a strongly moral position, rejecting a lover sensitively and tactfully. The poem was published soon afterwards, though almost certainly without Mary's permission.

Mary's letters to Sister Mar in Paris during this time were very different from the poem she wrote for Catherine Dashwood. Gossipy and deliberately ironic, Mary often delighted in expressing the outrageous to her sister just for the sake of doing so. There were lots of scandals for Mary to comment on. Since arranged marriages were the norm, extra-marital affairs were common among their mutual acquaintances. In June 1725, Mary wrote to Sister Mar about a particularly juicy piece of gossip where a man found his wife in bed with someone else. This led Mary to come up with a proposition. What if there were 'a general act of Divorcing all the people of England'? Every few years everyone would be forced to divorce. It would certainly save money, and probably ease heartache as well.[11] An anonymous essay entitled *On the Mischief of Giving Fortunes with Women in Marriage,* was probably also written by Mary. After a long satirical exposition, parodying legal language of the time, the essay proposed doing away with the dowry system altogether.

If women did not bring dowries with them into marriage, the essay argued, then men might not be tempted to marry simply for money.

A scandal closer to home for Mary was the court case about whether or not her friend Griselda Murray had been raped by Griselda's butler, Arthur Gray. In December 1721, the court trying the case had not believed Arthur's story and he had been sentenced to death by hanging. At the time Griselda's family were trying to work out what to do. They did not want to have on their consciences the fact that he was going to his death because of them. But they also feared that begging on Arthur's behalf for a more lenient sentence would imply that they were not wholly behind Griselda's account of events. Mary wrote a poem, her *Epistle from Arthur Gray to Mrs Murray,* in which Arthur Gray pleaded with Griselda to save his life. As Mary portrayed him, Gray was an unsuccessful suitor rather than a rapist. 'Since you will not love,' declared Arthur, 'I will not live.'[12] The normal power structures were reversed. Griselda held all the power. Arthur was the one to be pitied.

Mary may also have written another, far more incendiary poem about the scandal, *Virtue in Danger- A lamentable story how a virtuous lady had like to have been ravished by her sister's footman,* which was then widely circulated. If her Epistle had sought to defend Arthur as an honourable would-be lover, this bawdy ballad told a very different story. Here the rape definitely did take place. Griselda's mother, Lady Grizell, was portrayed as such a snob that it was only the fact the rapist was a mere footman that made her decide to take action. If Mary did write this second poem, she was making light of the crime, very much in line with how rape was viewed at the time. The events were an excuse for scathing satire. Griselda was given no sympathy whatsoever. In both poems Mary was using her skills as a writer to defend a convicted rapist; hardly, from a twenty-first century perspective, the actions of a feminist.

Mary and Griselda's friendship inevitably disintegrated as a result. Mary never denied having written the bawdy ballad. Many years later she wrote the words 'I confess it' in the margin of a published copy of the poem. And yet, unfathomably, she seemed surprised that Griselda turned against her. She wrote to Sister Mar (who remained friendly with Griselda throughout) expressing dismay that Griselda had refused to visit her. She later challenged Griselda on the subject. Griselda admitted that she was resolved never to speak to Mary again. A year later what Mary described as 'open warfare' broke out between the two. When they met by chance in Billingsgate market, Griselda started haranguing Mary. What Mary thought worse was that Griselda then turned to Mary's (unidentified, male) companion and warned him of Mary's reputation. This last accusation stung the most. Mary explained to Sister Mar that she had kept quiet at the time but that at a later date she had tried to reason quietly with Griselda. Apparently, Griselda admitted to her that she had acted foolishly. Whatever the facts of the case, the friendship had been destroyed.

From today's perspective Mary's attitude to Griselda seems anything but feminist. She sided with the man against the woman, despite the fact the woman had been a close friend of hers. She used a painful case as the subject of a bawdy poem, unsympathetic in tone to either of the protagonists. Consent was not a concept Mary really grasped and so she missed the far more serious implications of rape. In her defence, her writing about Griselda's case fits into a broader pattern. In everything she wrote she was exploring how women were treated in the world in which she was living. Her instinct was always to write in defence of the underdog, and usually, in the true-life stories she wrote about, it was the woman who was in that position. Here it happened to be the man.

Mary was a defender of women's rights, particularly within the institution of marriage. Instinctively she disapproved of sex outside its bonds, despite the reputation she herself was gaining during these years - mainly fuelled by Pope - of being sexually frustrated and lascivious. She wrote a short, eloquent poem in praise of constancy in a copy of the Duke of Wharton's edition of *Paradise Lost,* and later gave it to Maria Skerrett. Being constant was the only security that worked when nature itself was always so faithless, she argued. More than infidelity itself, though, she opposed the way that men held all the power when things did go wrong between the sexes. At some level it was this balance of power that interested her more than anything else. And her own marriage was an unusual one for the time in which she lived. She and Wortley had their own particular power-balance. She always saw herself as Wortley's equal, in part thanks to her intelligence, in part thanks to her social superiority to him, and also in part thanks to her observation of the different societies she had observed, travelling abroad. There is no evidence to indicate that Wortley disagreed with her on this all-important point of equality. The shadow of the state of Mary's own marriage falls across all of her writing. But she only grants tantalising glimpses as to how things really stood to those of us reading her today.

Chapter 11

Sister Mar

'My cure for lowness of Spirits is…galloping all day
and a moderate Glass of Champagne at Night'[1]

In Mary's lifetime mental illness was something little understood, often
treated with extreme cruelty. Mental health patients were frequently
locked up in asylums like the infamous Bedlam Hospital and visitors
were even invited to come and observe them for their own amusement.
When her own Sister Mar fell ill, Mary mustered all her strength to
ensure Sister Mar was protected. Mary herself also suffered from extreme
mood-swings throughout her life. When life-changing events occurred
such as the early death of her brother or her permanent scarring from the
smallpox, her mood inevitably dipped. But she was always able to regain
her enjoyment of what she called 'this golden now', unlike Sister Mar,
whose 'now' was very far from golden.[2]

Sister Mar had been subject to bouts of depression ever since her
teens. Her mother had died before she could remember her, her father
was a remote, critical figure who forced her into an arranged marriage
for his own reasons. Her much older husband, himself widowed with
a teenage son, then left her within a week of the birth of their only
daughter to travel to Scotland and lead the Jacobite rebels against the
new Hanoverian King George I, whom the rest of Sister Mar's family
supported. When that went disastrously wrong and Mar narrowly escaped
execution, she was compelled to go with him into exile in France. His
inherited estates were forfeited by the crown. In Paris, Sister Mar had to
endure creditors endlessly on her case and a husband who was forever
trying to play one political side against the other, without much success.
Nevertheless, she always supportive, always conscientious. She tried to
do the right thing by everyone, whether they were pro- or anti-Jacobite,
and to keep her own feelings in check. Mar described her to her stepson,
Tom Erskine, as 'a virtuous woman of very good sense and admirable

good equal temper', admired for her prudence and discretion.[3] In other words, she displayed exactly the personality type we now know is most likely to fall prey to clinical depression.

In July 1720, Mary was delighted when Sister Mar arrived back in England from France for a six-month visit. She was relatively unaware of the efforts their father, the Duke of Kingston, was making on Sister Mar's behalf to reclaim the Mar estates which had been forfeited to the crown. Back in Paris, Mar was beginning to take secret payouts from the English government in return for informing on his fellow Jacobites there. Provided he continue to furnish them with top secret information he would receive an annual pension of £2,000 (about £304,000 today). When he first found himself in exile in Paris Mar had earned himself the nickname Bobbing John for being equally obsequious to both sides, and now he was continuing with the same tactics, playing one off against the other. Sister Mar returned to her husband in Paris early in 1721. The two sisters would correspond with each other for the next seven years. Mary's letters were full of London gossip and humorous observations on the folly of mankind, using an easily decipherable code to cover up all her indiscretions.

Mary wrote often to her sister, requesting French lace, French porcelain and French fashions to be sent to England as soon as Sister Mar could arrange it. She even had a madcap plan at one point to travel to France and sell diamonds there. There was only a couple of years in age between Sister Mar's daughter, Lady Frances Erskine, known as Fanny, and young Mary. Their mothers were anxious to promote a friendship between them. For her part, Sister Mar had to be cautious as her letters were being intercepted. Mary found herself continually chastising her sister for not replying to her. She preferred not to think about how difficult life was becoming the other side of the Channel. Once she blamed her sister's silence on her enjoying 'the pleasures of Paris'.[4] Nothing could have been further from the truth. The letters from France grew fewer and fewer. What Mary failed to grasp was that Sister Mar's silence was the result of her sliding towards severe mental illness.

In 1724 Mar sent his wife and young daughter back to England again. By now Mar's pension from the English government had dried up and he had been pursuing an unsuccessful course of persuading the king to pardon him and give him back his forfeited estates. Now he adopted a new tactic. Mar asked the English government to allow his brother,

Lord Grange, to buy his estates instead. Grange would have total control over the income from the Mar estates but also crucially over Sister Mar's own allowance of £1,000 (£153,000 today). This was money from landholdings her father had given her on her marriage. Kingston, her father, was implacably opposed to Grange's involvement. Reconciling these two sides would inevitably prove an impossible task for Sister Mar, who arrived in England with her 8-year-old daughter Fanny on 19 May 1724.

Despite Kingston's best efforts to protect his daughter, the government permitted Grange to buy the Mar estates. He would now have control over Sister Mar's annual allowance, and also over a smaller allowance to which her daughter Fanny was entitled. He would be paid for his services out of the income the estates generated, and it was made clear he did not bear any liability for the situation. This was exactly what Kingston had dreaded. Although Grange was ordered to present annual accounts to Kingston, the ruling made it clear his primary duty was to pay off his brother's debts. Some land in Scotland owned by Sister Mar was to be given to Grange immediately as recompense for everything he was doing on her behalf. She had no power. As Grange put it: 'the valid Deeds or Deeds shall be made and granted by me and accepted by the said Lady and no otherwise.'[5]

Sister Mar's mission in London was threefold. Firstly, she had to press Lord Grange to pay her husband and herself some income from the estates. There were many debtors back in France whom Mar was doing his best to keep at bay. Secondly, she was to try to negotiate the pardon from the government for Mar's political past that he had sought for so long. Finally, she was to find the right bride for her stepson Tom Erskine, as a way of bringing some much-needed new cash into the equation. She moved into a house in Soho Square, which some friends loaned her. Letters began flying back and forth between Grange in Scotland, Sister Mar in London and Kingston at Thoresby in Nottinghamshire. It would be better for all concerned, Grange felt, if Sister Mar and Fanny went back to Paris. For their part, they dreaded returning empty handed. They needed to take back some cash.

At the end of June, Sister Mar travelled to Twickenham to say goodbye to Mary. It looked as if she could no longer delay her return. When her old friend Griselda Murray went down with a fever this provided a good excuse. Although Griselda had quarrelled with Mary, she and Sister Mar remained staunch friends. Sister Mar spent a week at Griselda's parents' home nursing her. From there she went to her father's house in Acton. Emboldened, she wrote to Grange asking for cash. She needed £3,000, she said (£460,000 today). He wrote back, explaining in a long-winded manner that Scottish tenants paid in arrears. Getting hold of this amount of cash would take at least a year, he warned. The only solution he could see would be to dip into Fanny's future inheritance. For Kingston, this was a red rag to a bull. Grange sent Alexander Raitt, who was employed as his agent, to Acton to try to come up with a solution. On 11 August, Raitt wrote that he was concerned Sister Mar might 'freat herself into a fit of sickness.'[6] For the first time someone was taking account of the toll this was taking on Sister Mar's mental health. Raitt managed to persuade Grange to pay Sister Mar an advance of £2,000 (£300,000 today). She and Fanny could now return to France.

Mary, who was still estranged from their father, knew very little of these machinations. The letters between the two sisters studiously avoided the subject. On her side, Mary was embroiled in the controversy caused by young Mary's inoculation. Tellingly, she shared virtually none of this with her sister. Mary's own quarrel with Kingston meant she could play no active part in his attempts to resolve Sister Mar's financial struggles. Other members of the family were invited to spend every summer at Thoresby, but not the Wortley Montagus. Meanwhile, back in France Sister Mar's husband had made a fatal mistake. He had shown a friend some of his personal papers, which proved beyond doubt that he had informed on the Jacobites in France to the English government. Unsurprisingly he was now cast out of the Jacobite camp. He tried writing threatening letters to James, the Old Pretender, to no avail. Then he even attempted blackmail, suggesting he would publish some of James' incriminating letters. He got nowhere. His wife's allowance had become all the more important as a source of income.

Kingston died in March 1726. Mary was at least present at his deathbed. He appeared to want to talk to her, perhaps as a gesture of reconciliation, but his second wife, Isabella, blocked any last-minute conversation. Sister Gower and Aunt Cheyne supported Isabella against Mary and the four women were still bickering at the moment of Kingston's death. His will had been carefully worked out. Mary received a slightly higher annual sum from his estate than her sisters, maybe as recompense for not having received a dowry. It included provision that the annual sum should not be passed on to her oldest son, so the row about 'entail' continued into the next generation. Kingston's death was treated with all the ceremony that surrounds the death of a public figure. An ugly dispute then arose when Isabella tried unsuccessfully to gain control of two of Kingston's grandchildren whose own parents were dead: Evelyn, Kingston's 14-year-old grandson and heir and his sister Frances Pierrepont. Instead Frances Pierrepont was sent to live with the infamous Aunt Cheyne.

Mary and Sister Gower both wrote to tell Sister Mar the news. Sister Mar had hoped her inheritance would prove a solution to the money worries in Paris, and she did receive land in trust, like both her sisters. But the will made it clear that Sister Mar would first have to discharge a loan of £20,000 which she had already received (£2.8 million today), before any further income was forthcoming. Her new estates in Lincolnshire, Wiltshire and Hampshire were to be held in trust so they could be passed to her heirs, but they would be excluded from inheriting if they were Catholic or if they lived anywhere other than in England. Kingston had maintained his iron grip from beyond the grave. Sister Mar had of course dreamed of more. On hearing this, Mary wrote her an unsympathetic letter. She was sorry for Sister Mar's illness and affliction she wrote, but she did not feel Sister Mar's emotions exceeded their father's feelings for her. Mary herself was caught up in the family quarrels back in England over their father's death. She would tell Sister Mar more when next they met, she wrote.

Mary's ignorance about mental health was evident in her letters over the next few years. She filled them with gossipy titbits. She revelled in the news that the infamous Rémond of South Sea Bubble fame had become engaged to a jeweller. She delighted in an anecdote about two lovers who kept their guest busy by asking her to play the harpsichord while they disappeared upstairs together. There were increasingly long gaps when Sister Mar failed to respond, which only made Mary angry. Occasionally Sister Mar would drop a hint that all was not well. In May 1727, Mary advised her to keep herself busy by galloping on a horse all day and drinking a moderate glass of champagne at night. In July, she wrote counselling her to fill her days as a diversion from 'those melancholy vapours which are the foundation of all distempers'.[7] She adopted the classic 'pull yourself together' approach. Keep busy. Minimise your hurt. Try not to dwell on your misfortunes. Sister Mar was too far down the road towards devastating breakdown to take heed.

Sister Mar wrote to Mary that she was fearful that, due to 'causes that you are too happy to have experienced', a time would come when she would need complete solitude. Once that happened then she imagined herself seeking some kind of oblivion 'to soften and assuage the pain of thinking.' She knew she was going under.[8] Their Sister Gower died the year after their father in June 1727. Now they were the only two left from the family they had been born into. George I died at the same time. His son George II's accession would have repercussions for them all. Mary's final letter to her sister in Paris in October 1727 described in hilarious detail all the various outlandish outfits worn by the elderly aristocrats at George II's coronation. It was easier to write anecdotes than to respond to her sister's pain. Sister Mar wrote back in November 1727 that 'I write to nobody nor have Spirits to go anywhere. Perhaps a letter from you may contribute to my cure.'[9]

Meanwhile Grange was continuing to press Walpole for a pardon for Sister Mar's husband, without success. As usual, the Mars were living in Paris way beyond their means. Although Sister Mar owned a house in Whitehall in her own right it was too run down to be let. Mar himself was physically unwell and his son, Tom Erskine, had resorted to gambling. Rumours began reaching London from people visiting Paris that there were fears for Sister Mar's mental health. By November 1727 this was plain for all to see. Mar took her to see doctors but there was no easy treatment. He began making plans for her to visit England for a second time, ostensibly to raise more money, but also presumably to absolve himself from having to care for her.

In January 1728, Grange's agent, Alexander Raitt, who had shown compassion towards Sister Mar in the past, travelled from Scotland to Paris so he could accompany her back to England. He waited there for six weeks until he judged that she had recovered sufficiently for them to cross the Channel. Mar would later express regret that he allowed her to travel when she was so unwell. He would never see her again. Sister Mar, Raitt, and her 12-year-old daughter Fanny arrived in England on 9 March 1728. As the *London Evening Post* reported, Lady Mar was 'so disordered in her Head, that it is believed she'll scarce ever recover her Senses.'[10] Rather than staying with Mary, she lodged in Marlborough Street. At last repairs were beginning to be done on the shabby, un-lettable house in Whitehall. Raitt carried with him a letter addressed to Sir Robert Walpole's brother. Sister Mar had never been interested in politics, it stated. Her husband requested yet again that he be formally pardoned and allowed to return. Even at this moment he was using her illness as a bargaining chip.

Mary was shocked to see for herself the condition her sister was in, severely clinically depressed and probably psychotic. Many years later Mary wrote that 'Madness is as much a corporal Distemper as the Gout or Asthma, never occasioned by affliction, or to be cured by the enjoyment of their extravagant wishes.' Since writing her earlier letter she had understood that a glass of champagne and a ride on a favourite horse had no bearing on recovery. She had also analysed that mental illness was no different from physical ailments such as gout or asthma. In both conclusions, she was ahead of her time. When she wrote that it was 'never occasioned by affliction' perhaps she was trying to rationalise, writing nearly thirty years later, that there was not one particular event that brought on Sister Mar's illness. Many separate events had piled pressure on her poor sister until she simply snapped.[11]

Two distinct sides were now beginning to form with opposing views as to what should be done. On the one hand there was Mar in Paris, backed up by his brother Grange and by his only son, Tom Erskine, newly arrived from Scotland. On the other there was only Lady Mary, now painfully aware she no longer had either her father or her Sister Gower to lend support. Although she had quarrelled with Kingston while he was alive, now he was dead she was determined to represent her family's perspective as forcefully as possible. The Scottish side feared that there was simply not enough money to go around. Things had been bad enough beforehand. Now Sister Mar's illness constituted a new drain on resources. From Mary's point of view, it was vitally important that Sister Mar had proper financial support for as long as she was unwell. Her need was greater than that of her exiled, traitor husband. Sister Mar was legally due her inherited yearly allowance, even if Grange had to administer it.

'Lady Mary has already begun to tamper with lawyers,' Tom Erskine wrote to his uncle in Scotland, 'you see what must be the consequences of this.'[12] He urged Grange to resolve things in person. Grange arrived in London in June 1728. First, he tried calling on other family members who might look favourably on his cause. When they successfully managed to avoid him there was nothing for it; he was forced to press his case with Lady Mary. Inevitably the meeting was a disaster. He found her spectacularly offhand and rude and she made it clear she blamed her brother-in-law Mar for her sister's illness and for the entire financial mess. Grange decided the only sensible course of action would be to move the patient to Scotland, where he could control things more easily. The Mars owned a property named Alloa House in Clackmannanshire and he could house her there. Griselda Murray and her parents agreed with Grange that this was an excellent solution. Grange even attempted to consult the psychotic Lady Mar, who as far as he could tell did not seem unhappy with the idea. The only person to whom he neglected to mention it was Lady Mary.

The plan was that Sister Mar would travel north by carriage, accompanied by Grange's agent Alexander Raitt, her young daughter Fanny, her stepson Tom, Griselda Murray and Griselda's mother. Grange himself would travel separately. They left London on 20 June 1728 and spent their first night just north of London in Barnet, at Griselda's parents' home. Lady Mar 'was well and easy and talked …about several past things and with good memory and judgement,' according to Grange.[13] Back in London Lady Mary learned of her sister's kidnap. She swung into action. The lord chief justice swiftly issued a warrant ordering Lady Mar's return. Mary, always a good horsewoman, rode north on horseback, intercepting the group in their carriage at Stevenage. She shoved the lord chief justice's warrant under their noses and forced them to turn around and head back to London, to her home in Covent Garden. Grange was beside himself with fury. The warrant specified that Lady Mar must be brought back to her own lodgings and he insisted it be carried out to the letter. So that same evening Sister Mar was moved again, this time from Lady Mary's house to the rooms in Marlborough Street. Inevitably everyone was exhausted and angry by now and the patient herself extremely distressed. Grange and Mary adjourned to a separate room to harangue each other.

Lady Mary's next move was to petition a body named the Commission of Lunacy to pass judgement on whether or not Sister Mar was insane. She needed a verdict which went her way if she were to win any future battles on her sister's behalf. After nine days' deliberating, on 12 July three commissioners and a jury of seventeen men found Lady Mar to be of an unsound mind. Grange and his lawyers argued that it was more proper for her to go to Scotland than stay in England and that in her lucid moments she agreed with them that this was what she wanted to do. They were forced to admit however that she was unable to care for herself. The commissioners ruled that she had been insane for at least four months and that there was no evidence she had been lucid at any point during that time. They had no explanation for what might have caused her illness except 'the visitation of God'.[14] Lady Mary next petitioned the Court of Chancery for her sister's custody. She won her case despite the judges' insisting that the trustees administering Sister Mar's affairs must be approved by Lord Grange. For his part, the furious Grange believed Wortley's friendship with the lord chancellor had swayed Chancery in Mary's favour.

Mary would need some payment from Grange for caring for Sister Mar. The next thorny issue was how much. Grange must have objected to the original figure mentioned because Mary wrote to the lord justice general in early 1729 arguing that she had been misrepresented as excessively grasping. £500 per year would suffice, she made it clear (just under £70,000 today, which sounds a large sum, but her sister needed full-time residential care). This sum was finally agreed in June 1729. It constituted half of Sister Mar's annual £1,000 allowance, and Mary generously accepted that Grange could retain the other half. Wortley and Mary signed the formal document agreeing the terms for their side and consenting to account for their expenditure, with Grange signing for the other side. For the next eight years Mary now had to produce a set of accounts twice a year to be sent to Grange confirming every last detail of what she had spent caring for her sister. At times Sister Mar was well enough to see friends such as Molly Lepell, and Griselda Murray, who inevitably continued to stir things. Mary also took on the responsibility of caring for Sister Mar's daughter, Fanny Erskine, whom she would bring up alongside young Mary.

It must also have fallen to Lady Mary to find somewhere for her sister to be looked after. Dr Richard Hale owned a small private asylum which he ran out of his own home in Hampstead. A newspaper soon reported seeing Sister Mar walking in Kentish Town, nearby. Private madhouses tended to be controversial places where people who were not insane at all were often held against their will. Hale's practice had a different reputation. He was an early advocate for allowing mental patients some physical freedom, for encouraging them to socialise and for treating them with respect. Rather than constraining them by force, he administered sedatives. He had worked at Bedlam for some twenty years and had been an expert witness during Sister Mar's Commission of Lunacy enquiry. Maybe this is where Lady Mary came across him. Only a few months after Sister Mar was put under his care, in September 1728, Hale suffered an apoplectic fit and died. For a time, it looked as if Mar might seize this opportunity to come to England and reclaim his wife, but perhaps the thought he might have to look after her put him off. She continued at the asylum under the care of Hale's successor.

For eight long years Mary kept the status quo while Mar and Grange made constant attempts to regain control of Sister Mar's income. Mary supported her brother-in-law's petitions to be granted a pardon, since this might mean he no longer needed the annual £500 he took from his wife's allowance. What she did not support was any notion that he should be allowed to return to England from his exile abroad. For his part he never felt he had enough money. The allowance should be split more in his favour, he argued. Too much of it went to Mary for Sister Mar's care. His point of view was seen as entirely reasonable by contemporaries, while Mary had to face vicious criticism for interfering and for being too controlling over her sister's life. 'She turns her very Sister to a Job,' wrote Pope.[15]

Stories abounded that Sister Mar had recovered. Several friends visited her and then reported to Mar in France that she was being kept against her will. On 13 April 1731, Lady Loudoun wrote about a visit of Griselda Murray's where Sister Mar apparently 'gave her a particular account of all that had happened to her,' despite her being in 'a poor little house with scarce clothes to her back'. Lady Loudoun pronounced herself determined to get 'this poor miserable woman out of her barbarous sister's hands'.[16] That same month Grange arrived in London to make a final attempt to get the situation reversed. He even persuaded Sister Mar herself to send word to the court that she would be happy to be sent to Scotland. As soon as Mary visited her, however, Sister Mar changed her mind again. It was obvious she had been coerced. Eventually Grange had to admit defeat. Mary had won the battle.

Fanny Erskine was in Aix-la-Chappelle with her father in 1731 when Grange lost this final attempt to win custody. Mar had been forced to flee to the Austrian Netherlands to avoid his French creditors. He railed angrily at Mary's controlling behaviour. Mary wrote a polite, carefully worded letter to Fanny about her mother: 'Quiet and Regularity is all that can be done for her in her present state of health.'[17] Fanny's loyalties were inevitably split, like many a child with warring parents. Next Mar began plotting a marriage of convenience between Fanny and Lady Loudoun's son, optimistically claiming that Fanny was sure to inherit money from her mother's side of the family in due course. 'It would be doing her wrong to call her a beauty,' he wrote to Lady Loudoun of his own daughter, 'but she may well be called a very gentlewoman.' Even here he was incapable of being loyal. He described Mary in the letter as 'that most unaccountable, mad, avaricious woman'.[18] If he could get Fanny married off, then they could use that as leverage to prise Lady Mar out of Mary's hands. Lady Loudoun wisely resisted his plan.

Mar died in May 1732 at Aix-la-Chappelle, shunned both by the English government and by the Jacobites, while his wife continued as a patient in Hale's private mental asylum. A contemporary of Mar's wrote that 'no man ever had a more glorious game to play and played it worse than he has done from first to last.'[19] Sister Mar's forced marriage had finally come to an end. Now her father was dead, Fanny began spending an increasing amount of time in Scotland with his family there. There was no love lost between Fanny and Mary, but it was an impossible situation for them both. In January 1732, scandal broke out when it emerged Lord Grange had arranged to have his own wife kidnapped and imprisoned, prematurely announcing her death. Mary's instinct that he was not a proper person to entrust with her sister's welfare had been proved correct. Regardless, Grange kept up the pressure on Mary, continually barraging her with complaints. The repairs to the house in Whitehall and the possibility of leasing it consumed him. For now, Mary's instincts were simply to protect her only sister and to do her best for her sister's teenage daughter.

In 1736 Fanny came of age. Wortley now urged his wife to relinquish all the responsibilities for Sister Mar to her niece. Doubtless he had had enough of the whole business. Mary had little option. Reluctantly she agreed. In 1741 Mary learned Fanny had married her cousin James Erskine, Grange's son, the previous autumn. This must have felt like the ultimate betrayal. In effect Fanny had given all the power back to Grange and the Erskines. Mary confessed she was not surprised: 'she had always a false cunning.' She railed against the bridegroom's 'impudence' at pretending this had not been a prime motive for marrying Fanny. Sister Mar herself wrote to Mary claiming she was responsible for the match rather than Fanny: 'which would be a very plain proof of her lunacy if there was no other,' as Mary put it. She wrote back politely and warmly, congratulating Sister Mar on her daughter's marriage and wishing the couple well. If there were ever any way in which she could help Fanny in the future, Mary wrote, she would be happy to do so.[20] With the benefit of hindsight, she had surely done enough. Fanny spent the rest of her life wrestling with the debts that beset her new husband's family and enduring the indignity of his infidelities.

Sister Mar herself did not die for another twenty years, still not recovered, aged 70. By then Mary was also an old woman and also unwell. They had not seen each other for many years. Mary's first instinct on hearing the news was to lament the fact she had been robbed of the chance of ever seeing her sister again and of giving her some comfort. Her elegy was simple: 'she was really honest and loved me.'[21] Sister Mar died penniless. All she left were requests that her two servants each be paid a year's wages and that Fanny give one of them a bible and prayer book. Even this was hedged with a request that Fanny find it within herself to forgive all the trouble her mother had brought her. To protect her sister, Mary had been forced onto the offensive. Rather than being thanked for her troubles, she had been vilified as money-grabbing and unhinged. She could only fight for so long before Mar's Scottish relatives won through. Yet thanks to Mary her sister was granted some financial security and was cared for with dignity and respect. Mary would not have recognised the label of mental health campaigner, but this was what she was.

Chapter 12

The Break with Pope

'What dire offence from amorous causes springs'[1]

Mary had weathered the turbulence caused by Pope on her return from Constantinople. For a time, the two kept their distance from each other but then they settled into a more conventional friendship, living as neighbours in Twickenham, with a large group of mutual friends and acquaintances. Mary was warned by Joseph Addison, as he lay dying, about Pope's potential to become a very vicious enemy; she should beware of quarrelling with him. At some time in the mid-1720s the two did indeed fall out. The reasons for the rupture are unclear to this day. But Addison was right. Deeply hurt, Pope used his pen to vent his anger. Although Pope had always admired Mary's assertiveness, paradoxically, it was this characteristic of hers which served to make things worse. Rather than passively accepting that his were the words of a flawed character, she decided to fire back. Inevitably a vicious war of words raged between the two of them for twelve years. Friends and relatives were drawn into the line of fire. Neither side would ever agree to a surrender.

Alexander Pope was an outsider. He had been born a Catholic and as such could never hold public office, attend a university or buy land. Unlike most of Mary's Whig friends, he was a Tory. During these Twickenham/London years, the Whigs consolidated their position as the ruling party. Pope disliked the increasingly powerful Sir Robert Walpole and was excluded from the political life which consumed many of his male friends. He never grew to a normal, adult, male height, but the Pott's Disease he had suffered as a child also disabled him in other ways. He was extremely sensitive to the cold, for instance, and always wore a flannel waistcoat and fur doublet, with a corset next to his skin, to hold himself upright. He could never travel very far. As a result, his life was a very particular one - rarified and pampered.

Dr Johnson said of him, 'He hardly drank tea without a stratagem.'[2] Although Pope was heterosexual, the life he led was more like the women of his acquaintance than the men. Inevitably his friendships were vitally important to him. He also knew how to use his sense of humour to endear himself to his friends. He described himself, with characteristic understatement, as: 'that little Alexander the women laugh at.'[3] He was different from Mary's other friends, both male and female. But Mary always gravitated towards outsiders.

Mary's attraction for Pope had always been her assertiveness, her confidence in also being someone different, defiantly unconventional. Pope tended to admire softness in the women he knew but in Mary it was her brilliance, her warmth and her creativity. When she was travelling, he wrote to her wishing that she would: 'appear to distant Worlds like a Sun that is sunk out of the sight of our Hemisphere, to gladden the other.' [4] The sun became the perfect metaphor for her. By the summer of 1722 he had met the very different character of Judith Cowper. Where Mary threatened him intellectually, Judith deferred to him. Where Mary was voluble and extrovert, Judith was retiring and humble. In a letter to Judith dated 18 October 1722 he compared the two women. While Mary was the sun, he wrote, setting too brightly, Cowper was the moon, shining with a dimmer, reflected light in 'Virgin Majesty'. Although Mary as 'sprightly Sappho' demanded his admiration, he preferred Judith's 'softer Wonder'.[5] Nevertheless, he remained dazzled by Mary's accomplishments. A mutual friend had written to Pope about a project of honouring Mary by writing a poem about her work on inoculation. Pope wrote back: 'immortality, if such a thing be in the gift of English poets, would be but a due reward for an action which all posterity may feel the advantage of.'[6] Unlike many of their contemporaries, he had grasped the magnitude of what she had done.

One explanation as to how the quarrel came about directly involved Hervey. Pope wrote to Dr Arbuthnot explaining that he, Mary and Hervey had all been together, when Mary and Hervey had asked Pope if he would join with them to write a satire. Pope did not disclose the target of this proposed collaboration. It may have been Griselda Murray. But whatever the poem was to be about, Mary and Hervey were already choosing to satirise a subject about which Pope felt very differently. When Pope refused, he reported that Mary and Hervey had taken offence and that this was the reason for their quarrel. When she was later asked about this, Mary denied it. The three of them had never physically been together in the same room, she explained. This feels like a technicality. The exchange could still have happened, even if the three were apart. Perhaps the story was founded in a germ of truth.

Another story, which was put about by Sir Robert Walpole's son, Horace, was that Mary borrowed a pair of bedsheets from Pope and returned them to him unlaundered. This was the cause of their quarrel, he explained. Horace later fixated on Mary's being filthy and unkempt, having been influenced by what Pope would go on to write about her. Another possible explanation concerns Pope's old nurse, who died in 1725. Pope had a memorial erected to her in Twickenham Church. An anonymous poem mocked this gesture: 'No wonder that he's so stout and so strong/Since he lugged and he tugged at the bubby so long.'[7] It was said that Mary had written these cruel lines and that this explained their falling out. They would certainly have offended Pope.

Another reason may centre on two portraits which Pope commissioned. In 1720 Pope asked Sir Godfrey Kneller to paint Lady Mary, and the resulting portrait would hang in the best room in his house for the rest of his life. However, four years later he commissioned their mutual friend Charles Jervas to paint its mirror image. This time the subject matter was Henrietta Howard and Pope hung it opposite Mary's in his best room. Mary had never been close to Henrietta Howard and this gesture may well have caused her offence. She may not have liked Pope's strong feelings for her, but her particular place in his affections was still important to her. Mary confided in a friend that she believed it was her friendship with the infamous Duke of Wharton which was the real reason that Pope fell out with her. Pope had felt pangs of jealousy.

The most widely accepted explanation is the one told by Mary's grand-daughter Lady Louisa. Her family always believed this was the reason why her grandmother fell out with Pope. Apparently, at a moment when Mary was totally unprepared for it, Pope approached her and made 'what romances call a *declaration*.' He was so ardent in his protestations of love for her that she found it impossible to be serious or even to be angry with him. Instead she burst into gales of laughter. This was the worst possible reaction she could have had. Pope was so hurt and ashamed by her response that from that moment on he became 'her implacable enemy'. It does seem unlikely that Pope would have revealed himself to Lady Mary in person like this. He was always extremely cautious about declaring himself in the flesh, despite his particularly flowery style on paper. Today we forget that this was how people expressed themselves in letters and so we tend to take Pope's ardour on the page at face value. But the image of Mary's laughing at him and his being mortally offended feels grounded in truth. Perhaps it is exactly what happened. We shall never know.[8]

Mary and Pope's social circle would nearly all be drawn into their vicious argument. Dr John Arbuthnot had been an important advocate of Mary's inoculation experiment, an unusual one in that he was a Tory. He was also a close friend of Pope's. Mary and Pope's mutual friend Lord Bathurst had made sure his children were inoculated but then a servant of his had died and the anti-inoculation lobby had used the death as evidence against the practice. In 1724 Bathurst, who was away from London, wrote to ask Pope if he had any news of Mary. Pope replied that he knew very little but would try for Bathurst's sake to find out a bit more. This implied that their argument had not yet taken place. Once it did, Bathurst would be one of only two of their literary circle who remained friends with both. The other was the older playwright William Congreve, who died in January 1729.

Mary's cousin Henry Fielding returned from studying abroad the same autumn and was enlisted by her to write poems supporting her cause. These were not for publication, but to help her vent her anger. She also wrote to Sister Mar about Pope. Sister Mar's descent into dementia would coincide with the public quarrel. Lord Peterborough who had secretly married Mary's lodger, sided with Pope, despite Mary's attempts to enlist his support. Her childhood friend, Henrietta, Lady Oxford, remained a staunch supporter of Mary throughout. Henrietta's husband, Lord Oxford, blamed Mary and endorsed Pope. But the friend who was most involved in the war of words was Lord John Hervey, whose intimacy with Mary Pope had always resented. Hervey was on Mary's side throughout.

By 1729, however it had happened, the friendship had evaporated, and the two erstwhile friends were now enemies. Pope wrote to a friend on 13 September complaining that Mary was libelling him: 'though my only fault towards her was leaving off her conversation when I found it dangerous.'[9] He was being deliberately disingenuous claiming this had been his only fault. Eighteen months earlier a poem of his was published, entitled *The Capon's Tale: To a Lady who fathered her Lampoons upon her Acquaintance.* Two of its verses were aimed straight at Mary. Pope had written the poem two years earlier in 1726 but in 1728 he expressly changed its setting from Wales to Yorkshire, where the Wortley Montagus came from. It told the tale of a sober yeoman who lived in Yorkshire, in other words Wortley himself, whose wife owned a hen which attracted lots of cocks. The innuendo was entirely intentional. The wife, like Mary, gathered round herself 'All the plum'd Beau-Monde', as Pope put it. She had so many chicks that she palmed some of them off on a 'feather'd Dupe', Pope himself. The final verse accused his former friend directly: 'Such, Lady Mary, are your Tricks/But since you hatch, pray own your Chicks.'[10] Pope's readers would have known exactly who Lady Mary was, and understood the accusation. The same month that Pope's poem was published, Sister Mar had arrived back in England, dangerously unwell, never to return. Although Mary must have read the poem, her attention was elsewhere.

Another longer poem of Pope's, *The Dunciad,* was also published the same year. In it the Goddess Dulness addressed the scurrilous publisher Edmund Curll, telling him always to blame other people when things went wrong. He should take his cue, Dulness explained, from Lady Mary: 'the sage dame, experienced in her trade,' who 'retails each batter'd jade/Whence hapless Monsieur much complains at Paris/Of wrongs from Duchesses and Lady Maries.' Pope's jibes at Mary contained in this couplet require a bit of unpacking for those of us reading the poem today. The 'hapless Monsieur' complaining from Paris was Rémond. Pope knew all about Mary's financial dealings with him. Prostitutes were often referred to as 'Duchesses' and Pope was implying that Mary behaved like a prostitute towards Rémond. They tended to give their clients syphilis. Pope was playing with words, making a subtextual connection for his readers in the know between 'pox' meaning syphilis and 'smallpox', the disease to which Mary was inextricably linked. The reference was only a couple of lines in a long poem, but it was chillingly unpleasant, nevertheless. An earlier draft of the poem included a couplet: 'See Pix and slipshod W - traipse along, / With heads unpinned and meditating song.' Pope eventually decided not to put this into the finished piece, but it showed the way his mind was working. Mary was slatternly, promiscuous and diseased.[11]

For the moment, Mary was too distracted by Sister Mar's fate and by the problems her son Edward was causing her to pay much attention to

The Dunciad. Other writers had their own opinion about Pope's poem. In a short piece of prose published in an anonymous pamphlet in June 1728, *A Popp upon Pope*, the famous poet was described as strolling in Ham Walks near Twickenham when he was set upon by two men who gave him a whipping in revenge for lampooning them. He was then rescued by friends who carried him home in their apron as if he were a baby. Mary might have had some input into this piece of satire, but at the time she had just stopped Grange's kidnapping of Sister Mar and was fighting to keep control of her sister's finances. Her sole authorship seems unlikely. There was even an unflattering reference in the piece to Dr Hale, whom Mary first met during the enquiry over Sister Mar's future. Mary would soon place Sister Mar in Dr Hale's care, so she would surely not have wanted to libel him. She might, though, have enjoyed reading the pamphlet.

When Mary's cousin Henry Fielding returned to England from studying abroad that autumn, she did confide in him about Pope. Just as she had done with Mary Astell, she set about writing parallel poems with Fielding, to express her feelings. She wrote one and he wrote two. In Mary's poem the goddess Dulness set up a headquarters in the grotto Pope had built for himself in Twickenham, decorated with shells. The poems were not for publication. For the moment, Mary was keeping her feelings private. In October 1729, she decided to write to Dr Arbuthnot to ask for his help: 'I leave to your judgement the character of those who have attempted to hurt mine in so barbarous a manner'. A verse satire, *One Epistle to Mr A Pope,* was being circulated among their friends. Pope claimed he had seen a version in Mary's handwriting and that it must therefore be by her. Mary suggested to Dr Arbuthnot that the real explanation for this was that Pope had been indulging in a bit of forgery. Mistrust and paranoia were already doing their damage.

The quarrel between the two had now become semi-public. In April 1732, the *Grub St Journal* published an anonymous play, *Mr. Taste, the Poetical Fop: or Modes of the Court, a Comedy,* which satirised them both. Pope was portrayed as the hunch-backed bad-poet-cum-translator Alexander Taste, who foolishly pursued Lady Airy. Mary had lost her M. She was a 'young widow of fortune, wit and merit, but strangely whimsical'. The play centred on Taste declaring his love and Airy laughing at him. Either the playwright had heard the story which Mary's family always told, or this play formed the basis for

Lady Louisa's later account. The truth was already becoming circular. The fact that the character of Airy was a widow was perhaps a jibe at the state of Mary's own marriage. Airy, the Lady Mary figure, had a friend called Phrodita, who was derided as being unfeminine and in love with her maid (Claude-Charlotte) and a sister called Lady Addle whose wealth her husband had taken and misused (Sister Mar).[12]

It was not in Pope's nature to let things lie. The following year he upped the stakes even further. His long poem, *The First Satire of the Second Book of Horace, Imitated,* translated and adapted the words of the Latin poet Horace, making it accessible to Pope's contemporaries. Two lines were clearly about Mary: 'From furious Sappho, a milder Fate/Poxed by her love, or libelled by her Hate.' Mary had been given the nickname Sappho in the past. As a teenager she had connected to the character of Sapho (sic) in the works of Madeleine de Scudéry. Both Pope and Lord Peterborough had written poems praising her and giving her the pseudonym of Sappho during the years when they were still friends. Here it was less flattering. Her lovers had been 'Poxed by her love.' She had given them syphilis. Yet again, pox and smallpox were elided. And they had been 'libelled by her fate.' Pope was accusing her of employing her pen to attack him, something she had so far only ever done in private.[13]

Yet again, she tried to appeal to friends. First, she turned to Lord Peterborough. He quickly made it clear that he had no wish to get involved. Pope called on him soon after Mary's visit and Peterborough wrote Mary a letter, giving a blow by blow account of his conversation with Pope about her. The letter read as if it were really ghost-written by Pope himself. The letter-writer condescendingly explained that the reference to Sappho did not refer to Mary at all. The writer had been thinking about 'some noted common woman', not her. Naturally, he refrained from giving the name of this 'noted common woman'. Mary did not write back.[14] Next she turned to Sir Robert Walpole, asking for his help. He obliged, writing to ask Pope to remove or alter the Sappho couplet from his poem. But Pope refused to grant Walpole's request. Mary had libelled him, he said. She had taken her own 'Satisfaction'.[15] Ten days later he wrote to someone else: 'You may be certain I shall never reply to such a libel as Lady Mary's.'[16]

Mary was becoming increasingly frantic. The next person she turned to was her friend, Lord Hervey. He had also appeared in Pope's reworking of Horace, characterised as Lord Fanny. Mary and Hervey decided to write a poem in response to Pope's attack: *Verses Addressed to the Imitator of the First Satire of the Second Book of Horace*. For the first time, a written response of Mary's to Pope's attack found its way into print. Its tone was uncompromisingly vicious. All its criticisms were the familiar ones levelled against Pope - that he was a Catholic, that he was disabled ('It was the Equity of righteous Heaven/That such a Soul to such a Form was given'), that he was a Tory, that he was a poor editor and a slapdash translator, that he blasphemed, that he libelled people ('You only coarsely rail, or darkly sneer'), that he was like the serpent in Genesis, that he was friendless, that he was a coward and that he was a traitor. Combined, they added up to an utter condemnation. The poem ended with a scathing curse. Pope would be destined forever to wander the earth, deserted by everyone, like Cain, the first murderer 'with the Emblem of thy crooked Mind/Marked on thy Back'.[17]

Although it found its way into print, the poem's authorship was shrouded in mystery. Hervey may well have arranged for its publication. Pope perhaps saw the manuscript and himself arranged to have it published, as a deliberate ploy to do Mary harm. For her part, Mary would almost certainly have planned for it be circulated among their friends rather than published. Publication could only lead to shame for her, as she knew from the past. Now it appeared in print she was standing right in the firing line. A newspaper advertising the poem's publication on 8 March 1733, stated that it was 'By a Lady', ignoring Hervey's involvement. A later advert went even further and described it as being 'By a Lady of Quality'.[18] The clues were there for all to read. Almost all of Mary's contemporaries, including Swift, Voltaire and Lord Oxford, her friend Henrietta's husband, pronounced it her work, not Hervey's. Today a manuscript of the poem with corrections in Hervey's handwriting proves that he was definitely involved. For the moment, though, Hervey escaped, his reputation intact. Mary, by contrast, had become just another common pamphleteer. She could no longer hide behind her rank. Everyone could see that she had resorted to using her pen as a weapon. The game had changed.

Hervey and Mary dealt with the public response to the publication of their poem in very different ways. Hervey seemed relatively relaxed about Pope's onslaught on them, describing it as a 'rotten egg'.[19] He defended his actions to Dr Arbuthnot. He had no wish to get into a 'paper war' with Pope, he told Arbuthnot. For him it was no more than that, simply a 'paper war'. At court, George II took Hervey aside and advised him not to write any more poetry: 'it is beneath your rank: leave such work to little Mr. Pope.'[20] Like Hervey, Mary also wrote to Dr Arbuthnot. The controversial poem was written without her knowledge, she protested, by 'a Gentleman of great merit, whom I very much esteem'. It would have been clear who she meant. Hervey could protect herself whereas she could not. She asked that Arbuthnot show her letter to Pope. Even if Pope guessed who the gentleman was, she wrote, he would never dare attack him. But she was not sorry, she said, that the poem had been written. If Arbuthnot did ever show Mary's letter to Pope, nothing came of it.[21]

Instead Pope attacked again. His *Second Satire of the Second Book of Horace* was published in 1734. Having decided against including Wortley in his earlier poem, he now characterised him as the miser Avidien. Alongside Wortley was his wife: 'For him you'll call a dog, and her a bitch.' Calling a woman a bitch had all the connotations it has today. Avidien, the Wortley figure, was so mean that when he was given gifts of partridges and fruit, he sold them on to raise cash, and instead lived off rabbits and roots, food which should by right have been reserved for the poor. The mud which Pope slung at Wortley here was destined to stick. The name and the reputation would follow Wortley to his grave. Looking back with hindsight over Wortley's papers, his household accounts show that he was generous to his servants and tenants, often giving them gifts such as partridges and fruit. There is no evidence of his receiving anything which he then sold on for cash. But Wortley's contemporaries did not read his household accounts. The poem described what it said would be a lucky day for Avidien and his wife, one when they found a lost bank note 'or heard their Son was drowned.' This was painfully close to the bone. Pope would have been aware that Mary and Wortley's son Edward had gone missing at sea a few years earlier but even he could surely not believe that they would ever have wanted Edward dead. His rage at Mary continued unchecked. [22]

Another tactic of Pope's in their war of words was to publish salacious material anonymously. He had written it, but he did not attach his name to it. This then allowed him to be far more unguarded and lewd than in the work officially attributed to him. The poem *Sober Advice from Horace* was published anonymously in December 1734. To put the reader off the trail, Pope included a dedication to himself. His readers were not fooled. The poem was all about sex. It opened by imagining Mary alongside 'Lord Fanny', among 'Pimps, Poets, Wits'. They were tainted by association with some of the nastiest in society. Later in the poem Mary appeared again, this time as the character Fufidia: 'With all a Woman's Virtues but the Pox/Fufidia thrives in Money, Land and Stocks.' As usual, Pope libelled her as having the pox - syphilis. He satirised her wealth and then alleged that although she normally charged ten per cent, men could have her body for free. She was sexually available, just like a common prostitute: 'A Lady's face is all you see undressed/ (For none but Lady M- shows the Rest).' Rémond was mentioned again as 'wretched Monsieur'.[23] Under the cloak of anonymity Pope's poisonous hatred boiled away unchecked.

Just five days later Pope had his far more elegant poem *An Epistle to Dr Arbuthnot* published, this time under his own name. In it their friend Dr John Arbuthnot urged Pope to be prudent when dealing with Sappho. The doctor implied that Sappho would go to any lengths, including the use of violence against them both, if they riled her. Pope portrayed himself in the poem as 'soft by Nature, more a Dupe than Wit'. Now he was soft, the characteristic which he loved most in women and Mary was by implication hard. He complained that she had slandered him for many years, without any provocation. The poem was even more damning of Hervey, whom Pope now called Sporus, naming him after a castrated young gay lover of a Roman emperor. Pope now had no qualms about castigating both Mary and Hervey - a woman and a gay man -using his own name.[24]

By now Arbuthnot himself was unwell. He and Mary began an elaborate game of mutual denial about Pope's latest poem. Arbuthnot supposedly assured her before publication that no one would think she was Sappho. Clearly this was untrue. The day after the poem was published, she wrote back to him, agreeing with him. There was nothing of her in the 'Lampoon of your ingenious Friend' but the problem, she explained, was that everyone in London would think that there was. She attacked Pope for 'the terrible malice he bears against the Lady signified by that name.' At the same time, she claimed to Arbuthnot that she was not the author of *Verses to the Imitator of Horace*. They both knew that to be a lie. She admitted to him that she wished Pope would stop libelling her. She remembered how William Congreve used to laugh behind Pope's back at all his poems when he was still alive. They were in a world of smoke and mirrors. Neither dared admit the truth. Arbuthnot died only a few weeks later. [25]

Far from giving up, Pope continued with his poisonous attacks on Mary. She was too clever for her own good, he wrote, someone who was plagued 'With too much Thinking to have common Thought.' She was physically disgusting: 'at her toilet's greasy task'. Her taste in fashion was questionable, dressed as she was in a sack, in 'diamonds with her dirty smock'.[26] When Pope decided to reissue all his earlier poems, he took out a line praising 'Lady Wortley's eyes'. Now it was 'Lady Worsley's' eyes he admired. At the same time, anonymous writers continued to revel in the spectacle of the two friends now having become sworn enemies. Pope was derided for his physical delicacy but, more damagingly, he admitted that he disliked Mary because of 'a Suspicion that she intended to ravish him.' Now Mary was being portrayed in published pamphlets as a would-be female rapist.[27] The argument had reached its nadir.

Both were damaged, but for Mary the anger and pain were more destructive. Pope could rise above it, where she was defined by it. The close circle of like-minded friends at Twickenham had been shattered. When Mary went to dine at the Oxfords' house, for instance, she had to check beforehand to make sure that Pope would not be there. While Henrietta, Lady Oxford, sided with Mary - they were distant cousins and old friends after all - her husband supported Pope. Contemporaries commented that Henrietta was far too dull to be a true friend of Mary's, but this probably explains why Mary always valued the friendship so highly. Mary's unpublished poem *Pope to Bolingbroke,* written at some point between July 1734 and June 1735, expressed her feelings towards Pope himself. He was a 'Toad-eater' with a soul full of venom. He was filled with envy at the smiling beauties who surrounded him. He deliberately lied about his sexual conquests. His life was one of retirement, eating broccoli and kissing his ancient nurse.[28] In fact, Pope's life was less changed by what had happened than Mary's. His reputation as a poet was untarnished. She would be destined to become merely a footnote for students of his work. He had won.

The fall-out had left Mary feeling isolated and paranoid. Many years later she met a young man named Joseph Spence in Rome. He was working as a tutor to the nobleman, Lord Lincoln and they struck up a bond. Mary talked to Spence of a malicious, gossipy story which had been spread about her back in London. It was said that the Sultan had shown his interest in seducing her by throwing his handkerchief at her, and that this was the reason she had been permitted to see the inside of the seraglio at Constantinople. She attributed this slanderous story to Pope, 'the wicked wasp of Twickenham', and pronounced herself relieved that his lies no longer had any bearing on her life, now she was far away from him in mainland Europe.[29] She would only feel totally safe again in 1744 when news reached her, while she was still in Europe, that Pope had died. For the moment, though, she was still living in England, between Twickenham and London. Twickenham had lost its magic because Pope had a house there too. London literary society, which in the past she had delighted in, had now largely turned its back on her. All she could do was lick her wounds. She had always been someone who loved making new friendships but significantly, this too no longer seemed to be happening. It felt as if she had already met everyone there was to meet. And everyone she knew had their own view on her quarrel with Pope. She was damaged goods. Middle-aged ennui had set in. She still had her family to occupy her, of course, but they brought with them their own set of trials and tribulations.

Chapter 13

Motherhood and Marriage

'it is married love only which can be delightful
to a good mind'[1]

Mary's two children could not have been more different. She wrote to Sister Mar in July 1727: 'My Girl gives me great prospect of satisfaction but my young Rogue of a Son is the most ungovernable little Rake that ever played Truant.'[2] She boasted that her son Edward was growing 'extream handsome', while young Mary had 'Sobriety and Discretion' on her side but 'I am sorry the Ugliness is so too.'[3] Mary's sharp tongue had got the better of her but young Mary was generally accepted to be plain, lacking the beauty her mother had enjoyed before falling prey to smallpox. Their daughter always reminded Wortley of his beloved dead sister Anne in looks, the sister who had been the reason for his meeting Mary. Edward was short, like his mother, but with his father's fair colouring. He clearly had great charm, despite his many character flaws. Young Mary was conscientious, dutiful and supportive of her parents, but when it came to her marrying Mary and Wortley would make serious, lasting mistakes. Edward, who had been a sickly, difficult child, grew up to be a troubled teenager. By the time he was of age his parents already despaired of his ever leading the life they would have wanted for him. Inevitably gossips branded Mary a bad mother.

While young Mary was educated at home, Edward was sent to Westminster School, like his father before him. At some stage, earlier than boys start at the school today, Mary dispensed with Edward's private tutor at home and enrolled him at Westminster. Fees were £20 a year for boarding at the time (just under £3,000) with a further five or six guineas for tuition (between £770 and £925). In 1720, when Edward was nearly 7, Mary attended a school play there in which Tom Erskine, Sister Mar's stepson, had the leading role. Perhaps she went as a prospective parent. Edward probably started boarding soon after. The school stood

128

right by Westminster Abbey, as it does today - a powerful reminder to pupils of their future importance in the public sphere- but it felt run down and many of its buildings were derelict. Dr Robert Freind became the headmaster during Edward's time as a pupil.

The culture at Westminster was a violent one. Corporal punishment was embedded in the life there. Edward would have suffered beatings for the slightest misdemeanour. In June 1722, soon after he arrived, a fight broke out with boys from other schools which was so serious that it left three people dead, including a sedan-chair operator who had been passing by and intervened. Again, just a year later two pupils fought a duel with penknives, in which one was lucky to survive from his injuries. In this cruel, bullying regime, the schoolboys were condemned to becoming either oppressors or victims.

Aged 13 Edward made an unsuccessful attempt to run away from Westminster and enrol himself at Oxford University. The following year he followed up with a far better-planned escape. He had 'gone Knight Erranting' as Mary put it in a letter to Sister Mar, putting a gloss on events as if Edward were some kind of medieval prince.[4] The truth was a much more stark wake-up call to his parents, if they had heeded it, that something was seriously wrong. Edward sold his schoolbooks to raise the necessary cash. Once he escaped the school, he walked in the direction of Whitechapel where he exchanged clothes with a street urchin. Then he continued to the River Thames. He planned to run away to sea. Perhaps he had good memories of the voyage back from Turkey when he was a boy. He found a troop ship in the East End and asked the boatman to let him on board, making up a fictional back-story. He was duly enrolled as one of the crew.

This was traumatic for his parents. They placed an advert in the *Daily Journal* offering a £20 reward for any information about him, admitting that he had run away and explaining that he was either on board a ship or had hired himself out to a tradesman or labourer. They were careful to appear conciliatory: 'If the Boy will return of himself he shall be kindly received and put to Sea, if he desires it.'[5] The urchin whom Edward had swapped clothes with was probably found but apart from that his parents had no other news of their son for several months. This time Mary kept the story from her sister in Paris. When she eventually did admit the truth, she wrote: 'Nothing that ever happened to me has touched me so much.'[6]

Life on board ship did not go as Edward had planned. Very soon his identity was discovered. Inevitably he was then prey to merciless teasing about being the 'Duke of Montagu'. The captain's grandson gave an account of the trip many years later. Apparently, the other crew members delighted in ordering Edward about: 'My lord, fetch this. My lord, swab the foredeck.'[7] Eventually Edward confessed the whole story to the ship's captain, who refused to believe him. He suggested the captain should ask him a question in Greek or Latin, to test whether or not he was genuine, but of course the captain was ignorant of classical languages. Next, Edward boasted that he was the first westerner to have been inoculated (which was not strictly true but was unusual enough to be a good means of proving his identity). He proudly showed the captain the scars on his arms. Unsure what to do, the captain moved him to his own cabin and gave him civilian clothes until the ship docked in Gibraltar. There the captain mentioned the story to the admiral of the Mediterranean Fleet who by chance had seen his parents' advert asking for help finding him and which also mentioned his inoculation scars. Edward was vindicated. In December 1727, he was put on a boat back to England and delivered home by Lord Forbes, a commander in the royal navy, a few weeks later.

The five months during which Edward was missing put his parents under an intolerable strain. The fact everyone in London was talking about the scandal only made things worse. When Mary did finally admit to Sister Mar that Edward had run away, she confessed she was thinking of coming to Paris to help herself get over things. Pope would use the story as yet another titbit to libel her with, as he stepped up his onslaught of her in print over the next few years. Edward returned in January 1728 and that same year Sister Mar travelled from Paris and Pope's vicious criticism of Mary in *The Capon's Tale* and *The Dunciad* both appeared in print. No wonder that by the end of the year she had worried herself into illness. This was to become a recurring pattern for her when life became exceptionally stressful.

Looking back on events later, Mary wrote that she felt she and Wortley were too lenient on Edward when he arrived back in London. They decided the best course of action would be to send him away to the West Indies. The Reverend John Forster was enlisted as Edward's tutor or 'governor'. He had been their resident chaplain, so must have felt like a safe pair of hands. Edward and Forster would not return for over two years and nothing is known of their adventures during that time. For Mary, her only son was banished into the unknown at a formative time of his life.

In 1730 Edward arrived back in London and immediately disrupted the status quo yet again. He announced that he had married a woman named Sally, allegedly a washerwoman. She was several years older than the 17-year-old Edward and the class difference between them was evident. Having married her he then left her almost immediately. Edward's behaviour patterns are often difficult to understand. Perhaps he did this to shock his parents and draw attention to his situation. Or maybe it started as being a love match, which quickly turned sour. Or perhaps even a drinking game or a dare. There were rumours in the press that Sally was a gold digger. Maybe she was. The Wortley Montagus were not unusual in having a son who was rake. Mary's father had been one too. He had raced through their inheritance and run up gambling debts, womanising and drinking to excess. Mary's nephew, Evelyn, Duke of Kingston, who had inherited the Pierrepont family fortune when his grandfather died, was turning out to be one as well.

Parents often solved these problems by marrying their wayward sons off to heiresses. Mary once made a half-serious quip to Wortley that Lord Cartaret, who had three daughters, might be prepared to marry an ugly one to Edward. By arranging his own shotgun marriage Edward had blocked this possible escape route. His parents did what they could. They tried to silence any speculation and found some money to support Sally. Although Wortley was by now one of the wealthiest men in England, he was under financial strain at the time. A series of strikes and poisonous rows between mine owners were making things difficult. He made sure to consult lawyers about his legal position, should he decide to disinherit Edward.

Four years needed to elapse before Edward came of age but already his father had no desire to meet him face to face. His parents appointed a new 'governor', this time a Scot named John Anderson. Any communication between father and son was either to go through Anderson or an agent called John Gibson of Richmond Buildings in Soho. Anderson managed to maintain good relations with everyone, but Mary was less enthusiastic about Gibson. She felt he made things worse by flattering Edward. Soon they sent their son abroad again. No letters of the time survive from Mary, but it is not difficult to imagine her feelings and in later life she admitted Edward had broken her heart. She and Anderson corresponded about Edward's progress. In June 1732, Edward and Anderson were in Troyes in the Champagne region of France, where Mary may even have visited him. Anderson's concerns focused on Edward's health. Although Edward was greedy, Anderson wondered if he was consumptive. In his late teens Edward went through a bout of religious fanaticism, praying for four or five hours a day. Anderson wrote that Edward's health had subsequently improved and that he seemed to be cured of his drinking habit, although he continued with his 'old intriguing disposition'.[8] His studies had not been going well and Anderson suggested they be allowed to move on. Mary arranged a sort of abbreviated grand tour for them both, first to Holland, then on to Switzerland and northern Italy.

Edward came of age in May 1734. He was now entitled to claim his £1,000 annual allowance (£160,000 today) from his paternal grandfather's legacy. He felt strongly that he was also due some kind of allowance from his parents. He may well have known that his father had already consulted lawyers about eventually disinheriting him, but there was no official word on that front. In the autumn he arrived back in England, leaving Anderson behind in Europe to deal with his debts. Wortley was up north as always, so Edward made his way to Twickenham. His mother stopped him at the doorway - the same doorway where she had greeted Maitland when he came to inoculate young Mary against the smallpox all those years ago. They could hear young Mary and her cheerful group of friends and cousins enjoying their amateur dramatics inside. Lady Mary made her position painfully clear. She was expressly forbidden to let him cross her doorstep, she told him. Reluctantly he withdrew. She then packed up and hurried to the house in Cavendish Square, but Edward followed her there. Reluctantly she conceded to a meeting with him at the house, but it went disastrously badly. Edward used all his flowery powers of persuasion, but she could not be budged. He made it bitterly clear that he held her responsible for blocking him from seeing his own father. Nothing was resolved.

There were two further terrible encounters over the next few years. One took place at a West End periwig-makers in St Alban's Street, where Mary and Edward met by chance. Again, Edward railed at her that she was preventing him from being reconciled with his father. At the second meeting Mary came up with the suggestion that he enlist as a volunteer in the Austrian emperor's army. Perhaps she was remembering the smooth Prince Eugene, the victor at Petrovardin, whom they had met on their way out to Turkey. Edward's response was to scream at her that having him enlist and ensuring he was killed would be a great way of getting rid of him. Mary was careful not to sink so low as to scream back. Instead she offered him bribe of £50 to leave the country again (about £7,000 today). Pope's literary reference to it being a good day for the Wortley Montagus if they were to discover their son had drowned surely came out of gossip about this incident. Edward did leave for Europe again but made it clear to his lawyers that they should continue to pursue his inheritance. As for Mary, she was 'quite fully persuaded that he can never make a tolerable Figure in any Station.' Inevitably she fell ill again. Hervey even reported that she was dying. She would recover, but nothing could alter the disastrous situation with her only son.[9]

Young Mary's story was very different. Unlike Edward, Mary's only daughter was educated at home, largely by her mother, who remembered the two of them finding contentment during these years. Young Mary may not have been beautiful, but she was talented. She could write poetry and sing and she particularly liked acting. Just as her mother had done at the same age, she wrote her own versions of classic texts in adolescent handwriting. The family's Armenian nurse had been replaced by someone who also liked Scudéry romances and would stay with them for many years. In later life young Mary would remember telling her mother that another girl had refused to be her friend and that this girl confessed she felt dull in comparison to young Mary, who came across as being very intelligent. Mary's response to this was immediate. Dull people would always despise clever ones, she told her daughter, so if young Mary ever felt superior about her intellectual prowess, she should remind herself that this came with a high price tag.

Young Mary's cousins played an important role in her life as an adolescent. Sister Mar's daughter Fanny Erskine, three years older than young Mary, lived with them from 1728, once it became obvious her mother could no longer care for her. Fanny's note to her young cousin that it was 'really quite odious of you to stay so long at Twick', rather than joining them in London, sounds just like a teenager today.[10] Fanny was often abroad, either visiting her father or, when he died, with his relatives. From 1732 Mary also found herself looking after Lady Frances Pierrepont, the only daughter of Mary's dead brother. When her parents had both died, Lady Frances had been sent to live with the infamous

Aunt Cheyne, but when Aunt Cheyne also passed away Lady Mary seemed to be the next best option. Lady Frances was five years older than young Mary, but they soon became confidantes.

Lady Mary often found herself critical of what she saw as the over-exuberant gang of teenagers who spent their time together in Cavendish Square and Twickenham. It consisted of her own daughter Mary; Lady Frances Pierrepont; Frances' older brother, the rake Evelyn, Duke of Kingston; and Lady Mary's two much younger stepsisters, Lady Caroline and Lady Anne, who were young Mary's age. Young Mary and Lady Frances wrote poetry and plays together, just as Lady Mary and Sister Mar had done when they were teenagers, fantasising in fiction about flirtatious encounters. They too invented classical names for themselves. Like Lady Mary's early pieces, these also demonstrated a great eye for detail. They sometimes featured older women, presumably modelled on Lady Mary herself, who were depicted as ugly and perpetually cross. This must have been how Lady Mary appeared to the two teenage girl cousins.

History repeated itself when Lady Frances found herself in a 'paradise' and 'hell' situation, as Lady Mary had done at the same age. Frances' 'paradise' was Philip Meadows, deputy ranger of Richmond Park, whom the girls called Phil, and her 'hell' was John Spencer, Sarah Churchill's venereal-ridden grandson, who on paper appeared a good match. Lady Mary viewed Phil Meadows as a fortune hunter. He pursued Lady Frances relentlessly. Lady Mary tried to enlist Frances' old brother, Evelyn, in her battle against Meadows but he declined to get involved. Frances meanwhile was adamant she would not marry John Spencer. On 23 April 1734, the day after her twenty-first birthday, Frances went with young Mary to the opera in Lincoln's Inn Fields. The two cousins were in one box and Phil Meadows in another. At the interval Frances claimed she was feeling unwell. Young Mary returned to the auditorium alone while the happy couple eloped. The London gossips fell on this piece of news with alacrity. One audience member wrote that France was right to run away: 'if she could not live without a husband, for nobody else would have cared for her notwithstanding her twenty thousand pounds.'[11] The couple were married two weeks later. Frances was probably already pregnant, since she gave birth to a daughter only seven months afterwards. Whereas for Mary her elopement had been a moment of high drama, for Frances it felt more like farce.

The young couple had little or no income and were reduced to living at Thoresby with Frances' brother Evelyn and his various mistresses. Evelyn would never have children. Frances and Phil eventually went on to have six. The Meadowses lived a life of genteel poverty, waiting for Evelyn to die, hoping they would inherit. Mary forever afterwards regretted the whole situation. She felt guilty that she and not done her duty by her beloved dead brother, caring insufficiently for his only daughter. She also believed Frances' lack of judgement related to her having been brought up by the childless, wealthy old Aunt Cheyne. Inevitably the affair coloured the relationship between Lady Mary and young Mary. Lady Mary felt her daughter should have done something to prevent the elopement. The anger between mother and daughter over what had happened would fester for many years.

In general, though, mother and daughter rubbed along well together, attending many social events in the London circles in which they moved. Young Mary enjoyed hearing the castrato Farinelli and accompanied her mother to the celebrations for the Prince of Wales' birthday. When young Mary was formally presented at court Lady Mary swelled with pride that she was commended by everyone. In the autumn of 1734 mother and daughter went to see a French play *Le Jeu de l'amour et du hazard* in the Little Theatre in the Haymarket, which was being run by Mary's distant cousin, Henry Fielding. Seeing it inspired Mary to write her own version of the play in English, *Simplicity,* in which the heroine swapped clothing with her maid, not realising that her suitor had done the same with his manservant. The piece was unusually warm and uncynical for Mary's writing. The jeopardy was straightforward; the lead character might just marry the wrong man. Now her 16-year-old daughter was growing up, Mary empathised with her in having to make difficult choices. The heroine had a kind, supportive father. This was a sympathetic portrayal of Wortley and contrasted sharply with the way Mary's own father had treated her at the same age. Lady Mary would later regret that she and young Mary had not been closer during these years.

Later that year, there were rumours in London that young Mary was engaged to Lord Perceval, son of the Irish Earl of Egmont. Lady Mary did not seem troubled by the thought of marrying her daughter to someone Irish and sending her off to live somewhere she herself had never visited. This had played a part in her own rejection of the Irish Clotworthy Skeffington, after all. Negotiations between the fathers began the following July, and Lady Mary was also involved, writing to Egmont's lawyers about young Mary's financial prospects. There were at least three other suitors, one of whom young Mary had kissed a couple of years before, and another, favoured by Wortley, who was one of young Mary's cousins, Sister Gower's son. Lady Mary liked Lord Perceval but her daughter, now 17, burst into tears at the thought of marrying him. Mary warned Wortley 'not to force his daughter...nor to marry her against her own consent.'[12] She remembered her own history.

Mary knew that Wortley was considering leaving his fortune to their daughter rather than their son by now, but the couple did not spell this out to young Mary. She was only 17 and the situation over disinheriting Edward was delicate. Perhaps because the future was undecided, Wortley was determined to get a good marriage settlement for his daughter, regardless of any wealth she might have in her own name later in life. To outsiders, it appeared that one of the wealthiest men in the country was being exceptionally difficult over how much her future husband would provide for her. This made the situation opaque and confusing. Lady Mary continued to favour Perceval and even arranged for him to meet with young Mary so he could make a proposal. She and her friends were more relaxed about lovers being left alone together than the previous generation had been.

Young Mary had other ideas. She had met the handsome John Stuart, Earl of Bute, in 1735, thanks to a shared a love of acting. Bute had already inherited his estate, but it was in Scotland and therefore not likely to yield the income that a London lifestyle demanded. Lady Mary gradually found herself won over by Bute. In the summer of 1736, she accepted him as young Mary's choice. Perceval then withdrew, perhaps because he knew that Bute was on the scene, but also because of Wortley's intransigence over finances. Bute's financial situation was worse than Perceval's, however, and Wortley dug in his heels. Where he had at least offered a small amount of money to Perceval, he refused any money at all to Bute. Mary disagreed with this strategy and things became increasingly tense between them. She was concerned about any life her daughter might have, condemned to relative poverty and living far from friends on the Isle of Bute. Lady Mary later admitted that she would have preferred for her daughter to remain single, just as she had wanted to do at the same age, but she felt pressure from the rest of the family so she made sure to warn her daughter of the perils of marriage.

She outlined her assessment of Bute's character. She believed him to be honest, she said, but hot-tempered. Not surprisingly this did not go down well with the young couple.

Wortley remained opposed to the marriage and gave the couple no money. Pope's satirising him as the miser Avidien does not seem so far off the mark in retrospect, but it simplified Wortley's complicated rationale for acting this way. Wortley accepted that the wedding would go ahead, but he and Mary were repeating some of the same errors which occurred around their own marriage. Bute and young Mary would start their married lives without financial security. Love alone was not necessarily seen as a valid reason to marry. But Mary and Wortley were also changing their tune for this next generation. They accepted the marriage, despite the financial negotiations not having been resolved. There was no need for this young couple to elope. Young Mary married her 'paradise' rather than making do with a 'limbo'.

The wedding took place in the parish of Marylebone on 13 August 1736. The bride was given away by her father. Mary heard her own daughter utter the famous marriage vows, the *paroles mysterieuses* as she later described them. But there was no wedding breakfast. An acquaintance wrote an account of events, taking umbrage at the way the Wortley Montagus had treated their only daughter. Once the young couple were settled, Mary went to have dinner with Bute's uncle, the Duke of Argyll, but Wortley refused to go with her. Soon the Butes did the only sensible thing and moved to Scotland. As an acquaintance maliciously put it, Bute had 'said he liked the young Lady and if she wold be content to live in Scotland he would marry her. She had said, anywhere rather than stay with her Mother.'[13] It must have felt messy and undignified for Wortley and Mary that they were at odds over such an important decision. As for mother/daughter relations, although they started well - Lady Mary was made godmother to the Butes' first child - the residue of hurt would soon come to pollute their future.

By 1736 both Mary's children had left home under strained circumstances. Her son felt like a lost cause, travelling Europe with a tutor just to keep at a distance the inevitable scandal that surrounded him. His father had already taken steps to disown him. Her daughter had married for love but as a result been denied the financial support Wortley could easily afford. She then retreated to live far away on the Isle of Bute at her husband's family home, which Mary would never visit.

137

Mary's own marriage had gone stale. Wortley and Mary's shared parenting of their only two children, rather than bringing them closer together, had driven them further apart. Wortley continued to spend time in the north, preoccupied by the family mining business. Twickenham, which had initially been a haven for Mary, was now tainted by Pope's campaign of hatred against her. She had fewer friends than before. Her favourite sister was unlikely to recover from mental illness and she could do nothing for her. Mary must have felt uncharacteristically redundant. She was 47 years old. Time for a mid-life crisis.

Chapter 14

Francesco Algarotti

'capable of making not only the most amiable but the most Estimable Figures in Life'[1]

In April 1736, the 47-year-old Lady Mary met the 24-year-old Francesco Algarotti and the meeting changed her life forever. Within two weeks of being presented to the young, cultured Italian she was madly, hopelessly in love with him. As she put it, just one tender glance and her soul melted: 'I faint - and find all Heaven within his arms.'[2] She had never felt this way before and she never would again. Lady Mary was particularly emotionally vulnerable that spring and summer. Negotiations were going on with young Mary's first serious suitor, Lord Perceval. Young Mary herself had recently met John Stuart, Earl of Bute and some time in this period she introduced him to her mother, not realising that Lady Mary was distracted by her infatuation with their Italian visitor. By the time Algarotti left that August, Mary's only daughter had married Bute, and Fanny Erskine had come of age and seized control of Sister Mar's affairs from her aunt. The quarrel with Pope continued and the Wortley Montagus' marriage was as cold as ever.

These facts alone do not give as clear a picture of Mary's emotional life during these few months as do the poems she wrote. In one she described herself looking at her new lover, Algarotti, as he lay asleep between the sheets: 'The plenteous silken hair, and waxen Arms/ The well turn'd neck, and snowy rising breast/And all the Beauties that supinely rest'.[3] Her poetry reached emotional heights she had never previously even attempted. It had become purely and simply a means of expressing her love. She found herself scribbling first drafts on scraps of paper and squirrelling them away from prying eyes. Algarotti's physical beauty she found overpowering. He was well-known for his good looks, but she also fell for his mind. She wrote to him: 'About manuscripts, statues, Pictures, poetry, wine, conversation, you always show taste, Delicacy and vivacity.'[4] Mary had found her soulmate.

Francesco Algarotti was born in Venice on 11 December 1712. His wealthy, middle-class family had homes in both Venice and Padua - hence Frederick the Great's nickname for him: 'the swan of Padua'.[5] As a contemporary put it: 'he is the son of a bookseller and the nephew of an apothecary, both of whom have their shops in Venice.'[6] It became clear early in his life that he would need to earn his own living. He quickly proved himself exceptionally able academically, studying first in Rome and then, aged 14, transferring to the University of Bologna. As well as being highly intelligent, Algarotti was strikingly good-looking, gregarious and highly sexed. His brother sent him a monthly allowance, but he raced through it. In 1735 he accepted Voltaire's invitation to visit him in Paris. Already he understood he needed a patron. He soon charmed Voltaire and started work on adapting the recently deceased Isaac Newton's scientific work, *Opticks or a Treatise of the Reflexions, Refractions, Inflexions and Colours of Light*.

From Paris, the young Algarotti then travelled to London, arriving in March 1736 on his own improvised grand tour. His aim in London, as it had been in Paris, was to enhance his reputation. He was beginning to see a future for himself as a writer and internationally renowned cultural theorist. Later in life he would also earn money as an art dealer. In the meantime, he depended on patronage and if this involved his giving sexual favours in return, he was happy to do so. He was armed with introductions. Voltaire had sent with him some writing to show to Queen Caroline. He had also recommended that Algarotti look up Lord John Hervey, Mary's great friend. The two met at court and struck up an immediate rapport. In the first week in April, Algarotti attended a meeting of the Royal Society, and only a week later he was shown the honour of being elected a fellow. For his part, Hervey was delighted with this new friend. He was at a turning point in his own life. His long-term lover, Stephen Fox, had recently decided to marry. At the same time, he was mourning the death of his mistress, Anne Vane. The timing of Algarotti's arrival could not have been better for him.

Hervey then introduced the 'swan of Padua' to Lady Mary. Voltaire and Abbé Conti may have also suggested they should meet. Algarotti would have been interested to view the ancient stone slab that Mary and Wortley had brought back from Troy. This may well have been the reason the handsome young Italian first went to Savile House in Twickenham. As she welcomed him into her home, Mary perhaps reflected that he was about the same age as her own son. Young Mary may also have been present at this first meeting. If so, she probably sang for them. Algarotti later went to pay homage to Pope at his Twickenham villa, taking with him another Italian visitor, Francesco Maffei. For obvious reasons, Mary was not there. Algarotti then visited Lord and Lady Oxford's library. The Oxfords may well have invited Mary to join them for Algarotti's visit. Henrietta continued to be one of her closest friends, after all. Algarotti had burst onto the social scene, teeming with ideas on art and literature. A great conversationalist, he was also a passionate lover of the good life. He particularly enjoyed fine wine. He was extremely handsome but, as Lady Louisa quoted Mary as saying, 'women see men with their ears.'[7] His looks were certainly a huge attraction but what Mary fell in love with was Algarotti's mind.

We have no way of knowing whether Mary and Algarotti slept together or not. Reading between the sheets (so to speak), whatever happened between them, the effect on Mary was so overwhelming, it feels as if for the first time in her life she was having fulfilling sex. Wortley's frequent absences would have made things easier. Algarotti was accustomed to seducing whoever showed interest in him, regardless of their gender. We do know that he would visit her most evenings in Twickenham. In April she wrote him her first, short note. Mary and Claude-Charlotte - who knew nothing of the situation - had waited three hours for him there in vain that Monday night: 'I believe some of your Martyrs have been canonised for suffering less.' If he were sufficiently repentant to ask for a pardon, she jested, then he could see her the following evening. In her letter Mary played with the idea that they were courtly lovers. He had sinned and he needed to repent, she playfully suggested. In a few, short words she had expressed more sexual desire for him than in all the protracted, overelaborate letters she had written to Wortley, during their courtship, twenty-five years earlier.[8]

Algarotti sought input from both Mary and Hervey, his two new friends, on his writing project, *Newtonianismo*. It took the form of a dialogue, set in an arbour, so Algarotti may well have been influenced by Mary's garden in Twickenham. In it the author discussed many subjects with a marchioness who displayed 'charms capable of inspiring thoughts and discourse little relative to philosophy'.[9] The marchioness described herself in the book as a 'citizen of the world', a phrase which Lady Mary would also later use about herself.[10] In the second volume Algarotti added a reference to inoculation, to stress how important the new scientific discovery was to women. Inoculation, he wrote, now preserved the charm of English beauties. The reference was flattering. For those readers in the know, Algarotti was making the link to Mary's inoculation campaign. He was also describing English women as beautiful, but the reference at the same time felt somewhat impersonal. Mary was not identified by name, after all. For Algarotti inoculation was merely useful in preserving beauty. He ignored the fact it also saved lives.

Where Algarotti's writing that summer was designed to be public, Mary's was intensely personal. In one poem she was about to reproach him when he appeared and: 'At that fair vision all resentments fly.' [11] Gone was her customary, ironic wit and in its place was pure, undiluted emotion. In another poem she described herself as waiting for Algarotti to come to her, totally infatuated by him, but disappointed when the sound she heard turned out to be merely the rustling of the wind: 'Can all the pleasures that he brings me pay/For the long sighing of this tedious day?' [12] In a third, of which Algarotti made a copy, she addressed him as Lindamira, the name she had used for a lover when she first began writing as a teenager. Some of her poetry she may have shared with him, but most was only for herself.

Unbeknown to Mary, Algarotti had also started sleeping with Hervey. Despite the closeness of their friendship, and Pope's hints about it, Mary tended to ignore Hervey's sexuality. He had confided in her his overwhelming sadness when his relationship with Stephen Fox had come to an end, but she seemed almost wilfully to miss the signs that Hervey and Algarotti were now lovers. Nor did she understand until much later in their relationship that Algarotti was mainly sexually attracted to men rather than women. Perhaps this spared her some heartache. It was hard enough that she found herself intensely jealous of all the women Algarotti met. To be jealous of both sexes might have been too hard to bear. Both Mary and Hervey started writing passionate letters to Algarotti in French, the traditional language of love.

By the middle of August, Algarotti was preparing to leave London for Italy. His book was completed, and arrangements needed to be made for its publication there. Mary grew desperate for him to come and visit her one last time before he left. She had lost her usual tranquillity, she lamented, and feared she would never find it again. The thought of his leaving filled her with terror. She begged him to 'forgive the absurdity that you have brought into being.'[13] Even at this moment she recognised that what she was experiencing was potentially comic, even absurd. Days before Algarotti left, the artist Jonathan Richardson, a friend of Pope's, did two quick pencil sketches of Algarotti's face. In one Algarotti faced the artist, smiling and benign like an English country squire, but in the other he turned his profile and his hooded eyes and beaked nose gave him the look of a malevolent bird of prey.

On 5 September 1736, Algarotti spent his last evening in England, taking supper with Mary. Hervey had pressed him to spend the precious time with him, but Algarotti had lied to Hervey about his whereabouts, saying he was dining with a third party. The two friends now found themselves pitted against each other as rivals for Algarotti's love. Their approaches to the young Italian were very different. Hervey was far more pragmatic. He knew Algarotti could never replace Stephen Fox in his affections, but simply provided a convenient substitute. Mary's feelings were far more self-destructive. Right from the beginning, she knew she was deceiving herself. Years later, writing about a younger man with an older woman, she wrote: 'no Man ever was in Love with a Woman of 40, since the Deluge.'[14] Mary wrote to Algarotti declaring that she would love him all her life, 'in spite of your whims and my reason',[15] but even now she knew that there was never any hope he would return her love.

In her first letter to Algarotti after he left, Mary enclosed a passage from Homer's *Aeneid,* comparing her own pangs to those felt by Dido. She admitted that she could have stopped him from going by making him a 'proposal' to pay him to stay. Already she was offering to buy his love. As it was, she admitted that she was spending hours in her study just thinking about him. She had invited someone to supper who innocently said that she had never met anyone as likeable as Algarotti. Mary did all she could to keep this guest with her, just to be with someone who could talk about him. She was aware Algarotti was sorry to leave London, she wrote, but she did not flatter herself that this was on her account. She regretted being a woman. If she had been a man, she could have travelled with him.[16] She confessed herself irrationally anxious that he might have drowned at sea, then she imagined him instead safely arrived in Paris, making fun of her letters with 'some beautiful Parisienne'.[17]

But Algarotti did write to Hervey. By now Hervey had discovered that the young Italian had spent his last evening in England with Mary, not him. In revenge, Hervey made sure to let Mary know that, unlike her, he had heard from their Italian friend. And, to rub salt in the wound: 'The Body you speak of has not mentioned you in his letters to me.'[18] Such was her desperation that, despite this, she did all she could to find out more from Hervey. She accosted him at court. Had Algarotti definitely arrived safely in Paris? What news could he give her? Mary and Hervey wrote different accounts to Algarotti himself of their encounter. Mary's letter to Algarotti gave her side of events in English, not French. This was business after all, not love. In his letter Hervey wrote that Mary seemed physically very changed since he had seen her last. She was in love, after all. She 'was as drunk before as wine can make one, and you have added Gin.'[19]

At some point Mary came clean to Hervey. She admitted that she had fallen in love with Algarotti, without realising that the person she was confessing to also happened to be Algarotti's lover. Hervey immediately wrote to Algarotti describing Mary as boasting that she had captured his heart. In truth, rather than a boast, it must surely have been a confession, an admission of vulnerability. Hervey would never tell her of his own affair with Algarotti in return. From now on, their friendship would be based on a lie. In a series of letters full of rhetorical flourishes and overblown metaphors, Hervey mocked Mary to someone he now knew was her lover. She had a particularly odd way of curtsying, he pointed out. Her overpowering feelings were surely less attractive, he wrote, than his own steady devotion. Not that Hervey had his own feelings as well under control as he implied. He wrote to Stephen Fox's brother that when it came to Algarotti: 'I write like a fool, think like a fool, talk like a fool, act like a fool; and have everything of a fool but the content of one.'[20] He wrote bitchily that by being absent the Italian was spared having his enjoyment of Mary's wit spoiled by looking at her face. Algarotti might have reflected that Hervey himself was no Cupid, but powdered and rouged, sporting a set of false teeth. Sitting in Paris, the young Italian was now receiving rival love letters from two middle-aged English aristocrats. He knew he could turn this to his advantage.

Astonishingly, despite this, Mary continued to see Hervey as a close friend. Algarotti by now had moved on to Milan - he had been in Paris only six days but had managed to visit Voltaire - and the two friends competed to receive letters from him. Mary had been careful to keep her feelings hidden from everyone else in her social circle. Even her closest friend, Claude-Charlotte, was kept in the dark, so Hervey provided a necessary outlet for her overpowering emotions. She would write to him the following year, thanking him for his friendship during this difficult time. The two rivals even took to writing poetry together about Mary's overwhelming infatuation for Algarotti, each contributing alternative verses. In Hervey's he tried to advise her to fall in love with someone else. This had been his tactic over his love affair with Stephen Fox, after all. She ended her poem: 'But Hunger never raised the Pain I feel/Which only one can give, and only One can heal.' A handwritten note, which Mary later scribbled over violently, ended with Hervey's: 'I'm tired of all this fine poetic Stuff/Now call for Supper, we have writ enough.'[21] Confessions of love can be boring things. Hervey was probably right to suggest a supper break.

On 29 September, Mary finally received her first letter from Algarotti. She decided to retreat to Twickenham, since it was guaranteed to be deserted at that time of year. People told her she was going to a wilderness, she wrote, but what they did not realise was that in fact she was leaving one: 'I choose to see nothing but trees since I cannot see the only Object dear to my Heart and Lovely to my Eyes.'[22] She had felt the same way about the trees at West Dean when she was banished there in her twenties during the Wortley courtship. She kept herself distracted by writing, just as she had done then. Even the gods were not as blessed as any woman who looked at Algarotti, she wrote. Whenever she thought of him: 'My Heart beats thick, my senses fail, /Disordered, blushing, cold and pale.' On the other side of the same piece of paper she wrote another short poem expressing her longing to experience 'cool Indifference' again. Another beautiful poem she wrote at the time took the form of a hymn to the moon. The 'silver Deity' guided her as she walked alone lit by moonlight.[23]

Next Mary decided to send Algarotti her portrait. She knew to do so was foolish, but she went ahead anyway. She probably had copied the Kneller portrait of herself aged 26, about the same age as Algarotti was now. She dispatched it to him in Venice in December 1736, accompanied by a poem, regretting the passing of time and the fading of her looks. It ended, plaintively: 'Look on my Heart, and you'll forget my Face.'[24] She sent a letter with it as well, telling him the picture was: 'wrapped up in poetry, without Fiction.'[25] The whole exercise was tinged with pathos. She later wrote: 'Fig leaves are as necessary for our minds as our bodies, and 'tis as indecent to shew all we think as all we have.'[26]

Even more boldly, the letter accompanying Mary's portrait included an offer to Algarotti: 'if your affairs do not permit your return to England, mine shall be arranged in such a manner as I may come to Italy.'[27] She would travel to his homeland to be with him. She admitted the suggestion she was making seemed extraordinary, but it had to be taken alongside the impression he had made on her heart. Algarotti, who was accustomed to having people fall in love with him, probably did not take her offer particularly seriously. The letter then continued with some far more matter-of-fact advice, in answer to a request he had made her about the best form of cataract operation for an elderly relation. Algarotti did not reply and for over a year their correspondence ceased. Maybe he did not know how to respond. Maybe letters have been lost. Or maybe he was simply preoccupied with his writing. He spent 1737 largely in Bologna, revising his book. Hervey wrote to him: 'I enquire often of Lady Mary what she knows of you. Sometimes she says she hears from you, sometimes that she does not; which is true I know not.'[28]

Having not seen Algarotti for over a year, with both her grown-up children away from home and a perpetually absent husband, Mary decided to challenge herself. For the first time she took work as a jobbing writer. The leading opposition newspaper at the time was called *Common Sense*. In December 1737 Mary began a series of nine articles about politics and public life, each printed on the front page of a new rival newspaper entitled *The Nonsense of Common Sense*. Although she chose not to be named as the author, Mary was nevertheless for the first time moving much closer to becoming a writer for hire. After all, she was infatuated with someone who was also a working author. Her printer was James Roberts, who had published poems of hers in the past. Now she wrote to him laying out her terms. She also scrawled on a printed copy of *Nonsense Number One*: 'all these wrote by me M.W.M. to serve an unhappy worthy man.'[29]

The nine articles, which were published over the next four months, took as their subject matter a variety of political issues of the day. Queen Caroline had died that year and in the first Mary responded to those who criticised the public mourning for her. People, Mary argued, would stop buying extravagant silk and start buying sensible wool instead as a result. She went on to criticise the working conditions of weavers. Her youthful idealism seemed to have returned. She did not mind risking Wortley's displeasure even if his involvement in life in Yorkshire meant that he would have known many of the wool-owners she was attacking.

Other subjects she tackled included an argument for replacing opera singers with robots; praise for low interest rates; a call for freedom of the press, in which she attacked the 'Race of Libellers' such as Pope; a hymn to liberty, where she questioned whether wealth and happiness could co-exist; and an attack on self-interest.

Her most interesting article in *The Nonsense of Common Sense* discussed the condition of women. She compared men's treatment of women with the more favourable treatment of their servants. She praised women who had done their duty to men. As the press had been attacking Walpole's second wife, her friend Maria Skerrett, maybe she was thinking of Maria. She suggested a picture gallery which rather than showing women according to their looks would show them according to their deeds. After all these were: 'Virtues of Choice, and not Beauties of Accident'.[30] She may have been regretting her decision to send her own portrait to Algarotti. Her deeds, not least her inoculation battle, were 'Virtues of Choice', after all.

Soon Mary's short excursion into the world of journalism came to an abrupt end. Maybe her reason for stopping was that she recognised that this kind of writing could not fill the emptiness that consumed her. It could not alter the fact that she was in a stale marriage with two grown-up children pursuing their own lives and that she was short of friends. Twickenham, which had been such a haven, was tainted by its association with Pope and by her sadness at Algarotti's absence. Her daughter and son-in-law returned from Scotland to London and presented her with her first granddaughter, also to be named Mary like her mother, grandmother and great-grandmother before her. Lady Mary was made the baby's godmother, but this did not fill the hole.

That spring there was renewed hope that she might see Algarotti again. His *Newtonianismo* had been published in Milan in December 1737 and the Catholic church had made it clear that he was no longer welcome in Italy, so instead he borrowed money from his long-suffering brother to return to England. He left in December 1737, accompanied by a new male lover of his own age named Firmacon. Mary wrote to him in English on 24 Feb 1738 to discuss the political situation. *The Nonsense of Common Sense* had perhaps helped her sublimate her feelings after all. She ended lovingly: 'I must necessarily be dull when the Sun and you are both so distant from me; may the spring bring return to you both.'[31] She was beginning to sound resigned to the situation.

On 15 June 1738 she wrote Algarotti another, very different letter, addressed to Paris, this time in French. She complained she had not heard from him for over a month, marvelled at the strength of her own feelings and acknowledged that she was deluding herself when she imagined that he thought of her sometimes in return. For the second time she made him an offer: if he could not come to England and if it pleased him, then she could come to Venice to 'settle in the States of the Signory for the rest of my life.' [32] Her plans were beginning to form. She likened herself to Homer's deserted Penelope, waiting for Odysseus to return. She praised his book, which she admitted she had read many times. Meanwhile Algarotti dallied in the south of France with Firmacon. He had a commission from Sir Robert Walpole to look for a painting by Veronese for Sir Robert to purchase. Mary may well have confided something of her unhappiness to Henrietta, Lady Oxford, who commissioned Carlo Francesco Rusca to paint her friend's portrait. Rusca depicted Mary cloaked in Turkish ermine, holding a book and leaning on a skull. Here was a woman who was evidently 50 years old but who was both stylish and learned.

Mary also made a new friend at this time in Henrietta Louisa, Countess of Pomfret. Although they had known each other previously it was only now that they grew close. Both were interested in interior decoration but careful what they spent on refurbishing their homes. They had met in several London auction rooms. The Pomfrets had ten children and money was short, so they had decided it would be cheaper to move abroad. This was what sealed the friendship. She might not yet admit it to her new friend, but Mary was thinking along the same lines. On 8 July 1738, Lady Pomfret went to take her farewell of Lady Mary before leaving for France. A warm, anecdotal correspondence began to develop between these two middle-aged women who shared friends, acquaintances and interests.

At same time Mary's closest friend, Claude-Charlotte, lay dying. Mary went to visit her daily, but there was nothing she could do. The struggle was long and painful. It eventually came to an end on 14 May 1739. The loss was hard to bear. Mary also had a painful and damaging quarrel with Lady Bute. The reason for the argument is unclear, but whatever happened Mary would remain convinced for many years that her daughter simply did not love her. The Butes headed north once more. Again, Mary was left alone. Much of her correspondence with Lady

Pomfret centred on the subject of how miserable life was in England. Algarotti remained in France, initially in Carcassonne and Toulouse, but by September, he was in Paris. They had now been apart for two years. Mary wrote to him in November 1738, swearing undying love as usual. She despaired that she would never hear from him again, she admitted.

In January 1739, Mary allowed herself to fantasise as before about a female 'Idol of a Parisienne, painted and gilded who receives…the homage that would make all my happiness.'[33] She wrote a poem about 'some giddy Girl' running to catch the prize which she had let drop. It did not cross her mind that any potential rival might also be male. When she again suggested moving to Venice Algarotti insisted that he would prefer to come to London. However, he would need some money for the fare. Hurriedly Mary wrote promising him that he could avail himself of any piece of her jewellery, but this unaccountably offended him. He wanted an open line of credit with her jeweller in Soho Square. She agreed.

In March 1739, Mary and Algarotti once again found themselves in the same city. As before, he successfully kept her in the dark about most of his activities. His new book on Newton was to be published in its English translation. Hervey acted as an unpaid publicist, sending copies to all the right people. Mary would have to be more circumspect. First Algarotti stayed with Andrew Mitchell, a barrister and fellow member of the Royal Society. Then he moved to St James's palace as a guest of Hervey's. Now Queen Caroline had died it was quickly evident he could not command the same favours, so he soon moved again to stay with Lord Burlington in Chiswick.

When Burlington outlived his usefulness, Algarotti found a new patron in Lord Baltimore, an officer in the household of the Prince of Wales, who had been appointed emissary to the Russian Court. Baltimore invited the young Venetian to accompany him to St Petersburg. Algarotti, who had begun thinking he might make a career for himself in the diplomatic service, accepted immediately and he and Baltimore set off for Russia together. Again, Algarotti's two middle-aged English lovers would send him rival letters during his trip. Most of Mary's do not survive, but Algarotti used his correspondence with Hervey to turn it into a travel book which was later published, inspired by what Mary had done with her *Embassy Letters*. True to form, he cannibalised them both.

Burlington's house in Chiswick was close to Twickenham and Mary and Algarotti must have met during this second visit of his to London, but neither of them documented what went on. By the time Algarotti left England again on 10 May, Mary was under the impression that he had agreed to her plan that she travel out to Venice and that they settle in the Italian city together. Predictably she said nothing of any of this in her letters to Lady Pomfret, whose life in Europe she was following with great interest. The plan was a bold one. It would mean a complete break with the life Lady Mary had been leading in England for the past twenty years, since her return from Turkey. Yet, she dared to hope that it might provide some kind of solution. As she wrote in a poem the following summer: 'I'm tired with this continual Rout/of bowing low and leading out.' [34]

Chapter 15

A New Life Abroad

'and so she set out with all the pleasure imaginable'[1]

Mary began making preparations for her new life in Europe with Algarotti, telling no one of her plans. Even Wortley seemed to think she was going to France, not Italy and for her health not for love. She began saying her goodbyes. She packed up thirteen different items of luggage, each marked with a bespoke MWM monogram, most of which were to be sent out to her later, once it was clear where she would settle. Three of the large boxes were full of her books and she smuggled others in elsewhere. The inventory alone of her books was twenty-three pages long. She included among them both the Italian and English editions of Algarotti's book *Newtonianismo* and poems by her old-friend-turned-enemy Alexander Pope. As she had always loved clothes, she took with her a bright red dress from Turkey, a hood, a laced hat and two velvet riding caps. She attended several auctions, including one in their old house in Covent Garden Piazza, perhaps dreaming of the new home she would be furnishing in Venice. She packed up four chairs, her needlework, two quilts, various items in gilt and silver and a box full of china. She would immediately regret not having taken her side-saddle and would write to Wortley to request it, along with more snuff, when French customs confiscated her initial stash. The entire shipment was valued at £500 (£78,000 today). She was clearly preparing for a whole new life abroad.

The prime motivation for Mary's trip was Algarotti. but she also found herself alienated from both children, whilst her husband was geographically absent and emotionally remote. She had suffered a painful and irreparable public quarrel with her erstwhile friend, Alexander Pope. Her closest friend, Claude-Charlotte, had just died a painful death. She increasingly disliked the climate in England. She had been suffering from gum disease and was sufficiently unwell to have given up riding, which had previously been one of her greatest pleasures. Her travelling for her health was of course a convenient fiction, but many people at the time went abroad for just this reason. Her letters to Lady Pomfret before she left indicate that she was indeed depressed and she had the example of Sister Mar to haunt her. Mary's spirits lifted immediately upon her departure. She had found in travel a cure for her low spirits, whatever the future would bring. She wrote to Lady Pomfret explaining that Wortley planned to follow her abroad in due course, but this was a well-chosen white lie.

On 16 July 1739 she wrote a brief note from London to Algarotti, who had now arrived in St Petersburg. Her words had an urgency and a determination very similar to the letters she had written to Wortley in the days leading up to their elopement twenty-five years before: 'It is not necessary to accompany such a proof of eternal Attachment with an embroidery of words.' She would meet him in Venice, she told him. She had considered arranging a *rendez vous* somewhere but decided it would be best to see him 'at the end of my pilgrimage'. It would be for him to answer her prayers and make her forget all the anxiety which surrounded her decision to leave. Perhaps at this moment she really did believe he could fulfil this role for her. Mary warned Algarotti that he must not write to her in London. She would be gone, and a letter sent there might have 'very unfortunate consequences'. If he did return to London once he had finished his current trip to Russia, then she took it for granted that he would not be staying there long.[2]

The day Mary left home, 25 July 1739, there was an eclipse of the sun. She set off with her two newly engaged servants, William and Mary Turner. Although the Turners had married just before leaving, they had deliberately not mentioned this to their new employer. Wortley's carriage took the three of them as far as Dover and was then sent back empty. Mary wrote a final, joyful note to Algarotti. She was leaving with a clear conscience: 'filled with faith and hope'. Her friends were weeping at her departure, but she was happy to 'take the leap for another world.' Before her, she explained, lay the Elysian Fields and happiness beyond imagining. She urged him to hurry to Venice: 'to repay me for all that I am sacrificing.' Even at this most exciting of moments there was an anxiety on her part that he might not repay her for everything she was giving up.[3]

Mary must have looked back on the parallel trip of she and Wortley setting out together for Constantinople, twenty years earlier. She made her way to Dover, stopping off to say goodbye to a friend in Blackheath. As soon as she left London, she started writing frequent, cheerful letters to Wortley, seemingly entirely untroubled by any guilt over leaving him. Perhaps she half-believed the fictitious tale she had spun him. Whatever her thinking, she instantly felt better. Whereas in her previous journey Mary had been travelling as the wife of a public figure, here her aim was to remain incognito. Nevertheless, impatient to get going, she decided not to wait for the packet boat, which sailed at night, but instead to hire her own vessel at the sum of five guineas (£825 today). Wortley would not be impressed.

Mary would pretend to Wortley throughout that she was unsure of her final destination. First, she travelled through France to Dijon, a journey of four or five days, and then she sailed down the Saône to Lyons, where she had been laid low with the 'flu on their way back from Turkey. In the past she and Wortley had found France impoverished and depressing, but this time everyone seemed cheerful and well fed. Her friendship with Claude-Charlotte in the interim had made her see France very differently. Her letters home were packed full of detail. She made sure in her correspondence with Wortley that she justified every item of her expenditure, always careful to report that she had spent wisely. She only informed him retrospectively on the anxieties she had that her money might be seized at the different borders she crossed. Almost as soon as she had crossed the English Channel she felt astonishingly recovered. She was: 'so much mended in my Health that I am surprised at it.'[4]

Although Mary had planned to travel incognito, it seemed that wherever she went she stumbled over fellow ex-pats, all of whom seemed remarkably friendly. As a middle-aged woman travelling alone, she must have stood out, but this was not necessarily a disadvantage. When she got into difficulties with customs or with foreign banks, her fellow travellers often proved themselves ready to step in and help her. She joked that she could not have been more followed had she been an Egyptian pyramid. In Turin she met Lady Pomfret's eldest son and she was quick to write to his mother, sending positive news of him, in marked contrast to her impression of one of her Feilding cousins, who also happened to be there. It was evident her plan to travel incognito was not going to work. Undeterred, she converted this into another excuse to

Wortley for constantly having to move on. She needed to find somewhere quieter, she explained, where she could be more anonymous.

By 6 Sept 1739 Mary was at the foot of the Alps, waiting to cross over via the Mont Cenis pass. She wrote a passionate note to Algarotti in French, comparing herself to Don Quixote. She admitted that nothing about the prospect frightened her nor distracted her from 'the sweet contemplation' of seeing him again. She included a few lines of poetry which she had written in English: 'Amidst this Chaos that around me lies/I only hear your voice, and see your Eyes.'[5] She was carried over the mountain pass on a seat strung between two poles, just as she had been before. In Turin she was stopped and threatened with being strip-searched for carrying snuff until some fellow English travellers intervened. Wherever she went, it seemed, people helped her, but still she was careful not to inform Wortley of this incident.

It was only when Mary got as far as Turin that she began to write to Wortley about the advantages of her travelling onwards to Venice. Rome she would avoid because the Old Pretender was there, she explained, and she wanted to make sure she distanced herself from the Jacobites with their connection to her brother-in-law. In Venice, however, she could live 'as quiet and as private as I please'.[6] She wrote to Lady Pomfret, who was in Siena, enthusing about the two of them meeting up in Venice. On the way she explored Milan, climbing enthusiastically to the top of the cathedral dome. She wrote home extolling the virtues of the Borrowmean Library there, which to her astonishment even allowed her to take books out. Her carriage broke down in the nearby city of Brescia and from there she took a boat down the river Po. By 25 September, she had arrived in Venice. Her leisurely journey had taken her in all about two months. When she did finally arrive, she was extremely careful in her letter to Wortley to include a reference to her regretting that this had not been her original plan. It was important, after all, to throw him off the scent.

Hervey knew the truth and she could write to him in a very different style. He wrote back eloquently. She had suggested to him that he travel out to join her, but he rejected the idea of 'jolting in Post-Chaises and lying in dirty Inns.' He described her flatteringly as a pilgrim with a staff in her hand and shells on her coat hem. The both knew the real reason for her pilgrimage, but he studiously avoided mentioning it. All he could do, he protested mockingly, was to send up a prayer to heaven for the purgatory that she as a travelling pilgrim would need to pass through before she entered 'the Gates of that Heaven your Piety deserves'.[7] Even then he eloquently acknowledged that a certain amount of waiting was going to be required until Algarotti arrived to join her.

Mary fell in love with Venice on first sight. She immediately went exploring the canals and palazzos. She loved the entire Venetian experience: the gondolas, 'the price of an English chair', the water lapping against the bridges, the 'clear bright sun' and the Grand Canal buildings fringed with green seaweed. She revelled in the fashion of ladies wearing 'a mask, price sixpence, with a little cloak and the head of a domino, the genteel dress to carry you everywhere,' which meant that it was 'the established fashion for every body to live their own way.'[8] She revelled in the anonymity it afforded her. Hervey wrote complimenting her that the descriptions of the city she sent him were better than Canaletto's paintings. Like Constantinople, Venice was extraordinarily diverse, and the range of different people Mary came across filled her with excitement. The city state was not a monarchy, like England, but an aristocratic republic. As such it felt quite close to Mary's own political ideal. She was not a monarchist but social status was nevertheless extremely important to her. She found herself constantly being offered boxes at the opera or the theatre, which delighted her. The air in Venice was wholesome, she stressed to Wortley, and it was remarkably cheap to live there. There was a man-of-war coming out relatively soon and Mary asked her husband to send out the rest of her belongings, hoping her boxes could travel out on it without risk of being seized by customs at Leghorn. Perhaps best of all, whereas in England her social circle had dwindled, here she was immediately a success.

Mary quickly found a palazzo to rent on the Grand Canal. She and Wortley knew the Italian Pietro Grimani from his time as Venetian ambassador in London and from their visit to Vienna. Now he was procurator of St Mark's, in other words one of the most important political figures within the Venetian Republic, and in 1741 he would go on to be made Doge, the highest office in Venice. He quickly came to visit Mary. He was a bit fatter than before but otherwise unchanged, she wrote home, and he sent Wortley his regards. Soon Mary was holding intimate literary evenings at her canal-side home. Grimani joined her for many of them. To her great delight, another of her visitors was her old friend Abbé Conti, whom she had not seen for twenty years.

She immediately started formally receiving new guests, including various ambassadors from different European countries. Despite the fact that Spain and England were on the verge of war she met the Spanish ambassador and quickly struck up a friendship with his wife. From arriving knowing only two people she soon found herself enjoying a whole new group of friends. Significant among these new acquaintances was the charming and elegant Venetian aristocrat Chiara Michiel, who would become one of her greatest friends, perhaps filling the hole left by Claude-Charlotte's death. She encouraged Lady Pomfret to visit, reporting that the social scene was excellent and there was very little vicious gossip and backbiting, unlike London.

Thousands of miles away, Algarotti was on the move again. He and his travelling companion, Lord Baltimore, left St Petersburg and headed through Germany where, at Rheinsburg, they met the 27-year-old Crown Prince Frederick of Prussia, the future Frederick the Great. Prince Frederick, who prided himself on his love of the arts, was married but had little interest in his wife. He was bowled over by Algarotti, who would have a profound and lasting effect on him. Baltimore hardly spoke any French, so Frederick and Algarotti were free to talk, undisturbed. Soon Algarotti was composing the libretto for a cantata which Frederick was planning to set to music. Frederick wrote to Voltaire of his new friend, whom he nicknamed 'the swan of Padua': 'He has lots of fire, of liveliness and of gentleness, which could not suit me better.'[9]

The visit lasted only eight days and in September, Algarotti and Baltimore travelled on to London for Algarotti's third and final visit there. He immediately looked up Hervey and confided in him just how wonderful Prince Frederick was: 'the most intelligent and amiable of men'.[10] This did not prevent his also starting, or maybe continuing, an affair with Andrew Mitchell, his host on his previous visit. Hervey wrote to Mary in November. Perhaps he realised he ought to let her know of Algarotti's whereabouts. 'Our Friend', he wrote discreetly, was in London.[11] Hervey had been careful, he explained to Mary, not to tell Algarotti that he had heard from her. After all, she had not given him any instructions to do so. He would follow whatever orders she sent him.

In Venice, Mary was not in a position to issue orders. All she could do, she felt, was wait. Apart from her correspondence with Wortley, she had little interaction with her family during these months in Venice. Her troubled son Edward had been to the city and departed before she arrived, leaving a trail of debts in his wake. He had used the name 'Montagu'. As a result, no one had made the connection between the middle-aged female traveller and the young rake. Grimani had simply assumed he was a confidence trickster. Mary concluded, quite rightly, that Edward had left under such a cloud he would not be back to bother her. Meanwhile her estrangement from her daughter continued. Lady Bute visited Wortley and sent out an unsealed letter to her mother with one of his. Mary's immediate instinct was to mistrust what she termed 'Scotch Artifice'. She complained to Wortley that Lady Bute was still treating her badly. She put her recent ill health down to the problems between mother and daughter and claimed her love for Lady Bute had been 'the passion of my Life'.[12] Even her maternal love for her daughter was now being used to distract Wortley from the real passion she had been feeling over the past few years. There was more truth in the rueful comment she made to Wortley that ''tis long since that I have looked upon the Hopes of continuing a Family as one of the vainest of mortal projects.'[13]

The Pomfrets had moved on from Siena to Florence. They began pressing Lady Mary to come and visit them there. Mary concocted an elaborate story to explain to them why she needed to stay in Venice, claiming that she had been waiting for Wortley to join her. That had always been their plan, she wrote, but his business in Newcastle had delayed him initially. Since then political difficulties with Spain had caused problems, though Mary continued to hope he would visit her in the spring and so needed to wait in Venice for his arrival. Meanwhile she wrote to Wortley that Lady Pomfret had been delayed by the illness of one of her daughters from visiting Mary in Venice but would be coming very soon. She could admit to neither her real reason for wanting to stay put.

In December Algarotti finally wrote to her, claiming not to have received any of her letters and suggesting that, rather than his coming to Venice, they might meet instead in Paris. Furious, she wrote back on Christmas Eve. She simply did not believe that all her letters had gone astray, she wrote to him. Even if that were the case, she found it extraordinary 'that you could imagine that I travel about the world in order to see carnivals and Festivals.' Surely he remembered their agreement that he come to live with her in the Venetian states? She had arranged her entire life so that they could do that. She could not simply travel to Paris, even if she wanted to. She ended with a flourish: 'It is certain that if I cannot make your happiness you cannot make mine. I do not intend to constrain you.' Her righteous indignation shone through.[14]

Hervey wrote to her from London a couple of weeks later. He reiterated that he had not said anything to Algarotti about her situation, as he had not yet had instructions from her on what to do. It feels unlikely this was true, given his past history of mocking her in his letters to Algarotti, and their hidden rivalry for Algarotti's affections. Hervey related how he had been forced to stop writing when 'our Friend' entered the room. Even without knowledge of the full facts, this must have been a painful image for Lady Mary. She had travelled across Europe to start a new life with someone who was at this moment entering the drawing room of one of her greatest friends back in London. Hervey went on to give her some advice. Just as a Venetian (in other words Algarotti) had made her forget every Englishman, so now someone from Piedmont, he suggested, might make her forget every Venetian. In other words, it was best to forget Algarotti. In part this was the well-meaning advice of a friend, but Hervey and Algarotti were doubtless sitting together in London, laughing at her behind her back.

Luckily, Mary was thriving in Venice by herself. Her palazzo had become the centre of a hugely enjoyable social circle. She revelled in the Venetian Christmas Eve celebrations and attended the high mass in St Mark's, excused as a non-Catholic from taking part in the service but nevertheless loving the spectacle. Meanwhile Wortley methodically sent out her remittance at regular intervals. She continued to reassure him that she was living relatively cheaply. She began writing again. *Carabosse* is her own ironic version of *Sleeping Beauty* where good and bad fairies competed to give gifts and the bad fairy won through. She had recovered her customary witty authorial voice. She dedicated the story to Abbé Conti and showed him her Rochefoûcault essay to admire. He had always been a particular supporter of hers and was now doing all he could to spread her reputation as a writer in Venice. She found the culture here favoured women far more than in London.

Venice began filling up for the carnival which ran from after Christmas to Ash Wednesday. Mary was delighted with the various Europeans to whom she was introduced, able to name-drop obscure European royal titles with ease. She liked the fact she was now living in a republic but spent her time sitting next to sovereign princes and being treated like a princess. To her surprise, she was celebrated wherever she went, as a particular feature of the social scene. As she put it: 'the Distinctions showed me here are very far above what I could expect.'[15] She was scathing about the young English travellers who stopped to pay their respects as they passed through Venice on the grand tour, likening them to the plagues of Egypt. and calling them 'the greatest blockheads in nature'[16], but she felt differently about James Stuart Mackenzie, Lord Bute's only younger brother. While relations continued frosty between Mary and her son-in-law, she and Mackenzie soon became very close. A lasting friendship would develop.

England did not have full diplomatic relations with Venice at the time, because the English government had taken umbrage at Venice's having received the Old Pretender's son, the Young Pretender, with full royal honours. Mary did not rate the English Consul, the 80-year-old Niel Browne. With the confidence of middle age, she was not shy in passing these kinds of judgements. In fact, she made offers to both to Wortley and to Sir Robert Walpole to send them intelligence reports about the situation in Venice. Walpole politely declined, using Hervey to write the refusal letter. Wortley, while making it clear he did not think she was somewhere where she would receive anything of relevance, did make provisions for her to send reports. They should not be in her own writing, he specified, and not be sent to him directly but to an anonymous source.

That spring Lady Pomfret kept up the pressure to persuade Mary to visit them in Florence, where they had rented a palazzo. The bad weather affected Mary's mood and she had to find ways of prevaricating until she knew what Algarotti intended to do. He was now suggesting they might meet in Geneva, in Holland, or somewhere in France. In February, she wrote twice to Lady Pomfret to say that the roads and weather made it too difficult for her to travel. The weather continued to be bad in March. Then the Ascension Day celebrations prevented her from leaving, she explained. In May the weather was bad again. In June it became evident that Mary's maid, Mary Turner, was pregnant and had been trying to hide this from her. This provided a perfect further excuse, for Mary could not travel without a maid. Not that Mary was overly supportive about Mary Turner's pregnancy, describing her to Lady Pomfret as 'the creature.'[17] Next it was the fault of all the many English who demanded to pay her their respects. They 'torment me as much as the frogs and lice did the palace of the Pharoah,' she explained.[18] Lady Pomfret, whose patience was being sorely tested by now, wrote angrily that Mary was just putting up excuses. Mary wrote back protesting that she could not possibly have got her own maid pregnant.

The Regatta finished at Easter but now Venice was preparing for the official Ascension Day celebrations. Mary accepted invitations to more balls, concerts and assemblies and the weather started improving. She went to the Arsenal to look at the *Bucentaur,* the gorgeously decorated boat used to transport the Doge out to sea on Ascension Day. The ceremony marked the Republic's 'marrying' the Adriatic Sea and the Doge dropping a ring into the water to signify the union. Mary went to watch the Ascension Day regatta from Grimani's palazzo, along with a great assembly of other people, all of whom were elaborately entertained. She wrote to Wortley to say that if it proved too difficult for the boat carrying her luggage to land at Leghorn, she could always go to Avignon in France to collect it. Perhaps she was making plans in case the only way of seeing Algarotti was for her to travel to France. She would need a cover story if that were the case.

In March, she wrote to Algarotti in a very different tone. She had chosen Venice as a place to settle, she explained, above all because it suited him. Her only desire was that they were close. She had found happiness here in Venice and new friendships: 'In brief, I am miraculously much better off than in London.' However, that did not mean Venice was the only answer. She would be happy to go somewhere else if he wished. She entreated him to consult his heart. Suppose he did come to Venice and settle there, even if he would rather not live in the same house as her, he could perhaps lodge nearby and they could see each other every day? If instead he wished her to move to a provincial town in France, then of course she would do it. What she wanted was a world where: 'we could live in Tranquillity.'[19] Now she was happier than she had been in London, she was able to attempt to negotiate. A compromise could perhaps be found. But she got no answer.

At the end of May, Crown Prince Frederick's father died. His immediate response was to summon Algarotti: 'I await you with impatience.'[20] Algarotti was at his side by the third week in June, discussing philosophy with the new emperor. Like Mary, Hervey was desperate for news. He wrote but got no reply. In June he wrote to Mary. He had lost 'my Friend Algarotti'. No need to avoid using their lover's name now. In July, Mary wrote Algarotti a hurried, angry note. She enclosed some of her writing, which, she explained, she occupied herself with in his absence, but she feared that his 'great visit' to Prussia, was 'doomed to be a great folly.' She also wrote to Wortley informing him that she would set out for Florence in the next few days. She could delay no longer. It was evident Algarotti was not coming.[21]

A letter from Mary to Lady Pomfret confirmed that, regardless of whether Mary Turner had given birth or not, she had decided she would come to see them in Florence. If the Pomfrets moved on to Rome then, Mary announced, she would be glad to accompany them. Mary Turner did give birth in early August and almost immediately the little party consisting of Lady Mary, William Turner, his wife Mary and the new baby set off for Florence. Lady Mary herself was suffering her familiar complaint of a swollen face. And a broken heart. For the next few years Mary would remain convinced that the Turners were only behaving badly so they could goad her into sacking them, and she would then have to pay for their voyage home. This fretting over servants was a very far cry from the romantic bliss she had imagined for herself when she set out from London. But there had been compensations along the way. Algarotti might have let her down, but she had rediscovered the joys of travel and fallen in love with the city of Venice. Next Florence awaited her.

Chapter 16

Finishing Things with Algarotti

'a very disagreeable Epoque of your Life'[1]

The Pomfrets, of course, knew nothing of Mary's real reason for being in Italy. They provided a convenient excuse to stay on, while she waited to see if she could engineer a reunion with Algarotti. What was due to be a month's visit with them in Florence extended to two months before she eventually set off again by herself, this time to Rome and to Naples, where Mary could pretend she was still waiting for her luggage to arrive by boat whilst looking for antique remains to send home to Wortley. Only Mary herself knew her real reason for keeping on the move. She needed to be reunited with Algarotti. In time she would see him again and her dream of time together in the land of his birth really would come true, but their meeting would not bring her the happiness she had been chasing. In truth, it was only her determination to remain civilised which prevented it from turning sour.

Mary set off from Venice to visit the Pomfrets in Florence in August 1740. The journey from Venice to Bologna was straightforward but the road from Bologna to Florence did not prove so easy. Finally, she arrived in what she had written to her hostess would be 'the promised land' and her friends welcomed her with open arms.[2] Lady Pomfret liked the historical connections associated with the Palazzo Ridolfi, the large house she and her husband had rented in Florence. Machiavelli had apparently lived there in the past. It was divided into separate apartments. The Pomfrets occupied one, while they installed Lady Mary with her servants in another, so their new guest was afforded some independence. The friends enjoyed sharing a social life in Florence and going together to see the famous sights. Lady Pomfret had put off visiting the Uffizi and the Pitti Palace until Lady Mary joined them. The two women also went to the comic opera together. They walked on

162

the Ponte Vecchio. They visited artists' studios. There was no time for Lady Mary to worry over her future with Algarotti. Her planned one month's visit extended to two.

Mary partly confided in Lady Pomfret about her unhappiness, although she kept what she said so ambiguous that she might have appeared to have been talking about her sadness over her son, not her lover. She showed her friend her essay *Sur la Maxime de Mr de Rochefoûcault,* and Lady Pomfret liked it very much, just as Conti had done in Venice. Unsure about Algarotti's whereabouts, Mary sent Hervey letter after letter, ingenuously asking him to forward them. Hervey attached a note with one saying he was sending Algarotti 'another letter from Sappho'. With his normal duplicitousness he wrote of Mary's letters: 'They seem to me like Sancho's geese and Banquo's kings, as if there was no end of them.'[3] Mary also wrote direct to Algarotti. She was making a short tour, she explained, whilst she waited to hear from him. On October 11, towards the end of her stay in Florence, she was: 'ready to go where you wish. I await your orders to regulate my life.' She clung to the notion that they still had a future living together as a couple. With this came a warning. She had been 'undecided' as she put it for a very long time, and she was clear that now: 'it is assuredly time for me to make up my mind.'[4] She would not wait forever.

Meanwhile, Algarotti was caught up in his ongoing affair with Frederick the Great. Like Mary, Frederick found Algarotti wary of emotional commitment. In a letter Frederick asked his lover to try his best to be open and sincere towards him, just the same requests that Mary was making. Algarotti had confided in his brother that he was discouraged as to whether Frederick would give him the financial support he needed. At the beginning of August, Frederick and Algarotti travelled to Paris, where Frederick fell ill. Voltaire visited them there and found a feverish Frederick, surrounded by several of his favourites, of whom Algarotti was only one. Frederick then travelled on to Regensburg to recuperate while Algarotti headed for Berlin. He had a plan. His hope was that by absenting himself he might prompt Frederick to realise how much he valued him. He began dreaming Frederick might perhaps give him a diplomatic position in England. Instead, at the end of the year, Frederick did finally send him a small amount of money and bestowed on him the title of count.

In Florence, Lady Mary was meeting many of the Pomfrets' acquaintances there. On her second day she met Lady Walpole, the prime minister's daughter-in-law. Lady Walpole had been married to Sir Robert's oldest son but was now separated from him. The Walpole family mistrusted her, as she had been unfaithful. She was in Florence with her lover, Samuel Sturgis. Mary was not impressed by Lady Walpole's flaunting of her relationship in this way, nor the couple's public arguments. Perhaps it made her reflect on her own situation with Algarotti. Mary would later make it clear to Wortley that she had been careful to avoid getting close to Lady Walpole, and that she mistrusted the weekly meetings Lady Walpole held where her guests were invited to discuss the folly of religion. Although Lady Mary herself was an agnostic, she felt that the ceremony of religion played an important role in maintaining civilisation and the rule of law. If Mary disliked Lady Walpole, the feeling was reciprocated. Lady Walpole did not think much of Mary's poetry and belittled Mary's taste in novels and romances.

At the same time Mary met Lady Walpole's brother-in-law, the 21-year-old Horace, or 'Hory' as Mary called him. Horace Walpole was in Florence as part of his grand tour. He had been inoculated as a child, thanks presumably to Mary's friendship with his father. Horace had opposed his father's second marriage. Mary had been a close friend of Walpole's second wife, Maria Skerrett, and instrumental in their relationship. Both Horace's mother and Maria Skerrett were now dead, but Horace could not forget the past. His own parents' marriage had never been happy. There were rumours that Horace himself was the product of an affair between his mother and Lord Hervey's brother, and Horace looked nothing like the rest of his family. Doubtless coming across Lady Mary in Florence dredged up all kinds of complicated thoughts and feelings for him.

Just before Horace was introduced to Mary, he had confided in a friend that he was due to meet 'a third she-meteor', who would shine alongside Lady Pomfret and his sister-in-law. The three would form, he wrote, 'a coalition of prudery, debauchery, sentiment, history, Greek, Latin, French, Italian and metaphysics'.[5] Horace tended to dislike women in general. He may well have been gay. If not, he was asexual. For him intellectual prowess was something men aspired to. Women should not. He made it clear that he did not rate Mary's writing: 'I like few of her performances,' he wrote, judging her style 'too womanish'.[6] But he hid this from Mary herself. She read him the *Town Eclogues* during her visit, and he took the trouble to add a seventh poem of his own, completing the cycle: 'as a Sequel to Lady Mary Wortley's Six'.[7] Inevitably his was very different in style.

Horace was at pains in his letters home to criticise Mary's behaviour during their time together. When she played at cards, he wrote, she cheated 'horse and foot'.[8] At an evening of country dancing held by the Pomfrets, Lady Mary apparently competed with Lady Walpole for the attentions of George Pitt, one of the young male guests. She even had the audacity to invite the young man to dance, rather than waiting for him to ask her. Everyone apparently laughed 'at her old, foul, tawdry, painted, plastered personage'.[9] As far as Horace was concerned, Mary had transgressed the normal social rules. Country dances were particularly active. She had danced vigorously despite being a 51-year-old woman. This, he felt, gave him licence to criticise.

Horace wrote a further particularly unflattering description of Mary's looks to a friend. She wore: 'a foul mob, that does not cover her greasy black locks, that hang loose, never combed or curled', and 'an old mazarine blue wrapper', which gaped open, revealing her petticoat. Her face he described as being swollen on one side. He hinted that this was due to the pox - or syphilis - continuing Pope's insinuations, which he had almost certainly read. Mary apparently inexpertly covered her face with white make-up to hide it. She had mentioned to Lady Pomfret that she had a swollen face at the time, but this was not due to syphilis. Instead, she was probably suffering from her usual complaint of the toothache. Her face was marked by smallpox scars, so her using make-up to hide them was understandable and not at all unusual.[10]

According to Horace, Mary was forced to leave Venice at the end of her visit. This was demonstrably untrue. Then, when she left Florence, he claimed her bedroom needed a special airing and that her sheets were bloodied. While at the country dance he had condemned her for being too old, post-menopausal, now her crime was that she still young enough to bleed. Apparently, she had also made sexual advances towards a suitor of one of the Pomfrets' daughters. Horace described her as having an insatiable sexual appetite. All this reeked of pure hatred on his part. None of it felt truthful. In fact, Mary's visit was deemed a great success by her hosts, who parted with her regretfully. Her friendly correspondence with Lady Pomfret continued. For her part, perhaps fortunately, Lady Mary remained ignorant of Horace's vicious loathing. She always felt her relationship with 'Hory' was a civil one.

On 16 October 1741, Mary then set off from Florence on a three-day journey to Rome, sending Lady Pomfret a polite thank you letter once she arrived. She had slept in a hovel on the way, she wrote, with only Mary Turner (and presumably Mary Turner's new baby) for company. She wrote to Wortley back in England telling him that she expected the Pomfrets to join her in Rome. Yet again, she was lying to him. Nothing in her letters to Lady Pomfret indicated that this was their plan. Her time in Rome was far more solitary than the social whirl she had experienced in Florence. She found rooms to rent in the Palazzo Zuccaro. It had a large garden, and this prompted her to begin exploring other gardens in the city, including that of the Villa Borghese, which she thought particularly delightful. She wrote to Lady Pomfret describing how she spent her days and included a short poem she had written in which she portrayed herself as a wounded deer, continuing to attempt to run, despite an arrow in her side. The poem had none of the emotional truth of her Algarotti love poetry. It did, though, show that she was prepared to admit something of her pain to her friend. Just writing about her feelings meant that they had begun to feel less intense, more received.

The dark and rainy weather in Rome in mid-November made Mary decide to move on again, this time further south to Naples. Wortley had suggested she might like it there. She was biding her time until she and Algarotti found themselves in the same city again, so this seemed as good a plan as any. James Stuart Mackenzie pressed her to return to Venice and even promised to come to Bologna to collect her, but Mary preferred to head on to Naples instead. Again, the journey was not easy. This time she decided to buy her own carriage, which overturned *en route*. In contrast to the Papal States, Naples seemed 'gay and Flourishing', even though the city was so overcrowded it was hard to find anywhere to stay.[11] The weather was warmer than in Rome and there was no need to light a fire, although this made her lodgings damp. The Neapolitan nobility she found friendly and she enjoyed the very fine opera there too. She met the son of the Spanish ambassador's wife, who had become her friend back in Venice. Her planned two weeks' stay extended to six and she even considered settling in Naples more permanently. However, the instability of the political situation concerned her. Besides, there still seemed to have been no news from Algarotti.

Naples interested Mary in particular because the ruins of an ancient city had recently been uncovered under the lava at Herculaneum. She was very keen to take a tour and applied to the King of Naples for the necessary permission. Earlier in the year Horace Walpole had been allowed to do so and she had probably heard him talk about his trip, but since Horace's visit a group of English tourists had arranged to have illegal copies made of some of the Roman treasures found there. As a result, access had become far more restricted. Mary never did get to see Herculaneum. On 5 December her luggage finally arrived from England at the Italian port of Leghorn. The original plan had been to have it sent straight to Venice but now she learned it could be dispatched to wherever she requested. Perhaps it could be shipped to her in Naples? Mary hesitated. The political instability dissuaded her. She would stay for the new year, but she then decided it would be more sensible to go herself to Leghorn to collect her bags, stopping off at Rome en route.

Lady Mary returned to Rome in January 1741. In Venice the friendship between James Stuart Mackenzie and Chiara Michiel was growing stronger and the two friends both put pressure on Mary to join them there. She declined. Perhaps Mackenzie, as Bute's brother, was instrumental in the letter Lady Mary now received from her son-in-law informing her that her daughter had given birth to their first son. The short note, neatly written, unlocked something in her relationship with the Butes. Very gradually the difficulties there would begin to improve, helped perhaps by the distance between the Butes in Scotland and Mary in Italy. Mary stayed in Rome for six weeks. She probably delayed her departure, hoping yet again to hear from Algarotti.

For his part Algarotti was in regular correspondence with Hervey in London. A cryptic note in one of her letters to Lady Pomfret implied that Mary had been trying to use her contacts to secure for Algarotti the role of Prussian ambassador to Venice. This would have answered her dreams and helped him as well. Instead Algarotti was sent by Frederick on a secret diplomatic mission to Turin to sound out its rulers, the royal court of Savoy, in the hope they would support Frederick's military ambitions. Both Algarotti and Frederick were now being treated for venereal disease. Presumably one of them had given it to the other. Naturally Mary knew nothing of this. Hervey did probably keep Mary informed of Algarotti's whereabouts. She learned that Algarotti was finally on his way to Italy, where they had agreed to meet two years earlier.

He would arrive in Turin at the end of January. His reason for being there, however, had nothing to do with her.

This second time in Rome proved more sociable than Mary's first. There had been severe flooding while she had been away in Naples and she spent time with her new acquaintances in Rome debating which might be the best town in Europe in which to settle. Lady Pomfret's daughter Lady Sophia gossiped to a friend that she suspected Mary would soon leave Italy and return to England 'to spend the rest of her days with old and odd Mr Wortley.'[12] Sam Sturgis arrived in Rome without Lady Walpole and, as Mary wrote to Lady Pomfret: 'the very face of a lover kicked out of doors'.[13] Reading the letter, Lady Pomfret jokingly accused her friend of having fallen in love with him. Mary wrote back indignantly. None of the men she had met on her travels interested her, she protested: 'Some figures are good, others have been ill made; and all equally indifferent to me.'[14]

Mary did though enjoy her role as someone whom all the young English gentlemen were encouraged to visit on their grand tour. She described herself to Wortley as their queen and they certainly paid court to her. She took the credit for being a good influence on their behaviour. When they were with her, she explained: 'there was neither Gameing or any sort of Extravagence.'[15] Although she did not compare the young men to their son Edward, the inference was there for Wortley to see. One of these young men visitors was Lord Lincoln, whom Mary claimed kinship with through their mutual ancestor, 'Wise' William Pierrepont. This, she explained to the rather non-plussed Lincoln, was why they shared a common interest in reading. Lincoln had fallen in love with Lady Sophia, Lady Pomfret's daughter, but would eventually make a pragmatic marriage to someone else. He shared Horace Walpole's attitude towards Mary and joked with him about her notion of their sharing blood. Horace wrote back to his friend that Mary's blood was 'poxed, foul, malicious, black'.[16]

Lincoln's tutor, Joseph Spence, felt very differently about meeting Lady Mary. He described her in glowing terms as 'one of the most extraordinary shining characters in the world'.[17] He wrote home to his mother detailed accounts of their various meetings and these letters counter-balance Horace's and Lincoln's. Mary and Spence talked on a wide variety of subjects. He was interested in her relationship with Pope. They discussed her elopement. Mary also explored with Spence her theory that men and women should keep their finances completely separate. This would stop the practice of men marrying for money, she theorised. She gave Spence a piece of her writing where, as in her letter to Sister Mar, she argued that parliament should dissolve all marriages at frequent intervals: 'the effect of this would be, that a multitude of slaves would be set free with us every seventh year.'[18] Although Mary had told him she thought it was possible for two people to be happy in the state of matrimony in theory, she regretted that this was an extremely rare situation: ''tis not quite impossible that this may happen, one time or another, before the world is at an end.'[19] She had shifted her approach from when she was writing her Rochefoûcault essay. She was not so indiscreet as to admit to Spence that her own marriage had disintegrated, but he could certainly have inferred that from their conversations.

In February, Mary set off once more, this time for Leghorn to collect her belongings. She wrote to Lady Pomfret, apologising yet again for not meeting up with her. As she sat writing, she explained, she was expecting at any moment to be summoned on board ship. Taking her luggage with her, she set sail from Leghorn to Genoa. Finally, it looked as if she might meet Algarotti. The passage was stormy. She had now been in Italy for a year and a half, successfully concealing her real reason for being there. Lady Pomfret wrote that Mary was 'wandering about Italy …to find some place where she may have six friends to pass the evenings with her.'[20] Her remark was kindly meant. She did not realise that her friend, who next left her luggage in Genoa and travelled on alone by road to Turin, was finally nearing the destination of her dreams.

Mary arrived in Turin on 16 March 1741. Algarotti could no longer avoid her. They would spend the next two months together and then they would part, their relationship at an end. What went on between them is of course shrouded in mystery. All we know for sure is that they both believed after two months that things between them were definitively over. Mary kept among the papers found at her death a fourteen-line poem written in Italian in Algarotti's handwriting. It was stored in her copy of the romantic novel, *La Princesse de Clèves*. Perhaps the novel reminded her of what happened between them. It told a tragic love story. The heroine was married but was in love with someone else. Her husband discovered her secret but subsequently died, leaving his widow free to marry her lover. But the marriage did not take place and instead she entered a convent. The author claimed to have learned about the nature of true love from this beautiful heroine, now a nun. As for the poem stored inside the novel, we do not know if it was written at that time and if so whether it was written by Mary or by Algarotti. It took the form of a meditation on the definition of love. Tantalisingly, it ended: 'True love, Maria, is what one guesses it to be.'[21]

Both Mary and Algarotti wrote to Hervey during their two months in Turin. As soon as Mary arrived, she wrote Hervey a letter which he noted was particularly cheerful and optimistic about her prospects. Another of her letters included a paragraph written in Algarotti's handwriting. Algarotti soon stopped writing letters of his own to Hervey. In one of the letters which Hervey wrote to Algarotti he signed off: 'my best respects and wishes attend your delightful companion.'[22] Hervey must have had mixed feelings about their spending time together without him. Hervey's son was visiting Turin. He went to pay court and even carried one of their joint letters back home with him for his father. Algarotti wrote eleven letters to his brother during his time in Turin, but they gave very little away as to what was really happening. His time with Lady Mary was 'not the least extraordinary' episode he wrote, deliberately using double negatives, in his own entire extraordinary life. Extraordinarily good or extraordinarily bad he did not say.[23]

We do have one single letter from Lady Mary to Algarotti, which probably dates from when they parted in May 1741. He would be angry with her, she wrote, for putting down in writing these words to him. As she saw it: 'I have begun to scorn your scorn, and in that vein I no longer wish to restrain myself.' She recalled the way, when she first fell in love with him, she could hardly speak, so fearful was she that she was probably boring him. Now, though, those feelings had gone. She had studied him, she explained. She had even used the book he was writing when they first met, the *Newtonianismo,* to understand the way light refracted through a prism. Just like that light, she had dissected his soul. She had to admit she had almost gone blind doing so, 'for these prisms are very dazzling.' His soul might be beautiful but the refracted light of his feelings towards her amounted only to indifference: 'because I am dull enough to arouse nothing better.' Mary was being exceptionally tough on herself. She did not flinch from what she saw as the truth and in doing so, she maintained her essential dignity. She realised that whatever spark there had been between the two of them had been extinguished.[24]

When they parted, Algarotti went to be with Frederick at his court in Potsdam and Mary headed back to Genoa. She had written to Hervey from Turin, which had been as he put it: 'a very disagreeable Epoque of your Life'.[25] She wrote again to him from Genoa and a third letter was carried back to England by his son. She craved his advice. He wrote back to her in June with a simple recommendation: 'your own Breast must be your best Cabinet-Council.' Mary must trust her feelings. She had intimated that the emotions of an elderly woman were unimportant, but he disagreed: 'the less one has left the more industrious one should be to manage and improve it.'[26] He quoted her some lines from Ovid. The best way to get over love, he advised, was to find someone else. This was Hervey's style but not Mary's. He rid himself of any feelings he still had for someone by forming bonds with other lovers. She would not, or could not, do that. In his own way he was giving her wise counsel. He may not have told her the full story, but nevertheless he had proved himself to be a friend to her when she needed him. What would she do now? One thing was certain. She had no intention of returning to England.

Chapter 17

Wandering Through Europe

'destiny must be followed, and I own, was I to choose mine, it should never be to stay perpetually in the same place'[1]

For the next few years Mary's life was peripatetic. The political situation in the region made things difficult for her. England had decided to support the heir to the Austrian throne, Maria Theresa, against Algarotti's patron and lover, Frederick the Great. Frederick fought the Austrians at the Battle of Mollwitz and was victorious on 10 April 1741, in what became known as the War of the Austrian Succession, just at the time that Mary and Algarotti were together. That autumn, when she and Algarotti parted, Mary went first to Genoa. Support for Maria Theresa was dissipating. Spain soon joined the war on the side of Frederick the Great, against the Austrians and the British, and began exercising its muscles over the Hapsburg-owned lands in Italy. As an Englishwoman, Lady Mary would no longer necessarily be safe there. She tried neutral Switzerland, but it was not to her liking. Next she went to Chambéry in France, but Spanish ambitions were not limited to Italy. Spain was soon at war with France too. Chambéry began to feel unsafe. Eventually Mary travelled to Avignon and settled there. Although situated in France, Avignon was owned by the Papal States, so it provided some kind of haven.

Three years later, in 1745, the Young Pretender began his campaign to regain the English throne for his father. The French gave him their support. Suddenly France and England were also at war. Mary found herself probably the only English person in Avignon who opposed the Young Pretender. Mrs Hay, an Englishwoman living there and said to be the Young Pretender's mistress, even began spreading rumours that Lady Mary was in fact a spy for George II back in England. Although Avignon was officially neutral, the political situation at the time caused food prices to double. Newspapers were no longer available and increasingly

172

Mary's letters went astray. She could trust no one. She wrote to Lady Pomfret that 'friendship in France (was) as impossible to be attained as orange trees in the mountains of Scotland.'[2] The Young Pretender's campaign went disastrously wrong, so by 1746 the streets of Avignon were full of Jacobite refugees, but instead of improving things this only seemed to make them worse. When Mary learned to her alarm that the French king had the right to seize all the jewellery and silver that she had planned to leave to her daughter on her death, she began to dream once more of returning to her beloved Italy.

At the start of this period, as soon as she had parted from Algarotti, Mary went to Genoa to find her luggage again. She decided to stay on there for the summer. She rented a lovely small palazzo by the sea for four months, deliberately avoiding the idea that she might consider returning home. She enjoyed the social life there and Wortley felt well-disposed enough towards her to increase her allowance. With an annual income of £1,100 (approximately £155,000 today) she was not short of money, but Italy was becoming dangerous. When Mary went to visit the consul in Genoa expressly to tell him about the rumours she had heard that the Spanish were very likely to invade, he belittled her anxieties, much to her annoyance. By mid-September she had had enough. She decided to head to Geneva in Switzerland, making it clear to Wortley that she would return to Italy once the political situation changed.

Mary and her servants travelled back to Turin and yet again crossed the Alps at Mont Cenis to reach the small Swiss republic of Geneva on 11 October 1741. Mary liked the city's lakeside situation but found it quiet, rather like an English country town. There was also a strong prevailing wind. It was, she felt, the exact opposite of Italy with 'no shew and a great deal of eating'.[3] She still feared a Spanish invasion and with prices in Geneva too high for her, Mary decided to move on. As she was reluctant to cross the Alps yet again, she chose the small French city of Chambéry as the next possible place to settle. She arrived there in November. Like Geneva, Chambéry was provincial, but her money went further there. It was also very sociable. The food and drink were good and the people companionable. She hired a new cook. Her health improved and she adopted the local habit of riding astride rather than side-saddle. Her letters increasingly went astray because political events were unfolding just as she had feared. She reported to Wortley at the end of November that the Spanish had indeed landed in Italy. By the beginning of March 1742, with the French army advancing towards Chambéry, it no longer felt safe. She decided to move on yet again.

Mary and her small household travelled next to Avignon, which they reached in May 1742, and which looked more likely to provide a safe haven for her. She reported that there were a lot of Spaniards in Avignon but that they seemed friendly. It was, she noted to Wortley: 'perhaps the town in the whole world where politics is least talked of.'[4] Ideal. She would stay in Avignon for the next four years and would even occasionally find it to her liking. Again, it proved expensive, but Mary rented an agreeable house at the top of the town. She was critical of the food in Avignon and of the wind, just as she had been in Geneva. She initially had concerns about her eyesight too, but gradually she was able to see more clearly again. A fever broke out in the city in February 1743, which she succumbed to, but she soon recovered. She also had more time to write now she was settled properly again. She probably drafted her allegorical fairy tale *Princess Docile* here and she wrote a rhetorical letter arguing forcefully for the education of women. As for the residents, she wrote to Chiara Michiel: 'People here know as little what Conversation is, as if they were fish.'[5]

Mary would often enjoy walking up to the ancient citadel of Rochers-des-Doms, above Avignon, with its magnificent views looking out at the countryside and back down over the city. When she praised the place to Wortley, she was careful to say the only better view in the whole world was that from Wharncliffe Lodge, the 'hovel' her father-in-law had lived in outside Sheffield. The Avignon city council heard how much she liked Rochers-des-Doms and, as a mark of their respect for such a famous English resident, in 1743 they granted her the use of a round tower there for the rest of her life. Delighted, she began work to improve it. She added a dome and a pavilion - alterations which would not cost much, she reassured Wortley. She moved all her books up to the tower for safe keeping and spent many happy evenings reading and writing, gazing at the view. On the inside of the tower she inscribed a verse, which she had translated from Latin, as her own fake epitaph, changing the gender of the subject from male to female, and praising a life: 'With decent poverty content/Her hours of ease not idly spent.' When she proudly sent the lines to Wortley he wrote back angrily. Why was she pretending that she had died? And that she had led a life of poverty? What would people think? Her intentions had been good, she reassured him.[6]

Mary's friends remained very precious to her during these years travelling through Europe, trying to find the right place to settle. The Pomfrets had returned to live in England in autumn 1741 but Lady Mary and Lady Pomfret continued to write to each other. Lady Mary's double friendship continued with Chiara Michiel and James Stuart Mackenzie, who she said had 'the heart of an Angel'.[7] Chiara's husband had been posted to Spain and Lady Mary wrote her many flowery letters about how the Spanish could not possibly appreciate her talents. In October 1742, Mary went on a special trip from Avignon to Lyons to meet Mackenzie and they wrote Chiara a joint letter from there. Mary's letters to Chiara about Mackenzie tended to alternate between concern about his lack of ambition and anxiety that he might be working too hard. In 1743 however, he fell from grace. He was enamoured of an Italian dancer in Venice, Barberina Campanini, and even proposed marriage to her. Wrongly, he assumed Lady Mary would approve. She did not. She made it clear that she felt Barberina should remain his mistress. She wrote to Chiara expressing her fears that Mackenzie was being duped. But he and Barberina remained unmarried. Chiara returned from Madrid to Venice in 1744.

Letters from friends back in England were also vitally important to Mary. Her correspondence with Hervey continued. She used him as a valuable sounding board. He sent her a parcel of books including Richardson's new novel, *Pamela*. On 18 June 1743, he wrote to her for the last time from his estate in Ickworth, knowing that he was dying, with characteristically gracious and complimentary words: 'May all your ways (as Solomon says of wisdom) be ways of pleasantness, and all your paths peace.'[8] He never did enlighten her on his real relationship with Algarotti. After his death his son bundled up all the letters Lady Mary had written to him and sent them on to her. She wrote back that if he had read them, he would have been surprised that her friendship with his father had been so long and so close and yet had always remained platonic.

In August 1744, news reached Lady Mary of the death of Alexander Pope. Neither Wortley nor Mary's old friend Henrietta, Lady Oxford, had wanted to tell her about it. They both remembered that Henrietta had supported Mary while her husband, Lord Oxford, had sided with Pope. Henrietta explained her silence about Pope's death by saying: 'I did not mention it, knowing the contempt you have for worthless people.'[9] Mary asked Henrietta to send her a copy of Pope's will and commented on it with apparent objectivity. Pope had taken his visceral hatred of her to his grave. If she had been hoping for an apology, or merely a mention, she would have been disappointed. Pope was buried in St Mary's Twickenham, near his old nurse, whose relationship with him Mary may well have satirised in verse in an attempt to hurt him. Fifteen years later, in 1757, in a similar vein, Mary would show a young traveller a commode in her house. It was decorated with a false back made of books, their spines showing they were written by Pope, Swift and Bolingbroke. The three writers were the greatest rascals, she told her visitor, and she had the satisfaction of shitting on them every day.

In general, though, Mary was careful to keep her response to the news as dignified as possible. Pope's death must have come as an enormous relief. Finally, there was an end to his implacable hostility. As she wrote to Wortley: 'since the Death of Pope I know no body that is an Enemy to either of us.'[10] That chapter in their life was over. Dealing with Pope had been a joint struggle for Mary and Wortley, something which had united them at least when so much else had divided them. Mary would also always remember the loyalty her childhood friend Henrietta had shown her throughout.

Henrietta's husband had died two years earlier, an alcoholic, in poor financial straits. Mary wrote at the time that she was 'vexed' at Lord Oxford's death, rather than being saddened at the news, and that Wortley would understand her response. This must have been in part due to concerns about her friend's unstable future, but also in part no doubt to Lord Oxford's having sided with Pope. The widowed Henrietta moved back to her childhood home of Welbeck Abbey, a few miles from Mary's family seat at Thoresby, determined to make it somewhere suitable for her heirs. Both friends expressed a wish that Lady Mary would one day get to see the many improvements. In 1744 Wortley heard that Henrietta planned to sell some manuscripts from her late husband's library which included poems very critical of his own family. He met with her to persuade her to suppress them. Mary was supportive from afar. She found Wortley's personality traits such as this easier to deal with from a distance.

Mary's servants were an important element in her life as a single woman abroad in such dangerous times. Just before the trip to Geneva William and Mary Turner came to her and gave in their notice. They were not prepared to cross the Alps yet again, they said. Instead, a Dutch ship would take them back to England. Mary was distraught at the prospect of losing them. All three had sleepless nights. That evening Mary wrote to Wortley asking if he could send out another maid from London. She could manage with someone European to carry out William's duties, she assured him, but she needed a lady's maid who was trustworthy and English. The next day the Turners decided they would stay after all. Lady Mary wrote a hurried second letter to Wortley.

Once they were settled in Avignon, Mary Turner gave birth to a second child, to Lady Mary's displeasure. The Turners promised her it would not happen again. Then William Turner suffered from what Lady Mary described as palsy, but which was probably a stroke. She attempted to help him by advising him that he should drink less red wine and eat less red meat. William took this well-meant interference rather badly. As he saw it, employers were always entreating their servants to eat and drink less. Later in the year Lady Mary arranged for him to visit a spa to treat his paralysis. She was doing her best to help, but in March 1744, the Turners gave in their notice for a second time. As William phrased it: 'he had rather be a chimney sweep in London than a Lord in France.'[11] They dared not tell their employer that Mary Turner was pregnant yet again. Lady Mary bowed to the inevitable. She graciously gave the Turners five guineas to help them once they returned to England (£880 today). For her part she accepted she would need to engage local servants. She immediately hired a Frenchman named Fribourg who stayed with her for many years.

Mary learned via her daughter that back in England her family home of Thoresby had burned to the ground in 1745. She took pride in not being hugely upset by the news: 'I thank God my Heart is so entirely detached from…(worldly possessions) that I never desire more than the small portion I enjoy,'[12] she wrote, rather sanctimoniously. Her relationships with both her husband and her daughter were very gradually improving. Distance helped. Mary grew increasingly anxious when Wortley's letters to her got lost, as he did about hers. He was often in Yorkshire, staying at Wharncliffe Lodge, and in 1745 he downsized to a smaller London house in Cavendish Square. That year he travelled to a spa in Germany for his health, but deliberately did not tell Mary. He preferred not to run the risk of meeting her face-to-face. They could keep up the pretence in their letters to each other that all was well between them, but being together would make it impossible to avoid confronting the truth – that she had left him and that she preferred a life of separation. Better not to open old wounds.

Lady Bute was living in Scotland at the family home of Mount Stuart, on the Isle of Bute. In Spring 1742 her second-born son died of a fever at just over a year old. Mary empathised from afar. Her own mother had given birth four times in four years, after all, and lost her life as a result. Relations with Lady Bute were still mistrustful. Mary wrote to Wortley of their daughter: 'She cannot have more than I have had; I wish the success may be greater,' as if she were envious of her daughter's lot and self-pitying of her own.[13] Gradually, things would improve. The Butes' next son, born in June 1744 would survive and grow up to become his father's heir. Lady Bute found life at Mount Stuart made her feel depressed. The couple were short of money and far from friends. Her letters in this state alarmed Mary. The shadow of Sister Mar hung over them both. 'The Melancholy Letters I have from my Daughter dispirit me so much,' she wrote to Henrietta, whose own daughter was friendly with Lady Bute, that 'I am hardly capable of thinking of anything else.'[14] When the Butes pleaded with Wortley for some financial help to enable them to move south more permanently, he was disinclined to lend assistance. He liked his own estate in Yorkshire, he argued, and saw no reason for them to leave theirs. In the summer of 1746 they moved south regardless, renting houses in Twickenham and London. Another child was born - eleven of their children would eventually survive - and Wortley gradually came around.

Wortley and Mary's son Edward continued to be a thorn in his parents' sides. He was still wandering round Europe, forever in debt. His returning to England would risk his being thrown into debtors' prison. Parliamentary immunity would protect him, so he wrote to his father asking his help in securing a parliamentary seat. Wortley was unenthusiastic. He wrote to Lady Mary of Edward: 'He ought not to entertain a thought of satisfying his Creditors any way but out of his allowance, be it greater or less.'[15] While Mary was in Chambéry she was asked whether she knew a confidence trickster who apparently had the same name as her. It emerged that Edward had asked for a temporary loan there and then never repaid it. Mary admitted she was related to this mystery stranger, but she did not explain that he was in fact her son: 'his pretended Enthusiasm is only to cheat those that can be imposed on by it.'[16]

In August 1741, Mary wrote to tell Wortley that she had received a letter from Edward asking for her help in dissolving his marriage. He hoped to make another, more financially advantageous match, he wrote.

Mary could not see this happening. She admitted: 'I expect nothing from him but going from one Species of Folly to another.'[17] Whatever Wortley did to help Edward, Mary believed it would never be enough. Their son would continue to play the victim with everyone he met. The question as to whether Edward would inherit his father's fortune hung in the balance. Mary wrote to Wortley as frankly as she could about this. She was indifferent to it as regards herself, she wrote, and she did not know whom he planned to name as his heir. That was for him to decide. Wortley had asked her to continue writing to Edward and she had done so by the last post. Edward enrolled that autumn as a student of oriental languages at the University of Leyden in Holland. On his arrival he found a bundle of letters from his mother awaiting him.

The following year Edward was back in England trying another tack to solve his financial problems: securing for himself a commission in the army. He began re-establishing connections with some of his wealthier relatives who might conceivably help him, including his father's cousin, Edward Montagu. Wortley was cautiously supportive of the army plan, although he made it clear he would rather his son fought abroad than was stationed in England, where temptation was likely to be closer to hand. He refused to meet his son, writing to him care of his agent, John Gibson. By March 1742, Edward was back in Holland. Letters continued to fly between Gibson and Wortley, who kept Lady Mary up to speed. Now their son was in Europe again, Wortley began putting pressure on Mary to meet him. Wortley was clear he remained as mistrustful of Edward as ever, but he wrote to Mary: 'I cannot imagine anyone so likely as yourself to give an impartial account of him.'[18] Whereas Wortley tended to describe Edward as weak, Mary disagreed. Instead, she saw him as set in his ways: 'I have never been mistaken in his character, which remains unchanged, and what is yet worse, I think it unchangeable.'[19] Meanwhile Edward wrote to his wealthy cousin, Edward Montagu, about his mother: 'she is much to be feared as a woman set upon a young man's ruin and much more still as a woman of superior genius.'[20] The prospect of meeting face-to-face filled both mother and son with dread.

It was agreed the two would meet at Valence, near Lyons. Mary and Wortley wrote elaborate letters to each other, laying the groundwork for any discussions. Mary assured Wortley that she would resist becoming overheated in their conversation: 'I see nothing but Falsehood and weakness through his whole Conduct.'[21] The elaborate arrangements for the meeting were finessed by Gibson. Edward needed additional financing for the journey and a servant to accompany him. His parents were unsure whether he was going to say he wanted a commission in the army or not, and if so whether they should be for it or against it. Mary began to feel surprisingly fired up at the prospect of finally seeing him again after all this time.

The meeting eventually took place in June 1742, not at Valence but at Orange, about twenty miles north of Avignon. The night before, Edward had stayed thirty miles north at the small town of Montélimar and managed to maintain the agreed fiction there that he was a Dutch officer named Monsieur du Durand, so as to preserve his anonymity. Mary wrote to Wortley immediately afterwards, describing the entire meeting. Edward, she reported, had lost his looks and put on weight. He looked older than his twenty-nine years. He had been keen to show off his command of languages to her. She had found him garrulous but not witty. She still feared his inclination to be influenced by the last person he has talked to: 'He has a flattering, insinuating manner which naturally prejudices strangers in his favour.'[22]

All the same, mother and son spent two whole days together and were able to talk relatively easily. The atmosphere was surprisingly un-acrimonious. Edward confessed that he was excited about going into the army and Mary went along with this. He attempted to flatter her but when he started saying that he would mend his ways she cut off his 'usual silly Cant'.[23] She made sure to stress to him his father's generosity and moderation. She lectured him on how he was too easily led and about how shameful it was always to live beyond his means. He accepted what she said. When she suggested he should have saved half his allowance when he was at Ysselstein in the Netherlands he blamed Gibson, who apparently had fixed ideas on how a nobleman ought to live abroad.

Edward then asked about Wortley's estate, posing the all-important question as to whether or not he would inherit when his father died. Mary replied carefully that nothing was settled. Edward made it clear that if he were made his father's heir then he would look after Mary. She took umbrage at this. She replied proudly that she did not believe that his father would leave her dependent on Edward, but even if that were his plan, she would never 'act against my Honor or Conscience' by lobbying Wortley on Edward's behalf.[24] In other words, she could not be bought. At this the meeting broke down. Caught in an inescapable cycle of recrimination and mistrust, it became clear that their relationship would never be healed.

Nevertheless, mother and son parted on seemingly good terms: 'he protesting to follow my advice in all things.'[25] She gave him £12 to cover the costs of his journey (£1800 today). He promised he would travel incognito, that he would write to her once he got to Paris and that he would only stay there only one night before heading to Flanders where he would await orders from his father. Instead he gave up his alias that night, admitting that he was really Edward Wortley Montagu, and boasting about his excellent relationship with his mother. Inevitably people assumed he was a confidence trickster. When he reached Paris, instead of staying only one night there as agreed, he lingered. Mary waited six weeks for a letter from him to arrive, despite his promise to write to her from Paris. She tried for ten weeks to get hold of an address for him, which eventually came via Wortley. Later that year Edward did return to London, but he was immediately thrown into prison for his debts. For her part, Mary anxiously sought reassurance from Wortley that she had said and done the right thing by Edward. She admitted: 'If he ever acts in a rational or sincere manner, I shall be much surprised.'[26]

Mary described the situation with Edward as being like losing a limb. In March 1743, she finally received a 'very foolish Letter' from him, the first since his return to England.[27] He continued to lobby to get a commission in the army and later that year he finally succeeded. The English were fighting with Austria against the French and Spanish, and Edward was given the relatively lowly post of cornet in the Seventh Hussar Dragoons. The king himself led his troops at the Battle of Dettingen - the last time a serving English monarch ever did so - but Edward arrived too late to join the battle. Mary wrote to Wortley that she had received word of their son's continued bad behaviour on the journey, but once he was with the troops Edward made sure to write his mother a letter. It was so eloquently phrased she assumed he must have had help with it. As she cynically put it, he wrote to say: 'nothing had been done without him, when I know nothing he has done.'[28] In 1744 Edward was back in London again and joined the Turkish Club there. His early life in Turkey always played an important part in his life. It was only now that Mary learned the full story of how Edward had not kept his word when they parted in Orange. Furious, she wrote to Wortley: 'I wish you would consider…that tattling and lying are qualities not be forgiven even in a chambermaid.'[29]

In May 1745, Edward finally took part in military combat, at the Battle of Fontenoy. The English and the Austrians were defeated by a larger French army, but Edward acquitted himself well. His mother was wracked with anxiety that he might have been killed: 'I cannot so far forget that I am a mother as not to be under concern for my Son.' [30] A month later she still had not seen a list of the casualties. The account of the battle he finally wrote to his mother failed to impress her. She despaired of his 'Idle vain way of talking of himselfe'.[31] He claimed that he had been thrown from a horse due to cannon shot, whereas she suspected that his fall had been due to the blast from the cannon rather than the shot itself. She was right. Wortley was more encouraged by events than Mary. Later that month Edward was transferred to the Royal Scots Regiment, given the rank of Captain-Lieutenant and made aide-de-camp to the English commander-in-chief. Clearly his fellow soldiers thought he had done well, even if he did behave rather grandly towards them. At this, Mary was motivated to write Edward a far kinder letter: 'I wish nothing more than that your future conduct may redeem your past.'[32] The following year he and his regiment were all captured by the French and imprisoned at Liège. For once his parents could not attribute his misfortune to his poor behaviour.

The difficulties of dealing with their son gave Mary and Wortley a reason to stay in touch with each other, as they wrestled with how to deal with him. To a lesser extent the same was true of their dealing with the Butes. Mary had by now been away from England for seven years. She had become accustomed to life by herself, celebrated as the famous literary figure abroad, making friends as she travelled, enjoying the books her family sent out for her but detached from life back in England. She had no wish to return home. For his part, Wortley seemed to have accepted this. He was careful to make sure their paths did not cross, even when he himself travelled to Europe. Avignon had served its purpose and provided a resting place for Mary for a few years. But increasingly she longed to return to Italy. Venice was her spiritual home. She wanted to get back there.

Chapter 18

Count Palazzi

'Madam, be less hot-headed; think of your danger'[1]

Avignon was becoming increasingly unsuitable as a place for Mary to live. By 1746, aged 57, she was determined to return to Venice. But Spanish troops were posted at all the borders between France and Italy and she could not travel to Venice by herself as a single woman. Friends suggested to her she could do with a secretary. Maybe she could find someone to combine these two roles? She came across an Irishman named Sir James Caldwell in the Languedoc and struck up one of her characteristic immediate, intense friendships with him. He looked as if he might help her but then, as quickly as he had made his offer, for reasons of his own he withdrew it. By June she was back in Avignon. The streets were flooded, and her eyes were so inflamed that she could neither read nor write. She had had enough. She became all the more determined to set off as soon as she could and by August, she was on her way.

The means of travelling to Venice presented itself in the person of the 30-year-old Count Ugolino Palazzi. He arrived in Avignon in July 1746 as the Gentleman of the Bedchamber to the Prince of Saxony. Mary had met the Prince's tutor in Venice a few years earlier. Mainland Italian nobles such as Palazzi were barred from holding any state office in Venice, so Palazzi's working as a gentleman of the bedchamber was entirely proper and would have given him impeccable credentials. Mary found herself confiding in the young man of her passionate desire to return to Venice. To her surprise and delight he offered to escort her there.

Palazzi suggested they should stop off on the way to visit his mother at their family home in the small Italian city of Brescia. Situated a hundred and eighty kilometres west of Venice, Brescia formed part of the neutral

Venetian territories and was therefore safe from any military incursion while the War of the Austrian Succession continued to rage. Mary's old friend Grimani was now Pope, which made it feel all the more secure as a destination. Mary readily agreed. They were just about to set off when Palazzi admitted that he needed a loan of 300 sequins (£23,000 today) if he were to accompany her. He would, he assured her, repay the money as soon as they reached Brescia. This was a large sum and Mary entertained a few doubts about the wisdom of lending it to him, but she agreed. After all, she had loaned Algarotti money in the past, whenever he had asked her. She was perhaps flattered by Palazzi's attentions but also, more importantly, she needed him to escort her to Venice. Her relationship with Algarotti had been a romantic one, whatever its complications. With Count Palazzi she was embarking on something altogether darker.

The little party travelled by sea from Avignon to Genoa. Mary did not have official papers, so she kept a low profile in the inn where they stayed the night. Next they travelled by coach over the mountains heading eastwards. In one of the passes they came across a battalion of Spanish troops, retreating from their Austrian enemies. Since the English were allied with the Austrians against the Spanish, this was potentially extremely dangerous for them. Palazzi's tactic was to lie. Mary was a Venetian aristocrat, he explained to the Spaniards, on her way to meet the commander of the Spanish army, Don Philip. Impressed by this tale, the Spanish soldiers accompanied them to the nearby town of Serravalle. They arrived as night had fallen, only to discover that Don Philip himself was already lodging there. Luckily the town was packed full of Spanish troops, all refuelling ready for their next foray, and rumours were flying that the Austrian army was about to arrive, so no one took much notice of Lady Mary and Palazzi.

All the inns were full of wounded Spaniards, so Palazzi persuaded one of the innkeepers, who was himself making preparations to flee the town, to allow Lady Mary to spend the night in one of his bare bedchambers. There was no furniture and no supper, but she still had her freedom. The next day an Austrian battalion did indeed enter the town. Since the Austrians were allies of the English, Palazzi immediately went to the commanders and revealed to them Mary's real identity. Delighted, they gave Mary and her party food and drink and made them welcome. A couple of days later a guard of Austrian Hussars even escorted them out of the town towards Italy. Palazzi had negotiated his way through a dangerous situation with aplomb. No wonder Mary increased her trust in him.

Once they arrived in Brescia Mary wrote to Wortley back in England telling him that she had decided to stay there for a time. The journey had been expensive, she explained, but worth making. Since leaving Avignon her eyesight had begun to improve. She knew the city of Brescia a little bit, because seven years earlier her carriage had broken down there on her way from England to Venice. The count pressurised her to stay with his mother, the widowed Countess Palazzi. The countess' house stood in the Piazza del For, off the large Roman forum. Mary was aware she had to find the right occasion to ask the countess for a refund of her loan to Palazzi, so this seemed a sensible course of action.

When the two women finally met it immediately became evident the count was so in debt that Lady Mary could not possibly ask for repayment. To complicate matters, Mary was suddenly struck down by a terrible, mysterious fever, which laid her low for two whole months. The symptoms indicate that this was malaria. Mary had hoped to move from the countess' house to her own lodgings in Brescia, but this was now clearly impossible. As she put it: 'I think myself in natural decay. However, I do what I am ordered.'[2] Marooned here, Mary's spirits flagged. She wrote to Henrietta back in England: 'My Life is useless to the World, and (allmost) tiresome to myselfe.'[3] The illness was dragging her down. Henrietta replied: 'I wish you could with Ease live in your Native Country.'[4] There was still no question of her returning home.

That autumn Count Palazzi travelled south with Mary to the family's country house in the large village of Gottolengo near the river Po, to recuperate. The village was about 20 kilometres south of Brescia and had approximately 2,000 inhabitants at the time. The houses were densely packed within the square shape of the village's crumbling medieval walls. Mary was shocked to see the dilapidated, ruined state of Palazzi's house. If she had known this before setting off, she admitted, she would never have agreed to go there. But: 'I found the country air was very salubrious for me, and I hoped to recover completely in a short time.'[5] Then she would be on her way. She asked Palazzi's advice about what she should give his mother as a thank you gift. Taken aback, he railed against his mother's behaviour, but then admitted that a gift of money might be acceptable. Meekly,

Mary handed over 200 sequins for him to give to her (£15,000 today). She never heard whether it reached its destination.

In November, Lady Mary was invited to celebrate Martinmas with one of Palazzi's aunts in the nearby village of Cigole. Palazzi made it clear his aunt would be extremely disappointed if she refused. Mary was still very weak from her illness but reluctantly she agreed. The count insisted she bring her servants with her. Her French Huguenot maid, Mari Anna, who had taken over from Mary Turner, would look after her clothes and her manservant Fribourg would wait on her at table. Palazzi reassured her that her house in Gottolengo would remain secure. He could vouch for the trustworthiness of his manservant. Against her better judgement, Mary set off. She enjoyed the evening in Cigole but began to feel unwell during the meal. She called for her carriage, but her hostess was insistent she stay the night and showed her to a specially warmed bed.

The next day, when Mary finally returned to Gottolengo, her house had been burgled. Her most precious possessions had been stolen, including all her jewellery, which she had kept in locked boxes. Palazzi's servant was nowhere to be seen. Distraught, Mary retired to bed with a fever. The count came to her the next day, explaining that he would need money if he were to make enquiries about the burglary on her behalf. She handed over the forty sequins he requested (£3,000 today). Three days later he returned empty handed, pointing the finger of suspicion at his brother, the Abbé Palazzi, who had been at the dinner with them and whom he described as 'a very bad man'.[6] The Abbé was indeed a well-known criminal, but Mary did not know this. She scolded the count for being so disloyal to a family member and said nothing to him of her own suspicions. If Palazzi had taken her possessions, she rationalised to herself, then he would soon disappear back to Saxony, where he had lived in the past, and set himself up with the proceeds. Instead, he stayed in the area.

Another of Palazzi's aunts, Madame Roncadelli, visited Mary at Gottolengo to commiserate with her on her losses. She was the widowed sister of Palazzi's late father: 'a respectable elderly Lady who had lived honourably and had the reputation of a saint.'[7] The two of them drew up a list of all Mary's lost jewels, to be sent to the local shopkeepers in case anything turned up. Although she doubted anything would come from this, Lady Mary was impressed by Madame Roncadelli and the two formed an emotional bond. After all, Mary was always well-disposed towards European middle-aged ladies. She failed to grasp that for Madame Roncadelli family ties might be stronger than these expressions of friendship. Meanwhile Mary's malarial fever gradually abated, cured, she said, by quinine.

Mary kept her letters home vague about the count having persuaded her to purchase his country house in Gottolengo. As she recovered, she found herself intrigued by the history of her new surroundings. She wrote to Wortley that the villagers thought the origins of the village were Roman whereas she could see clearly that they were Gothic. No parish records existed before the region became part of the Venetian territories, 300 years earlier. There had been a fire in the village and when Mary arranged to have the courtyard of her house levelled, it revealed fire-damaged bricks. She had locks put on the doors of her house and glass in all the windows. With her furniture still in Avignon, she resolved to buy herself an armchair. Everybody else in the village only had wooden, armless dining chairs rather than anything comfortable. The count also managed to procure for her a large quantity of tapestries, more than she needed, but he was insistent the collection could not be broken up.

Once spring came, Lady Mary hoped to move on. But the count put increased pressure on her to stay, claiming he would be totally dishonoured if she left. She let slip that, although she liked the house, she regretted not having a garden. Immediately he found someone to sell her some land nearby which had previously been an old vineyard. It was on a little peninsula above the River Oglio and she set about creating a garden for herself there, fixing up seats of turf in its bowers. Her furnishings finally arrived from Avignon, in a terrible state of repair. Several pieces of furniture had been lost, along with some of her china and four snuff boxes, one of which was inset with precious stones. Palazzi feigned anger at this and threatened to have the courier who had delivered them shot. Lady Mary only laughed. Her possessions were not worth committing murder for, she told him. She paid Palazzi the 200 sequins the agent had apparently demanded to cover his transport expenses (£15,000 today). Maybe the attention she was receiving from Palazzi was flattering and she enjoyed the company. For whatever reason she seemed wilfully to ignore what was really happening.

Mary wrote to her married daughter, Lady Bute, in July 1748 describing her routine now she was settled in Gottolengo. She rose at 6.00 am and after breakfast set off to her garden to supervise the people working there. Then at 9.00 am she inspected her dairy and her poultry stock. She was proud to keep silkworms, a common industrial crop in the region. At 11.00 am she studied for an hour before taking lunch at midday and then sleeping until 3.00 pm. In the afternoons she and some local priests played cards together until it was cool enough to either walk in her wood, go for a ride or take a boat on the river. She admitted to her daughter that she sometimes wished to have a bit more conversation but 'the commerce of the World gives me more uneasiness than pleasure, and Quiet is all the Hope that can reasonably be indulged at my Age.'[8] She asked that her son-in-law send her out a book on practical gardening, since this was also a favourite pastime of his. Her books had arrived undamaged from Avignon and kept her busy, as always. Presumably they were not thought worth stealing. She was delighted when others were sent out from England. Palazzi she described as merely an irritant, who spoiled her horses by riding them too hard and who had a tendency to break her chairs.

In 1749 Palazzi came to her, claiming he had finally found a way of making amends for the money she had lost. He suggested a property deal. His plan was that she should buy a life annuity in a house close to Brescia owned by a 90-year-old man with no children. Once the old man died, which would surely be very soon, the property would be hers. Mary explained that she did not want to get into property speculation in a foreign country. At this Palazzi flew into a rage, shouting at her that she was depriving him of his only way of making reparation. The next day the elderly owner of the property (or someone claiming to be him, as Lady Mary shrewdly put it) arrived, trembling and bent double. He had with him the valuation of his house along with the deed of sale. Mary meekly signed in the presence of a notary and two witnesses and duly paid the first annuity.

In March 1750, Lady Mary fell ill with the ague (probably a reactivation of her malaria) and was advised by the local doctor to travel north to the spa town of Lovere on the banks of Lake Iseo, forty-five kilometres north of Gottolengo, beyond Brescia, to drink the waters and convalesce. She wrote to her daughter that the quality of the waters and the way the houses were built into the hills reminded her of the English spa town of Tunbridge Wells. It was, she wrote, 'certainly one of the prettyest places in the World'.[9] She threw herself into the cultural life in Lovere, enjoying the operas which played three times a week, as well as concerts and balls. Mary had forgotten how much she loved music. Her days in Lovere soon fell into a pattern. She would take the waters first thing, then travel by boat to some part of the lake and have a stroll in the mountains before returning to play at whist with her fellow visitors or enjoy a concert.

And so, the next few years took on their own rhythm. Mary would spend the winters in Gottolengo and the summers in Lovere, stopping off at Brescia every time she made the journey. She found great contentment in these years, despite the shadow of Palazzi hanging over her. She described herself as remarkably contented to occupy herself with her 'Huswifery'. She encouraged the local people to make butter and soon they proved to be as good at it as her. She introduced 'Custards, Cheesecakes and mince'd Pies, which were entirely unknown in these Parts, and are received with universal applause.'[10] The local people in Gottolengo even wanted to put up a statue in her honour, until she was forced to tell them that her religion did not permit such a thing.

At one point Mary had to scotch local gossip about the true nature of her relationship with Count Palazzi. In March 1750, the Count came to her in a great fright with news that the local administrator of justice in the province of Brescia, the *podestà*, had written to the countess complaining that Palazzi was holding Lady Mary prisoner. Always sparky in a crisis, Mary replied that she was happy to testify that she was there of her own free will. Two hours later one of the *podestà*'s officers arrived to interview her. The count then insisted that Mary make the journey to Brescia where she was required to reassure the Palazzis' many guests that it was 'very natural that a Lady of my age should choose retirement.'[11] Again, she was happy to go along with the situation, and even deny in public the coercive control the count was exerting over her.

In June 1750, Mary's teeth started aching painfully and a neighbour sent for the local surgeon. When he examined her mouth he paled visibly, thinking gangrene had already formed. He hurriedly called the best dentist in the area, who travelled from nearby Cremona and operated immediately, cauterising her gums: 'my Tongue being infected and so swell'd that I could not utter one word, though I was in perfect Memory and Senses.'[12] Luckily she began to feel better the very next day and her fever dropped, but she was advised to recuperate in Lovere. Here she met Dr Baglioni, someone for whom she would grow to have enormous respect. He persuaded her to buy herself a second little house in Lovere, which she later enlarged so her servants could sleep there with her. Inevitably Count Palazzi was involved in this purchase. Palazzi suggested she deposit all her remaining capital with a banker in Brescia named Francesco Ballini, described by Palazzi as: 'a man of unblemished integrity, and of great wealth'.[13] When she announced she planned to visit Ballini for herself the count told her that Ballini had crippling gout and could not see her just now. From then on, anything she received from London, particularly her allowance from Wortley, she paid straight over to Ballini, who sent her detailed accounts at regular intervals.

Letters from Wortley, Lady Bute and her friend, Henrietta, Lady Oxford, were relatively rare and her own to them often went astray. She failed to grasp that they were being intercepted. The long silences meant that Mary would work herself up into a frenzy of anxiety over how her friends and family were doing until a letter or a parcel of books would suddenly arrive from England and her peace of mind would return. She devoured Richardson's *Clarissa,* and also *Tom Jones* and *Joseph Andrews,* both written by her cousin, Henry Fielding. Back in England the Butes' fortunes were improving. In 1748 Bute went to the races in Maidenhead and by chance met the Prince of Wales, Prince Frederick, whom Dr Maitland had travelled out to Hanover to inoculate. Mary had also written her bawdy poem about his sharing a mistress with Hervey. Bute and Prince Frederick immediately struck up a friendship. Bute found himself staying with the Prince and Princess of Wales that night at their estate at Cliveden, where they discovered a shared a love of gardening. Soon Bute had been made the prince's First Lord of the Bedchamber and a friendship developed between the two wives. When Prince Frederick died suddenly three years later his widow, Princess Augusta, appointed Bute tutor to their 13-year-old eldest son, Prince George, the new Prince of Wales. As the Butes' financial situation improved, they moved to Kenwood House on Hampstead Heath and later to a house in South Audley Street in Mayfair.

When John Anderson, her son's old tutor, visited her in Brescia, Mary fantasised that his new pupil might make a suitable match for one of her granddaughters back in England. She wrote to her daughter about the importance of female education. She clearly imagined that her granddaughters would not be given dowries when they married and were likely to grow up to be 'Lay Nuns' for whom books and reading would be important.[14] Mary wrote that she disapproved strongly of pretending that looks in a woman were of no significance. Beauty gave a woman agency, she argued, but intelligence was all-important. In the animal kingdom females and males were equally intelligent, so why would this not be the case for humans? She advocated the importance of studying, particularly Latin and Greek, which were seen as a uniquely male preserve. For herself, she toyed with the idea of writing a political history of modern times, but if she did put pen to paper, nothing survives.

The years passed. In spring 1751 Count Palazzi's mother died very suddenly. The same year Mary herself also fell ill again at Gottolengo and travelled to Lovere to take the waters. Three years later she became even more dangerously ill and Dr Baglioni was sent for once more. This time Mary was preparing herself for death. Baglioni promptly arranged for her to travel north to Lovere. When they reached the foot of the lake, he had her bed transferred from the coach onto a small boat, so she could travel more peacefully and avoid the road. At Lovere she drank the waters and for the first time in her life tried swimming, aged 65. She began to recover. She pronounced herself in agreement with the local people whose nickname for Dr Baglioni was the Miraculous Man.

The Count lodged near her in Lovere but even he could not ruin her summer by the lake that year. Dr Baglioni suggested she hire a secretary. He found Doctor Bartolomeo Mora who turned out: 'on experience to be gentle and sincere'. He would remain in service to Lady Mary for the rest of her life.[15] It was Bartolomeo Mora who began the task of looking through the backlog of all Mary's paperwork while she stayed on in Lovere to recuperate over the winter. He broke the news to her that she was indeed being deceived by Count Palazzi over the annuities she was continuing to pay to the 90-year-old man, who was still very much alive. This finally made Mary realise that it would be wise to escape Palazzi's control and move on to Venice, as she had originally planned. First, though, she needed to travel to Gottolengo, to pack up all her furniture. Palazzi insisted on escorting her. Like Mary, his health was poor. When he fell more seriously ill, she found herself allowing him to stay with her in Gottolengo, bedridden, for two whole months. Her plans to move on were yet again delayed. As she put it: 'I believed him to be poor and observed him to be stupid and supposed that he too was being swindled as he was swindling me.'[16]

Lady Mary's old friend Henrietta, Lady Oxford, died in December 1755. She left Mary a substantial bequest of 400 sequins (£30,000 today) but as always, the count became involved. Mary wrote to Wortley and to Henrietta's son-in-law proposing to use the legacy to commission an engraved diamond ring. Yet again both her letters mysteriously went astray, and Mary soon heard from a contact of Palazzi's offering to arrange for the ring to be commissioned and sent out from England on her behalf. At this the scales finally fell from Lady Mary's eyes. When she thought back over the years, Palazzi had always found a way to prevent her leaving for Venice: 'My chaises were broken, my Horses lamed, my Maid taken ill, the rivers in flood.'[17] In effect he was now holding her prisoner. Aware that very few letters were getting through, the truth dawned on her: they were being intercepted. Palazzi was increasingly isolating her. Even now she failed to grasp the full extent of the power he was exerting over her, but she could finally see that she was in danger.

Next Mary was summoned to the bedchamber of a local priest who whispered to her that he might be able to recover all the jewellery that had supposedly been stolen when she first arrived in Gottolengo. The jewels had apparently been pawned but could be redeemed, at the cost to her of 12,000 sequins (nearly £1 million today). Lady Mary just laughed. Her jewellery was not worth that much, she told him. A few days later a mysterious, hooded monk appeared at her house, bringing with him a large trunk, which she recognised as one of Palazzi's, full of the stolen booty, including the missing furniture from Avignon and the jewelled snuffbox. Mary virtuously pointed out to the monk that a large cross of emeralds and a diamond ring in the hoard were not hers but agreed to guard them until the rightful owner was found. An hour later Palazzi sent word that the cross and ring were his. How much would she be prepared to pay for her belongings, he asked? They did a deal.

Although Palazzi seemed finally to accept that Mary was leaving for Venice, he begged her to take a detour en route to the home of his aunt, Madame Roncadelli, who lived in Pontevico, ten kilometres east of Gottolengo. Reluctantly Mary agreed, since she liked and trusted Madame Roncadelli. Before leaving she needed to take out 4,000 sequins, which she currently had deposited with her banker, Ballini (about £300,000 today). Palazzi offered to take the funds out on her behalf, in exchange for a ten per cent commission. She meekly agreed and then set off to Pontevico. The going was slow, and she and her servants were forced to stay the night at a merchant's house, only to discover the next day that their carriage had been sabotaged.

Undeterred, they had a new wheel made and travelled on. They were only a short distance from Madame Roncadelli's house when a strange man approached, brandishing a huge gun. Dr Mora shrieked, convinced he was about to die. Lady Mary found herself laughing at Mora's hair, which was all standing on end. The man with the gun presented Mary with a letter from the count. In flowery language Palazzi wrote that he had been compelled to cash in all Lady Mary's savings and use them to pay off his own debts. He begged her pardon. Furious, Mary hurled the letter at Dr Mora. At that precise moment Madame Roncadelli's carriage arrived to convey them to her house.

At Madame Roncadelli's it became obvious that they were there because Lady Mary needed to be informed of the full extent of the count's deceit. All the money banked with Ballini had indeed disappeared. Worse, the two houses Mary thought she had bought in Gottolengo and Lovere were not hers for the long term. She had only leased them. Once she left the area, their ownership reverted to Palazzi. Lady Mary protested that they had drawn up contracts clarifying her ownership. She began opening the pouches where all the contracts were stored, only to find they had been replaced by blank sheets of paper. Next Madame Roncadelli produced a document which she asked Lady Mary to sign, stating that Mary had lived entirely at the count's expense for the past ten years. Strengthened by her anger, Lady Mary tore the document into little pieces: 'saying in a loud voice that they meant basely to swindle me.'[18] Dr Mora started trembling with fear, his hair on end again, whispering to her: 'Madam, be less hot-headed; think of your danger.'[19] After a further sleepless night the two sides reached an agreement and Lady Mary signed a much watered-down document. As she rationalised it, if she did not sign, she would never get away. It was not the truth as she saw it but the honour of both parties had been saved.

Reluctantly, she agreed that the count could accompany her as far as Mantua. Having said goodbye to him there, she travelled on to Vincenza, only to find him lodging at the same inn. Again, she extricated herself but when she was only a mile from Padua he emerged, claiming he had organised a lodging for her. When she travelled on to Venice, he did the same thing. At this she doubled back to Padua without telling him, but he turned up again. Finally, there was nothing for it. Mary, who had resisted confrontation for so many years, was forced to talk to him. Where were the title-deeds to the two properties she had bought, she demanded, and what was the name of the merchant who had handled her precious legacy from Henrietta? Palazzi could produce neither. He retreated to Gottolengo. She had finally rid herself of him.

It was only in August 1756, once she was safely away from the province of Brescia and starting to settle to a new life in Padua and Venice, that Mary began to take steps to prosecute Palazzi for the embezzlement which had gone on. A friend of Chiara Michiel's encouraged her to write an account of the various events, her *Italian Memoir*. While this was cathartic, Mary eventually decided not to take further action against the count. She must have rationalised that very little could be achieved; her own position was too compromised, after all. Plus, there was the signed document back in Pontevico. Later, as a result of his many violent crimes, Palazzi was banned from the Venetian dominions. He went on to spend several years in prison. It had been a lucky escape. Mary had lost large sums of money, along with her confidence and her integrity. But she was still alive.

Chapter 19

Growing Old Abroad

'a sentimental old woman, what a Monster'[1]

The 67-year-old Lady Mary settled in Padua and Venice for the next five years, in much better health than she had been when she lived in the Po Valley. The house she rented in the parish of San Massimo in Padua was where she went to read and recuperate. It became the equivalent of her home in Twickenham during her marriage, or of Thoresby when she was a teenager. She described herself as finding enormous contentment there: 'like a Mouse in a Parmesan cheese'.[2] The botanical gardens in Padua, the oldest in the world, became a favourite place. Venice was where she went for socialising and stimulation, just as London had been in her early life. She bought a house with a small garden there and hired a lame gondolier to ferry her about. Originally, she made sure she was in Venice for the annual carnival, but later she preferred the city out of carnival time. Although Venice was expensive, she loved its parties and concerts. She delighted in the parcels of books which arrived from England at both homes and found herself writing again. She continued work on her fairy story, *Princess Docile,* the ironic tale of the perils awaiting a princess who was too passive - perhaps as a way of laying the ghosts of her years under Palazzi's domination – and kept a notebook of maxims.

The British Resident in Venice - an official diplomatic post - was John Murray. Mary called on his wife when she first arrived in the city. Soon she found herself disliking Murray himself intensely, finding that the ageing rake was 'always surrounded with Pimps and brokers, who are his privy councillors.'[3] He personified a libertarianism and sexual promiscuity prevalent in Venice at the time which had not been the cultural norm when she lived there before and to which Lady Mary found herself strongly opposed. Casanova, for instance, often recounted the story of how he had watched John Murray and his mistress making love, only fifteen minutes before the mistress died of syphilis, her face half-eaten away by the disease. Murray was also well known for ensuring all the young men who arrived from England on their grand tour had had their first sexual experience before they left Venice. The elderly Lady Mary was highly critical of all this lasciviousness. She formed another enemy in Joseph Smith, the British Consul, an ally of John Murray's. Smith was in his eighties and recently widowed. Murray and Smith disliked Mary just as much as she disliked them. She ascribed this to their being envious of her many friendships. Mary had always been someone who evoked either great fondness or great hatred in other people. As she grew older, this propensity only seemed to be increasing.

The hostility from Murray and Smith made life difficult for Mary. Her letters from England were sent to Murray, as the British Resident, for him to forward to her. Inevitably this made her paranoid. Whereas previous residents had shared their English newspapers with Lady Mary once they had read them, Murray stopped the practice. He also did his best to prevent the young English noblemen on their grand tour from visiting her. In 1758 Murray and Smith started putting about rumours that Mary was pro-Catholic and pro-slavery. This must have felt exceptionally galling when Mary remembered how she had remained so loyal to the English cause throughout her time surrounded by Jacobites in Avignon. Word also reached her that the two men were gossiping about her having exploited the Armenian nurse she had brought back with her from Turkey, claiming she had insisted the young woman leave her husband and family to travel to England. Isolated and with time to dwell on all this, Mary began to fixate on the fear that these slights might harm the Butes back in England, now her son-in-law was becoming an increasingly important public figure. She felt protective towards Wortley too. She wrote to Lady Bute asking her not to mention any of this to her father.

That autumn Joseph Smith loaned Mary his copy of Robert Dodsley's *Collection of Poems,* which included several of hers. Some of the *Town Eclogues* had been included and Mary wrote 'mine' by them. The bawdy footman's poem to Griselda Murray which rumour had it was by Lady Mary was also in the collection and she wrote 'I confess it' alongside it. So far so good, but Dodsley had also included a poem about a woman who was over-keen on a younger man. Many years previously back in England a friend of Mary's had become besotted by a handsome young man and Mary had written the short poem in the person of the embarrassed male lover, *Answer'd by Me. M.W.M.* to help her friend overcome her feelings: 'Good Madam when Ladyes are willing/A Man must needs look like a fool.'[4] Dodsley's collection named Sir William Yonge as the love-object and implied that Mary herself had been embarrassingly over-amorous towards him, not that the poem was written to help out a friend. She was furious and wrote to Lady Bute to say so but concluded that 'silence and neglect is the best Answer to defamation.'[5] She was glad witches were out of fashion, she pronounced, or else her enemies in Venice would say she was one.

Despite these problematic foes, Mary also had many friends in Venice and Padua. She rekindled her friendship with Chiara Michiel, who was back in Venice under an informal house arrest due to her husband's political activities. When they were apart the two continued their lively correspondence in French, which they kept up for the rest of Lady Mary's life. Mary also became close to General William Graeme, whom she had first come across during her years in the Po Valley, when he arrived in the region as the new commander-in-chief of the Venetian military forces. Graeme brought with him a younger colleague, Colonel William Hamilton, who soon also endeared himself to Lady Mary. Hamilton would go on to marry Lady Emma, Nelson's mistress, in later life. For now, he was a nicely mannered young soldier. His superior, General Graeme, was connected to Lord Bute by marriage. Perhaps this link gave Mary the idea of asking Graeme if he would be the executor of the will that she started drawing up in 1757. Graeme was then called away on military service and so his executor role was never formalised.

Bute asked Graeme if he could send news back to him in London about his eccentric mother-in-law, and when Graeme returned to Venice in 1758, he sent Bute a detailed account of his findings. Mary's health he feared was poor, he wrote. He had attempted to persuade her to return home, but she told him she was wary that the climate in England would be bad for her. This sounds like a well-worn excuse. He also reported that he was sure Mary's servants were cheating her behind her back. She was very fond of 'baubles', apparently. Graeme promised Bute that he would: 'once more see if it is possible to make her think of going home and write your Lordship again upon this subject as soon as I can conjecture what her intentions are.'[6] Mary, of course, had no idea he was sending these reports on her back to England. She might have been more guarded with him, had she known.

Mary even crossed paths again with Francesco Algarotti. He had retired from service with Frederick the Great in 1753, pleading that he was unwell, and since then had been living in a village ten miles from Padua. He had written to Mary from there when she was living in the Po valley, but she had not replied because she had heard a false rumour of his dropping dead from a stroke. Perhaps this explained her decision to find a house for herself in Padua, rather than just settling in Venice. General Graeme was also in correspondence with Algarotti and once she learned that he was definitely still alive, Lady Mary started sending Algarotti some of her writing. He in turn then sent her some of his. In the spring of 1757, they finally met once more, at a mutual friend's supper party in Padua. Anticipating their reunion, she wrote to him: 'What things I shall have to tell you!'[7] In her informal journal, her *Commonplace Book*, she wrote a note to remind herself 'to wear jet bracelets when I see Al.'[8] The years had passed, and their eccentric relationship was now a distant memory, but the letters she wrote to him once they met were still outrageously flirtatious. For his part, he kept the relationship formal, preferring to commune with her about all things cultural. To their credit, the two continued their friendship in person after the initial reunion and when Graeme came to visit Lady Mary in Venice in May 1758, he brought with him a letter to her from Algarotti.

May 1758 also proved an auspicious month for Lady Mary because of the arrival in Venice of a couple who immediately struck up the greatest of friendships with her: the Scottish lawyer, Sir James Steuart, and his wife Lady Frances. While Mary was someone who prided herself on having close friends, this was a friendship on a different level. The Steuarts were Jacobites, exiled from England for Sir James' part in the Young Pretender's 1745 uprising. They initially moved to Tübingen in Germany but had now travelled to Venice for Sir James' health. Maybe because Murray and Smith had spread malicious rumours that she was pro-Catholic, Mary, who had previously always stood firm against the Jacobite cause, decided that she was not going to let these political differences impinge on her relationship with the Steuarts. Murray, for his part, refused to visit Sir James and his wife, since they were Jacobites. That can only have endeared them all the more to Lady Mary. Enthused that they shared the same surname as her daughter and son-in-law, albeit with a different spelling, she flew to meet them. Immediately nothing was too good for them. They were without a servant. She found them one. Sir James' indisposition required a strict daily routine. Mary changed hers to accommodate them. Next she insisted they move into her little palazzo in Venice. Then she sent them to stay at her house in Padua. By late May she had joined them there.

The three spent an idyllic summer together in Padua. After so many years of loneliness, finally Mary had the close companionship she had so often craved. Sir James used the library in Padua to research the book he was writing, *An Inquiry into the Principles of Political Economy*. When it was finished, he would dedicate it to her, to her great pride. That summer in Padua she wrote that she delighted in observing Sir James and Lady Frances so contented in their life together as a couple and even introduced Sir James to Algarotti. When the Steuarts finally left for Tübingen again at end of August, her spirits sunk low, not helped by the storms and torrential rain that caused the river to burst its banks, cutting Padua off from the rest of Italy. She and the Steuarts would keep up a fond and lively correspondence for the rest of her life. She poured out her thoughts and feelings, explaining: 'I desire you would sink the critic in the friend, and never forget that I do not write to you and dear Lady Fanny from my head but from my heart.'[9] When Lady Fanny felt sad about their situation in Tübingen, Mary's letters back exuded positive energy. Sister Mar's fate still hung over her. In time she would write to her daughter to see if Bute might be able to procure a pardon for Sir James for his Jacobite activities and a return to England. She even planned to spend the summer of 1759 with the Steuarts in the Tyrol, until she gradually realised that the journey would be too much for her: 'now age begins to freeze.'[10]

Other friendships were also renewed. Bute's brother, James Stuart Mackenzie, was appointed the British Envoy in Turin. Mary longed to meet his new wife, Lady Betty, there. 'When summer approaches,' she wrote to Mackenzie, 'I shall be inventing schemes for that purpose.'[11] She heartily approved of the match, and longed for a reunion between herself, Chiara and Mackenzie, just like old times. She yearned to travel further afield again and looked back on the days when the Alps seemed to her merely molehills, compared to the challenge they presented now. Deprived of seeing Mackenzie again, she nevertheless used their correspondence to petition him for a promotion for Graeme's subordinate,

William Hamilton. As the political situation changed in England and the war in Europe eased, letters to and from England were far more likely to arrive. Mary began a correspondence with someone she had inoculated as a child, Wilhelmina Tichborne, a spinster of Lady Bute's age. She met the young architect, Robert Adam, on his grand tour, and continued to enjoy her role as grand dame of the circuit, despite Murray's attempts to prevent it.

Back in England, the Butes' fortunes continued to rise. Mary's son-in-law was appointed Groom of the Stole to the young Prince of Wales in 1757, despite opposition from George II, who mistrusted Bute's influence on the young future king. Pamphlets circulated rumours that Bute was having an affair with the Prince of Wales' mother, Princess Augusta. Although this gossip was almost certainly untrue - the Butes' marriage continued to be strong - it inevitably threatened to be damaging. Mary wrote from Italy giving advice: 'the real interest of Prince and People cannot be divided.'[12] His mother-in-law must have felt like an unnecessary distraction to the ambitious Bute. As a Tory, his political affiliations were very different from hers. He supported William Pitt the Elder, the new prime minister, who had changed allegiance in Europe and now supported Prussia against Austria. This was the reason why correspondence with England had become much easier. Mary took advantage of the situation to write increasingly frequent, emotionally open letters to her daughter. She hit upon the idea that Bute should give the young prince a gift of furniture made out of Venetian glass and fixated on sending jewels back home to her older granddaughters. On 12 August 1757, Lady Bute gave birth to her eleventh and final surviving child, Louisa, who would grow up to become her grandmother's first, informal biographer.

The correspondence with Wortley continued. Even he could not now fail to be impressed by his son-in-law and he wrote to Mary praising him. He added to this a complaint that her letters still continued to get lost. It was vitally important to secure their safety, he reminded her, as pedantic as ever. In November 1757, he sent word that he had been taken very ill. Lady Mary's thoughts immediately turned again to the thorny problem of his will. In August 1758, General Graeme and Colonel Hamilton visited Mary in Padua to bring news of the Butes back in England and reduced her to tears. Mary wrote to Wortley about the pride they both felt in having a son-in-law like Bute: 'It is a Satisfaction I never hoped, to have a Son that does Honor to his Family.'[13] The irony of the contrast between their son-in-law and their own son was not lost on either of them.

For Edward too things improved for a short time, but the fundamental problems remained unresolved. Once he was set free as a prisoner of war, Edward returned to England. Whereas in the past he had petitioned friends and relatives to get into the army, now he petitioned them to leave it. His cousin, the Earl of Sandwich, secured for him the safe parliamentary seat of Huntingdon. Other family members stood aside to vacate the seat for him, and there were no other candidates, so in 1747 he became a member of parliament, which provided him with the necessary protection from his debts. Edward and Sandwich got on well and Edward travelled as Sandwich's secretary to France to secure the peace deal at Aix-la-Chappelle. The treaty which brought to an end the War of Austrian Succession was signed there in October 1748. Such a position as Edward's required funds, and he pressed both parents for an increase in his allowance from them. His father travelled out to Paris so that father and son could be presented together at the court of Versailles. Wortley made sure he did not write to Mary about this turn of events. As always, he resisted any kind of reunion with his wife. But for the first and only time in his life he felt some pride in his son.

By the end of 1750 Edward was in London again, his relationship with his father back to normal. Horace Walpole observed Edward on the London social scene and wrote of him: 'His father scarce allows him anything: yet he plays, dresses, diamonds himself.'[14] Although as a member of parliament Edward was immune from debt, he drifted into a new friendship with the notorious highwayman, James McLean, who had previously robbed Horace Walpole in Hyde Park. Edward and McLean gambled extensively together, and Edward even agreed to be McLean's second in a duel. Soon McLean was sent to the gallows.

In the summer of 1751 Edward embarked on a bigamous marriage, since his first marriage still stood in law, this time to a friend of McLean's, Miss Elizabeth Ashe - known as The Pollard Ashe because she was very short in height - who herself had already been married three times. He returned to Paris, taking his new wife with him. There they embarked on a career of swindling, gambling and extortion, threatening physical violence towards anyone who owed them money. Soon Edward was arrested for gambling with a loaded dice. He was imprisoned in the Châtelet but after eleven days' petitioning was released on bail. He returned to London yet again to ask his father for more money, leaving his new wife behind. Word of this reached his mother in Italy. 'The only way to avoid disappointment,' she wrote to Wortley, 'is never to Indulge any Hope on his Account.'[15]

In 1754, Wortley ensured that Edward was given the rotten borough of Bossiney in Cornwall as his new parliamentary seat. Edward probably never attended the House of Commons, since he never made a maiden speech, and he certainly never travelled to Cornwall to visit his constituency. Instead he started writing. In 1760, he sent his mother a book he had written, a long and pompous historical study entitled *Reflections on the Rise and Fall of the Ancient Republics adapted to the Present State of Great Britain*. One of his previous tutors inevitably also claimed ownership. A letter from his first wife, Sally, also reached her, asking for yet more money. Wortley's health began to fail towards the end of the year and Mary became increasingly concerned he might fall under the influence of the wrong people and be persuaded to nominate Edward as his heir.

George II died in 1760. At the time of his death Bute was out riding with the Prince of Wales near Kew. Bute immediately took his pupil to the royal palace to hear the news officially from the prime minister. Bute's own position hung in the balance, but the new king, who himself was only 22 years old, quickly made his favourite a Privy Councillor and then gave him a succession of increasingly better posts. Far away in Italy, Mary was delighted. 'I bless God I have lived to see you so well established,' she wrote, 'and am ready to sing my *Nunc dimittis* with pleasure.'[16] Her thoughts were turning towards her own death. Although she had many friends in Venice and Padua, she found increasingly that she missed her family back in England. At a concert in Venice, the hostess's daughter sang beautifully. A man sitting next to Lady Mary whispered in her ear that he had heard her daughter sing when he was in London. At this Mary found herself unable to contain her emotions. She started to cry uncontrollably. When her sobbing grew so loud that she threatened to disrupt the concert, there was nothing for it; she had to leave the room. At the end of 1760 she found a lump in her breast. She knew from her friend Mary Astell exactly what this meant. In the past Lady Mary had written 'I should be troublesome if at London,' but now she was not so sure. [17] Perhaps, after all these years abroad, the time had come to return home.

Chapter 20

London Again

'the wretched remnant of life'[1]

Wortley died on 21 Jan 1761 at his house in Cavendish Square in London. The news did not reach his widow in Venice until the following month. She probably heard it from the much-hated Murray. It must have been galling that Murray knew before her. She must surely have been prepared for the notion that Wortley would die first. He was eleven years older than her, after all. Despite this Mary wrote of her profound shock at the death of the husband she had not seen for twenty-two years. What she dreaded above all, she explained, was to see 'my Family torn to pieces…at my Time of Life. I desire nothing but peace and Retirement.'[2] The reason for this tearing to pieces was Edward. As Wortley's only son, under normal circumstances Edward would have been his heir, but Wortley had long been wary of passing his hard-earned wealth to his rake of a son. As Mary wrote to her daughter: 'I never will join with your profligate Brother.'[3]

Wortley's will was highly unusual. He left Mary an annual allowance of £1,200 (£180,000 today), in effect continuing their arrangement of many years. He also allowed her to keep all her belongings, including her furniture, silver, jewels and books. Tellingly, these had theoretically belonged to him all this time. To Edward he left a new annual allowance of £1,000 plus his existing allowance of £600 per year (£240,000 per year today). Once Mary died, Edward would then receive her allowance as well. This feels generous, but Edward was enormously in debt and he had expected much more. Wortley left to his legitimate grandchildren £2,000 each (£300,000 each approximately today). The rest of his fortune, estimated at £1.35 million (over £200 million today), he left to his daughter, Lady Bute, for the remainder of her life. On her death his fortune was then to pass not to her oldest son, but her second son, James Archibald,

203

who would take the surname Wortley. It felt as if Wortley's arguments as a young man about 'entail' were being rehearsed all over again. He was determined to control his fortune from beyond the grave. Lady Bute's eldest son, Lord Mountstuart, would inherit his father's estate when Bute died, but his grandfather Wortley was much wealthier than his father, so his younger brother James Archibald would inherit far more than him.

In February, Mackenzie sent Mary the will from Milan. He wrote to his brother, back in England, that Mary was anxious and confused: 'she is so undetermined about everything she makes fifty resolutions every day and changes them before night.'[4] Mary could not sleep for worry. Her eyesight, as was so often the case, worsened. Bute felt it would be best if she stayed in Venice, but England was calling Mary. On reading the will, Mary's immediate response was to take offence that it implied she had been squirrelling money away, when this was not the case. Overall, though, she was happy with it. However, news soon reached her that Edward had decided to contest it, not in his own name, but in hers. His argument was that, as his parents had eloped and his mother had no marriage settlement, she was entitled to a third of Wortley's estate under the old dower tradition. Presumably his reasoning was that this money would eventually pass to him, or more likely that the whole will would be declared void and he would then inherit the entire estate. In England rumours abounded that he would be successful.

The emotional strain on Mary was enormous even before she received the sad news that her Sister Mar had died. All the complex emotions surrounding the struggle over the care of her favourite sister must have come flooding back. She would never see her again. Mary became paranoid about Murray's enmity towards her, and convinced that General Graeme, who in the past she had asked to be the executor of her own will, had now come under Murray's influence. She was convinced all her letters were being opened and her servants spied upon. She also began fixating on the fact there was no mention in the will of the allowance she received from her deceased father. Would that continue? Mary's main anxiety, though, was Edward. That month she wrote to her son-in-law: 'I know nothing of those infamous libels my son has produce'd in my name. I dare be poor, I dare not be dishonest. I own I am weary of fighting with one hand ty'd behind.'[5] It felt as if she was engaged in an epic struggle. She wrote to her daughter confirming her loyalty and reiterating that she wanted the will to stand. In March, she wrote to

Edward, 'my unhappy and Guilty Son', care of Lady Bute. The letter was short and angry: 'You have shortened your Father's days and will perhaps have the Glory to break your mother's Heart.'[6] These were not the words of someone undetermined. Mary was clear that she mistrusted her son and disliked what he was doing.

Mary was becoming increasingly determined that the time had come, after twenty-two years, to return home to London. The Butes, she felt, needed her support against Edward. 'I will set out for England as soon as the Weather and my Health permits,' she wrote to Lady Bute in February.[7] The plan began to form. She would cross Italy, stopping off in Turin to see Mackenzie and Lady Betty and finally meet her oldest grandson, who was staying with them. Then she would cross the Alps into France via the Mont Cenis pass as she had done in the past. Yet England and France were still at war, so gradually Mary came around to the idea that it might be better to cross the Alps at the Brenner Pass in the southern Tyrol instead and travel home through Germany and Holland. There might also be an opportunity to go by way of Tübingen and see her friends the Steuarts again. But she delayed, deterred by the weather and fearing the bustle of London. Whichever route she travelled, she was old and sick. And Mackenzie had held out the promise that he might perhaps first come to Venice to see her.

Lady Mary's physical and mental health were both deteriorating. News from England was slow to reach her, and she continued to mistrust Murray, who was one of her main sources of information. Bute's uncle, the Duke of Argyll, at whose house Mary had dined soon after the Butes' wedding, died on 15 April. As a result, Bute decided he would rather have his brother, Mackenzie, back home, looking after the family's affairs, than continuing as British Envoy in Turin. But no one thought to tell Mary. When she finally heard the news it only served to increase her paranoia. She had been counting on Mackenzie's visit and now he would not be coming, nor would she get to meet Lord Mountstuart. She became all the more resolute about heading home. Her anxiety began to focus on where she would live once she arrived in London. She had always sent her letters to Wortley care of his banker, and she realised she did not even know Wortley's address there. Her manservant Fribourg announced that he would prefer to go back to Avignon rather than accompanying her to England but her Huguenot maid, Mari Anna, and the faithful Dr Mora both agreed to go with her.

In September she set off. She parted for the final time from her old friend Chiara Michiel, who wrote that she was astonished at Mary's extraordinary courage. Lady Mary was 72 years old and had breast cancer. The journey itself would be arduous and England was at war with France. As Mary wrote to Sir James Steuart: 'I am dragging my ragged remnant of life to England. The wind and tide are against me; how far I have strength against both I know not.'[8] She travelled north, through the Dolomites, lodging at a miserable inn on the Brenner Pass and then to nearby Innsbruck, where she got hold of a Hungarian passport from the Austrian officers there. She wrote from Augsburg to the Steuarts, who had left Tübingen for Antwerp, asking their advice as to where to go next. She eventually decided to travel by way of Frankfurt and Cologne, where she had stopped on her trip out to Turkey with Wortley, then she headed for Amsterdam. She was perhaps planning to hand over her precious *Embassy Letters* into the Steuarts' safe-keeping. Mary Astell had urged her to ensure they were published once she had died, and she would have thought the Steuarts the perfect people to ensure this happened.

From there Mary travelled to Rotterdam, another city she had visited on her journey out to Constantinople as a young woman. In November she wrote to Sir James: 'I begin to think we resembled two parallel lines, designated to be always near and never to meet.'[9] His health continued to be poor, so she would need to travel to Antwerp to see him. But she lingered two months in Rotterdam. Its Calvinist tradition suited her at this stage in her life, she wrote. The Irishman Sir James Caldwell made contact with her to ask for her patronage. She had last met him in the Languedoc when it looked like he might accompany her from Avignon to Venice, before Palazzi volunteered to do so. Now Caldwell was hoping for an Irish peerage. Mary also met an evangelical preacher named Benjamin Sowden here in Rotterdam. When it became evident that she would not be seeing the Steuarts again, she pressed into his hands her two-volume *Embassy Letters* with their preface by Mary Astell.

For the moment, Mary knew she needed to get back home. Time had run out for a reunion with the Steuarts. She began looking to hire a boat to take her all the way up the Thames, to dock in central London. In November her daughter rented a house for her in Great George Street (now St. George Street), just south of Hanover Square. Mary wrote to Lady Bute that she could not remember the street. What if the air there did not agree with her? The anxiety over practical arrangements masked a much deeper fear. What would it be like for mother and daughter to see each other face to face after a gap of twenty-two years? They had argued before Mary left. The relationship had certainly improved over that time, but their only contact had been by letter. The recent controversy over Wortley's will only threatened to make things worse. As Mary put it: 'God send us a happy meeting, notwithstanding the lyes that have been told.'[10] She also knew that she was returning home to die. She confessed: 'I heartily wish you may close my Eyes, but to say truth I would not have it happen immediately.'[11] She longed to see her grandchildren, and particularly her granddaughters, several of whom were now at marriageable age.

The frosty weather in Rotterdam delayed her. She would need to wait until the temperature improved. She wrote to the Steuarts promising them to continue petitioning on their behalf for a political pardon for Sir James. She assured Lady Frances that she would make sure she gave a hearty welcome to any of their relatives who made their way to her in London. On New Year's Day 1762 she set out, but the ice was still impenetrable and she was forced to turn back. Rumours were spreading that the Anglo-French Seven Years War was finally coming to an end, so the roads were crowded with army officers heading home. Realising she needed help, the ambassador in The Hague finally allocated a packet boat for her private use.

Mary arrived in London in the middle of January. She probably stayed with the Butes in their South Audley Street house for a few days before moving into the rented Great George Street house on 27 January 1762. No record survives of the family reunion. Mary met her many Bute grandchildren. Their eldest daughter Mary was the only granddaughter she had ever set eyes on until now. That alone must have made the return to London worthwhile. Her son-in-law's star had continued to rise since George III had been crowned king. Pitt the Elder and the Duke of Newcastle, both disliked by the new king, were ruling in coalition. Newcastle, now an old man, had been a significant political figure when Mary was younger, and a supporter of Sir Robert Walpole in the past. The king was putting pressure on both Pitt and Newcastle to make Bute Northern Secretary and a British, rather than simply a Scottish, peer. While Pitt was keen to continue the Seven Years War against France and to maintain support for Britain's ally, Prussia, Bute and the king both wanted to bring the conflict to an end. As a result, in October 1761, Pitt resigned as Prime Minister. For the time being Newcastle took over, but Bute could feel that the top job was within his grasp. With the situation so delicate, it was little wonder that Bute had preferred the idea that his eccentric mother-in-law stay put in Venice. Now she was back in London, she would need to be managed.

Bute was, as his youngest daughter described him: 'the most insufferable proser, quite unconsciously'.[12] That would not have posed a problem for Mary, who always enjoyed flowery speech. All her initial fears of his suitability as a son-in-law had long since disappeared, particularly now his star was so clearly in the ascendancy. Lady Bute was known as rather a forbidding figure. She too must have had mixed feelings about seeing her elderly mother again. During Lady Mary's twenty-year absence England had become far more socially conservative than when she left it. London was ablaze with the damaging but unfounded rumours of Bute's affair with Princess Augusta.

The only family member not present was Edward. He had left for Venice just as Lady Mary had vacated it. In her words to him: 'You say you know Venice. I am sorry to say Venice knows you, and I know all your Criminal Extravagancies,'[13] Mary made it clear she felt the Butes were being far too generous to Edward. Lady Bute had agreed that her brother could continue as member of parliament for Bossiney and benefit from the status and protection it gave him. The Butes also settled on Edward an estate worth £8,000 (£1.2 million today). No doubt they felt it better at this moment to give him some financial security and keep his mouth tight shut. They did not need the slightest whiff of impropriety at such a delicate time. This was not Mary's style. As she put it: 'I am not to be bribed, flattered or bullied, and have always detested Hush money in all shapes.'[14]

Mary found the experience of returning to London life overwhelming. So many people wanted to pay their respects that the sound of the many voices in her little 'harpsichord-shaped' rented house deafened her. Lady Louisa remembered her jesting: 'I am most handsomely lodged. I have two very decent closets and a cupboard on each floor.'[15] The lack of space alone contrasted sharply with her palazzo in Venice. Horace Walpole soon came to visit. On 2 Feb 1762 he wrote to his friend Montagu:

> 'I have seen her; I think her avarice, her dirt and her vivacity are all increased. Her dress, like her languages

is a galimatias of several countries; the groundwork, rags, and the embroidery, nastiness. She wears no cap, no handkerchief, no gown, no petticoat, no shoes.'[16]

When he told Lady Mary that her face had hardly changed, she was so flattered she playfully boxed his ears. Her Venetian-influenced dress style differed from the fashions in England and he joked that she had left all her clothes in Venice.

Many of her friends had not lived to see her return. Hervey and Lady Oxford had died many years before. Her old friend Lady Pomfret had passed away just a month previously. Lady Pomfret's eldest daughter, Sophia, had died in childbirth. Lady Mary made sure to visit Lady Pomfret's second daughter, Lady Charlotte Finch, who wrote: 'she… was Vastly entertaining, very oddly dressed, but retains a great deal of beauty especially in her eyes.'[17] Mary was delighted when she at last got to see James Mackenzie again. Hervey's son, whom she had met in Florence, visited her too and so did Sir James Caldwell, who was still pressing for an Irish peerage. Soon Mary was not only receiving guests at home but also accepting invitations elsewhere. She was reunited with her late brother's only son, Evelyn, Duke of Kingston, and met the young Sir Joshua Reynolds. As her great-nephew, the son of Sister Mar's daughter Fanny Erskine, put it: 'a Beauty and Wit of the two last preceding Ages had arisen from The Dead.'[18]

Meanwhile Mary's son-in-law was achieving his ambition, thanks to the power-broking of Newcastle. Soon Mary would become the mother of the prime minister or as Horace Walpole jokingly referred to her, 'the Queen Mother'.[19] Newcastle had become embroiled in a controversy over whether to continue a subsidy which was being paid to Prussia. Bute opposed it. Realising that his power was waning, Newcastle finally resigned on 26 May. The king immediately made Bute prime minister and First Lord of the Treasury. Bute's family, his mother-in-law included, were doubtless proud of his success, but the tensions continued. He remained an unpopular figure. The newspapers portrayed him as a conniving Scottish Tory, who supported the Jacobites, and who had no interest in protecting the English and their hard-won victories from the costly Seven Years War. Mary commented on the surprising turn of events where the king himself was very popular and the government less so. She had never seen such a thing before, she wrote. She would not be at all surprised, she admitted to Chiara Michiel, if she now saw nutmeg growing in English fields, so topsy-turvy was the world. Horace saw Mary again at a niece's house. This time she seemed to be dressed more conventionally and he admitted she was more discreet than he would have expected: 'but she is woefully tedious in her narrations.'[20]

Initially Mary's thoughts turned to making her way back to Venice, but it quickly became evident that this was out of the question. Chiara Michiel handled her anxieties with both compassion and style. She knew her friend would never make it back to Italy. Mary must have taken the decision not to have a breast removed, to get rid of the cancer. She would have remembered all too well the terrible pain Mary Astell had suffered. In May, she caught a gastric 'flu which was doing the rounds. Dr Mora and Mari Ana also suffered. Her nephew Evelyn was forced to cancel a dinner because there were not enough healthy footmen to wait at table. That same month Mary's tumour burst. In her final letter to Chiara Michiel she used the word 'Adieu' for the first time: 'Adieu my Beautiful and worthy Friend; be assured that I am with the most perfect devotion entirely Yours.'[21]

The constant stream of visitors continued, everyone keen to take their own leave of her. As Horace Walpole put it: 'She behaves with great fortitude and says she has lived long enough.'[22] Her doctor would have attempted to ease her pain with opium and hemlock. One day both her daughter and her son-in-law, the prime minister, were visiting her when Sir James and Lady Frances Steuart's only son was announced. He was now a young army officer, whom she had never met but often discussed with his parents. Delighted, she chased all the other visitors out of her bedroom: 'My dear young friend has come to see me before I die, and I wish to be alone with him.'[23] The sparky flirtatiousness with young members of the opposite sex, which Horace had criticised so vehemently in Florence, continued unabated.

On 23 June, Mary wrote her will. She did so in her own hand, and left two copies, written out in full. In it she left almost everything to Lady Bute. She gave to Lady Oxford's daughter the diamond ring she had commissioned from the legacy which Lady Oxford had left to her. Her other rings she bequeathed to Chiara Michiel. To Mackenzie she gifted a snuffbox. The faithful Dr Mora was given £500 (about £73,000 today). Each of her servants received a year's wages. Mari Ana was also given her travelling expenses back home to France and all Lady Mary's clothes and linen. Most controversially, Mary left the sum of one guinea (£155 today) to her son Edward. After all his father, she felt, had amply provided for him, and he would inherit her own allowance automatically on her death. By giving him something, however small, she probably thought she would prevent him from contesting the will.

Mary died on 21 August 1762 in her house in Great George Street. She never stopped petitioning the Butes on behalf of both James Steuart and James Caldwell, right up until her death. She was buried the next day with no ceremony in the vault of Grosvenor Chapel, South Audley Street, just by the Butes' house. They clearly wanted to dispose of her remains with as little fuss as possible, no doubt relieved that her time in London had proved uncontroversial. Bute's premiership would only last ten months, before he retired from public life to his estate in Hampshire, where he pursued his love of botany. The Butes' many children nearly all married and had children. Some of their lives turned out well, some less so. Edward, as unconventional as ever, converted to Islam and became a devout Muslim. His illegitimate child Massoud – probably a foster son - was renamed Fortunatus and was Lady Mary's only black grandchild. When Edward read that his washerwoman ex-wife, Sally, had died, he advertised for a pregnant woman, whom he could marry in order to cut his nephew, James Archibald Stuart, out of the Wortley inheritance. He was not successful. James Archibald Stuart, later Stuart-Wortley-Mackenzie, was made Baron Wharncliffe. His descendants are still alive today.

Lady Mary's reputation grew rapidly soon after her death, immediately her *Embassy Letters* were published. On her death bed she had fretted about their fate. She hoped that the Reverend Benjamin Sowden in Rotterdam would make sure they found their way into print. He approached the Butes with the manuscripts after her death and accepted Lord Bute's offer to buy them from him for £200 (about £28,000 today). He must have felt he had done his duty. The Butes made no attempt to find a publisher. As luck would have it, though, before he took the letters to the Butes, the Reverend Sowden had met two English travellers in Rotterdam who expressed interest in having a look at them. So he had allowed them to read the two-volume manuscript overnight. Unbeknown to Sowden, the travellers had worked overnight to transcribe a copy. They then made sure to find a publisher. Mary would have loved the drama of this tale and its happy ending. Her wish did come true. In her preface, Mary Astell had urged Lady Mary's first readers to: 'offer her the Palm which is justly her due, and if we pretend to any Laurels, lay them willingly at her Feet.'[24] They obliged. Her published letters were instantly a best-seller and inspired a whole new vogue in all things Turkish.

Lady Mary's daughter, Lady Bute, had always been a cautious, conservative figure - like her father - and she pronounced herself unenthusiastic about her mother's propensity 'to record as certain facts stories that perhaps sprang up like mushrooms from the dirt.'[25] So as soon as Lady Mary died the Butes took steps to recover all her other letters, to prevent publication. Mary had also given Lady Bute her diaries, ranging over fifty years, from before her marriage right up to her last days. Lady Bute was the only person who ever got to read the many volumes in full. Reluctantly she allowed her youngest daughter, Lady Louisa, to read a censored version. Lady Bute then made sure to burn them all, before her own death in 1794. Lady Louisa was faithful to her mother but even she understood how destructive an act this was. As a child she was always scolded if ever she expressed interest in reading a book and warned that she should be careful not to grow up to be like her wayward grandmother. However, when Lady Mary's great-grandson, Lord Wharncliffe, began the task of compiling Lady Mary's unpublished work in 1837 and ensuring it made its way into print, Lady Louisa's *Biographical Anecdotes of Lady M.W. Montagu* were published alongside them.

The work has continued since then. A further edition appeared in 1861. In 1907 Emily Morse Symonds published Lady Mary's first full-length biography using the pen name George Paston. The irony that a full 150 years after Lady Mary's own death a woman would still have to pretend to be a man for her work to be acceptable would not have been lost on Lady Mary herself. The American academic and literary historian Robert Halsband carried out a huge amount of much-needed spade work in the 1950s and wrote a far more comprehensive, properly sourced biography. He also collected all Lady Mary's letters and edited her poems and prose. His successor, the Canadian academic Isobel Grundy, then wrote a hugely impressive, admirably all-encompassing biography in 1999 and made sure even more of Lady Mary's writing was published. Yet today Lady Mary still remains someone relatively unknown outside academic circles. Her writing is usually read merely as a footnote for students of Alexander Pope.

And yet Mary's story resonates all the more powerfully three hundred years later. As a scientist (a word first used in the nineteenth century) she played a key role in finding a cure for smallpox. Although she had never studied science formally, she observed the folk practice in Turkey, carried out an experiment there on her own son, and then worked out that the same practice could be applied in England. She went on to use her admirable skills as a social networker to market this new-found cure and to argue in print that doctors were wrongly medicalising the process. For this she got little thanks in her own lifetime and even as late as 1957 the academic Genevieve Miller's history of smallpox expressly played down her role. Two monuments, an obelisk at Wentworth in Barnsley and a statue with an inscription singing her praises at Lichfield Cathedral, are easily missed. The first was put up by a friend of Horace Walpole's, who was rumoured at one time to be romantically linked to Mary's granddaughter, Lady Louisa. The other was endowed by a female descendant of Sister Gower's. 'Thus by her Example and Advice,' it explains, 'we have soften'd the Virulence and escaped the danger of this malignant Disease.' 'Soften'd' feels a particularly un-Lady-Mary-like description of her actions. She herself never went to either Wentworth or Lichfield.

Ironically, Lady Mary is more fêted in mainland Europe. In the Pantheon square in Rome - somewhere she only visited for a short time - she is commemorated on a bench alongside Zhand Xiahun, Elizabeth Garrett Anderson, Louise Merzeau, Nzinga Mhandi and Frida Kahlo as part of a Women's Memory Project. The town of Lovere on Lago d'Iseo in Northern Italy has based its entire marketing campaign around Lady Mary's describing Lovere as one of the prettiest places in the world. Her words are quoted proudly in Italian throughout the town. A walkway by the lake is named after her, as is a residential street. In both cases it feels as if Lady Mary's memory is being used to fulfil other people's agendas. Her scientific legacy is not mentioned.

She was far more than these memorials imply. Her spirit and tenacity coloured her entire, adventure-filled life. She refused to accept the rules of the world she was born into. Her feminist writing questioned the conventions of the time around the institution of marriage. The irony she used in her writing about divorce only served to highlight the importance of her message. She pointed out the imbalance of power that existed between the sexes and questioned a world where a woman's money automatically became her husband's. Her travelling helped her look at these questions from a very particular, original perspective. Her account of meeting Turkish women in the *hammam* in Sophia was rightly seen as groundbreaking as soon as it was published. She decided against divorce for herself, but she followed her dream, nevertheless. Although her love for Algarotti was never reciprocated in the way she had hoped, she found happiness living an independent life in mainland Europe and revelled in her unique position there. Joseph Spence rightly described her as a 'comet of the enlightenment'.

Not that her life was an easy one. She was someone who invariably evoked great passions in others, both for and against. Meeting the famous Alexander Pope and his circle when she was only 26 years old felt hugely exciting for her. It seemed she had made it. She then had to contend not only with contracting smallpox and losing her looks but also with Pope's unwanted attention. She managed to dampen his ardour for a time, but he became a powerful enemy when things eventually did go wrong between them. The story bears telling for a #MeToo generation. She had a burning intelligence, just like Pope. Like him, she had a prodigious writing talent. She had powerful friends and aristocratic connections on her side. And yet Pope was still able to do her enormous damage. In the war between them, it was he who emerged victorious. Nor was he the only man she found hard to handle. Rémond successfully terrorised her with his threats to reveal everything to Wortley over the South Sea investments she had made for him. And Palazzi used extortion against her for ten whole years at a time when she was vulnerable, living a lonely life in mainland Europe and determined not to return home to England. She never found intimacy easy. Ultimately it worked better for her to write warm letters to Wortley back in England, but to live a contented life as a single person.

Mary was a strong woman before the term was invented, who showed remarkable courage throughout her life. She chose to elope rather than be press-ganged into a marriage she could not countenance. When she knew she had contracted smallpox, she shut herself up in her London house and got on with battling the disease all alone - and survived. She accompanied Wortley across a war-torn Europe to Turkey, something most women of her generation baulked at. When she learned about inoculation in Turkey, she decided to have both her children protected. She fought to save Sister Mar, who had fallen prey to mental illness, from the men in the family who saw her sister's incapacity as a means of financial gain for themselves. She stood up against Pope. She set off for a new life in Venice with Algarotti, telling only one person (Hervey) what she was planning. When it became evident that she and Algarotti would never live together as she had hoped, she deliberately sought him out and brought things to a close with enormous dignity. When the situation with her son, Edward, was particularly bad, it was she, not Wortley, who agreed to meet him and try to find a solution. At the end of her life, knowing she was dying of breast cancer, she travelled hundreds of miles across war-torn Europe to see her daughter's family again.

Only a fraction of Mary's writing still survives. So much is lost. We do, though, have the image of her unbuttoning her stays in the *hammam* in Sophia so as to show the other women the whalebone cage underneath. We have her account of sitting on a verandah in the Constantinople January sunshine, heavily pregnant, her feet warmed by her *tendour*, writing poetry in praise of the new world in which she found herself. We have her walking and talking with the young Maria Skerrett, her 'little thread satin Beauty', in leafy Twickenham, weighing up whether or not Sir Robert Walpole's intentions were honourable.[26] We have her galloping to catch up with the coach trundling its way northwards, brandishing the lord chief justice's warrant she had obtained to prevent Grange from abducting Sister Mar. We have her description of the delights of playing cards every evening with the priests in Gottolengo or inspecting the butter-making in her dairy house by the River Po. We have her happiness in later life in her palazzo in Padua, 'like a Mouse in a Parmesan cheese'.[27] And sobbing uncontrollably at a concert in Venice when a neighbour mentions the daughter she has not seen for twenty years. And holding steady the same daughter, young Mary, at a moment which will change the course of life in the western world, while cautious old Dr Maitland makes the necessary shallow cuts on the little girl's wrists and ankles.

Appendix

Following in Mary Wortley Montagu's Footsteps

Many of the places Mary knew can still be visited today: in England Borbach Chantry, which formed part of the parish church at West Dean in Wiltshire still stands, although only the stable block survives of the house itself; Wharncliffe Lodge in the village of Wortley near Sheffield is privately-owned but it is possible to walk through the park and look at it from the outside, with its magnificent view over the Peak District; Middlethorpe Hall just outside York is a country house hotel; Castle Howard where Mary took refuge for a few weeks after Queen Anne died is open to the public; in Twickenham Mary's home Savile House no longer exists, but Pope's grotto can be visited and Kneller's house still stands.

In Sophia, Bulgaria, there are several bath houses like the one Mary visited. Edirne in Turkey (Mary's Adrianople) is also worth visiting as is Pera, the suburb of Constantinople where she lived in the embassy (the site of today's consulate). In Venice the Palazzo Foscari, which was her home there, is now a branch of Burger King near the station. In Florence it is possible to rent an apartment in the Palazzo Ridolfi, where Mary stayed with the Pomfrets. The Palazzo Zuccaro, where she lodged in Rome, is at the top of the Spanish Steps and now houses a library. In Avignon the Rocher-des-Doms ancient citadel where she was granted the use of a round tower can be visited, although the tower itself has been destroyed.

In Brescia, the Piazza del For contains the house belonging to Count Palazzi's mother, where Mary was struck down with malaria. The small town of Gottolengo where she settled for ten years and cultivated her garden still prospers, as does the town of Lovere on Lake Iseo, where Mary is remembered fondly and her endorsement of it being one of the most beautiful places in the world is still used in the town's marketing. Several streets are named after her and a lakeside walkway is called the Lunge Largo Mary Wortley Montagu in her honour. The botanical gardens in Padua which she loved can be visited still. Great George Street, where she died in the rented 'harpsichord-shaped house' is today called St George Street. Her funeral took place in Grosvenor Chapel, South Audley Street, where the Butes lived. Although Mary never visited Lichfield, the cathedral there proudly displays its memorial to her.

Bibliography

Abbreviations

BL Eg - Egerton Manuscripts, British Library

Bute - The Bute Archive at Mount Stuart

CL - *Complete Letters of Lady Mary Wortley Montagu,* ed., Halsband, Robert, (Oxford, 1965-7)

CB - Commonplace Book, Sydney, Australia

E & P - *Essays and Poems and Simplicity a Comedy,* eds. Halsband, Robert, and Grundy, Isobel, (Clarendon, Oxford, 1977)

HMS - Harrowby Mansucripts, Sandon Hall, Stafford

HP - Hertford-Pomfret Corr. - Correspondence between Frances, Countess of Hartford (afterwards Duchess of Somerset) and Henrietta Louisa, Countess of Pomfret, between the years 1738 and 1741, (Phillips, Richard, 1805)

Hervey - Hervey Manuscripts, Bury Archives

Hunt - Huntington Manuscripts, The Huntington Library, San Marino, California

Mar and Kellie - *Report on the manuscripts of the Earl of Mar and Kellie preserved at Alloa House. NB.* (London, 1904)

MS - manuscripts

MWM - Mary Wortley Montagu

Mundy - Mundy Manuscripts

PRO - Public Record Office

RW - *Grundy, Isobel, (ed.), Lady Mary Wortley Montagu: Romance Writings,* (Clarendon Press, Oxford, 1996)

trans. - translation

Wal Corr. - Walpole, Horace, *Correspondence, (*ed.), Lewis W.S. et al., (Yale University Press, 1937-82)

WhM - Wharncliffe Manuscripts, Sheffield Archives

Works by and about Lady Mary

France, Linda, *The Toast of the Kit-Cat Club: A life of Lady Mary Wortley Montagu in Eleven Chapters,* (Bloodaxe, 2005)

Grundy, Isobel, *The Verses of Lady Mary Wortley Montagu*, (PhD Thesis, University of Oxford, 1971)

 - 'The Politics of Female Authorship: Lady Mary Wortley Montagu's Reaction to the Printing of her Poems,' in *The Book Collector,* 31, (London, 1982)

 - (ed.), *Lady Mary Wortley Montagu: Romance Writings*, (Clarendon Press, Oxford, 1996)

 - 'Editing Lady Mary Wortley Montagu,' in Hutchison, Ann (ed.), *Editing Women,* (Toronto, 1998)

Lady Mary Wortley Montagu: Comet of the Enlightenment, (OUP, 1999)

Halsband, Robert, 'New Light on Mary Wortley Montagu's Contribution to Inoculation,' in *Journal of the History of Medicine and Allied Sciences,* VIII (OUP,1953)

 - *The Life of Lady Mary Wortley Montagu,* (Clarendon Press, Oxford, 1956)

'Walpole versus Lady Mary,' in *Horace Walpole: Writer, Politician and Connoisseur,* ed., Smith, W. H., (Yale University Press,1967)

 - 'Virtue in Danger,' or the Case of Griselda Murray,' in *History Today*, (Longman, London, October 1967)

 - 'The Lady's Dressing Room,' explicated by a contemporary,' in Miller, H.K., Rothstein, E., Rousseau, G.S., (eds.), *The Augustan Milieu* (Oxford: Clarendon, 1970)

Leslie, Doris, *A toast to Lady Mary,* (London Hutchinson, 1954)

Montagu, Lady Mary Wortley, *The works of the Right Honourable Lady Mary Wortley Montagu,* ed., Dallaway, James, (Longman, London, 1812)

 - *Original Letters…to Sir James and Lady Frances Steuart; also, Memoirs and Anecdotes of those Distinguished Persons,* (Greenock, 1818)

 - *Letters and Works*, ed., Wharncliffe, Lord, (London, 1837)

 - *Letters and Works*, ed., Thomas, W. Moy, (Bell, London, 1898)

 - *Complete Letters of Lady Mary Wortley Montagu*, ed., Halsband, Robert, (Oxford, 1965-7)

 - *Essays and Poems and Simplicity a Comedy*, eds. Halsband, Robert, and Grundy, Isobel, (Clarendon, Oxford, 1977)

Paston, George, *Lady Mary Wortley Montagu and her Times*, (Methuen, London, 1907)

Pierrepont, Lady Mary, *Indamora to Lindamira*, ed., Grundy, Isobel, (Edmonton, Alberta, 1994)

Works by Lady Mary's contemporaries

Addison, Joseph, *The Letters of Joseph Addison,* ed. Graham, Walter, (Clarendon Press, Oxford, 1941)
  - *Spectator, Volume 8,* (Tonson and Draper, 1714)

Algarotti, Francesco, *Letters from Count Algarotti to Lord Hervey and the Marquis Scipio Maffei*, (Dublin, 1770)

Anon, *The Reports of the Committee of Secrecy to the Honourable House of Commons Relating to the Late South Sea Directors*, (London, 1721)

Applebees Journal

Arbuthnot, John, *Mr Maitland's Account of Inoculating the Smallpox Vindicated by Dr Wagstaffe's Misrepresentations,* 2nd edition, (London, 1722)

Astell, Mary, *A Serious Proposal to the Ladies, wherein a method is offer'd for the improvement of their minds*, (Richard Wilkin, England, 1697)

Burges, James, *An Account of the preparation and management necessary to inoculation,* (P. Vaillant, London, 1754)

Daily Journal

Daily Post

Dumont, Jean, *A New Voyage to Levant,* (London, 1696)

Fielding, Henry, *The Modern Husband,* (London, 1732)
  - *The History of Tom Jones*, (London, 1749)
  - *The Adventures of Joseph Andrews,* (London, 1742)

Frederick III of Prussia, *Oeuvres de Frédéric le Grand*, (Berlin, 1850)

Gay, John, *Trivia or the Art of Walking the Streets of London*, (London, 1716)
  - *Poems on Several Occasions, (*Dublin, 1752)

Gentleman's Magazine

Goldsmith, Oliver, *She Stoops to Conquer,* (1773)

Grub Street Journal

Graham, John Murray, *Annals and Correspondence of the Earls of Stair,* (Edinburgh, 1875)

Hertford-Pomfret Corr., *Correspondence between Frances, Countess of Hartford (afterwards Duchess of Somerset) and Henrietta Louisa, Countess of Pomfret, between the years 1738 and 1741,* (Richard Phillips, 1805).

Hill, Aaron, *A Full and Just Account of the Present State of the Ottoman Empire,* (London, 1709)
 - (ed.), *The Plain Dealer,* (London, 1724-5)

Howard, Henrietta, Lady Suffolk, *Letters,* (ed.), Croker, J.W. (John Murray 1824)

Howgrave, Francis, *Reasons Against the Inoculation of the Small-Pox. In a Letter to Dr Jurin,* (London, 1724)

Johnson, Samuel, *Lives of the English Poets,* (ed.), Birkbeck Hill, George, (Oxford, 1905)

Jones, Erasmus, *Pretty Doings in a Protestant Nation,* (Roberts, London,1734)

Jurin, James, *A Letter to the Learned Caleb Cotesworth…Containing a Comparison between the Mortality of the Natural Small Pox, and that Given by Inoculation,* (London, 1723)

Kirkpatrick, James, *The Analysis of Inoculation: Comprising the History, Theory and Practice of it,* (London,1754)

Llanover, Lady, (ed.), *Autobiography and Correspondence of Mary Granville, Mrs. Delany,* (London: Richard Bentley, 1861)

London Evening Post

Macky, John, *Memoirs of the Secret Services, (*London, 1733*)*

Maitland, Dr Charles, *An Account of Inoculating the Smallpox*, (London, 1722)

Mar, Earl of, *Report on the manuscripts of the Earl of Mar and Kellie preserved at Alloa House. NB.* (London, 1904)

Marlborough, Sarah Duchess of, *Letters of a Grandmother 1732-1735*, (ed.), Thompson G.S., (Cape, 1943)

Massey, Edmund, *A Sermon against the Dangers and Sinful Practice of Inoculation,* (London, 1725)

Massey, Isaac, *A Short and Plain Account of Inoculation with some remarks on the main arguments made use of to recommend that practice, by Mr Maitland and Others,* (London: W. Meadows, 1724)

Pope, Alexander, *Full and True Account of a Horrid and Barbarous Revenge by Poison, On the Body of Mr Edmund Curll,* (London: J. Roberts, 1716)
 - *Works*, (ed.), Warburton, William, (London, 1751)

*Works, (*ed.), Warton, Thomas, (London, 1797)

The Works of Alexander Pope; with a memoir by the author. New edition. (ed.), Croly, George, (Adam Scott, London, 1854)

Alexander Pope Correspondence, (ed.), Sherburn, George, (Oxford: Clarendon Press,1956)

Poems, Twickenham Edition, (London and New Haven, 1939-64)

The Poems of Alexander Pope, a one volume edition of the Twickenham Pope, (ed.), Butt, John, (London: Methuen, 1963)

Prose Works, (eds.), Ault, Norman and Cowler, Rosemary, (Oxford: Blackwell, 1936, 1986)
  - http://www.en.utexas.edu/Classes/Moore/neoclassical/neoPoetry6. htm (2020)
  - https://oll.libertyfund.org/titles/pope-the-complete-poetical-works-of-alexander-pope (2020)
  - https://www.poetryfoundation.org/poets/alexander-pope (2020)
  - https://www.quodlib.umich.edu (2020)

Richardson, Samuel, *Sir Charles Grandison*, (London, 1753)

Scudéry Madeleine de, *Artamene or The Grand Cyrus,* (Geneva: Slatkine, 1972)

Sheridan Richard B., *The Rivals, (*London, 1775)
  - *The School for Scandal,* (London, 1777)

Sloane, Sir Hans, *An Account of Inoculation,* (London, 1767)

Smith, D.N., (ed.), *Letters of Thomas Burnet to George Duckett 1712-1722,* (Oxford, 1914)

Spence, Joseph, *Anecdotes, Observations and Characters of Books and Men Collected from Conversation*, (ed.), Osborn, James M., (Oxford, Clarendon Press, 1966)
  - *Letters from the Grand Tour/Joseph Spence,* (ed.), Klima, Slava, (Montreal, 1975)

Steele, Richard, *Correspondence,* (ed.), Blanchard, Rae, (OUP, 1941)

Steele, Richard et al., *The Tatler, 1709-11*, (ed.), Bond, Donald F., (Oxford, 1987)

Stuart Wortley, Violet, (ed.), *A Prime Minister and his son, from the correspondence of the third Earl of Bute and of Lt.-General the Hon. Sir Charles Stuart, K.B.,* (John Murray, 1925)

Voltaire, *Letters on England*, Hancock, Leonard (ed. and translator) (London, 1980)

- *Lettres Philosophiques,* translated by Fletcher, Dennis, (Grant and Cutler, 1986)

Wagstaffe, William, *A Letter to Dr Freind; shewing the Danger and Uncertainty of Inoculating the Small Pox*, (London, 1722)

Walpole, Horace, *Correspondence, (*ed.), Lewis W.S. et al., (Yale University Press, 1937-82)

Unpublished Source Material

Bristol Manuscripts, Bristol

The Bute Archive at Mount Stuart, Isle of Bute

Commonplace Book, University of Sydney, Australia

Egerton Manuscripts, British Library

Egmont Manuscripts, Historical Manuscripts Commission

Finch Manuscripts, Leicestershire Record Office

Halsband Manuscripts, Columbia University, New York

Harley Manuscripts, British Library

Harrowby Manuscripts, Sandon Hall, Stafford

Hervey Manuscripts, Bury Archives, Bury St Edmunds

Huntington Manuscripts, The Huntington Library San Marino, California

John Murray Collection, London

Manvers Manuscripts, University of Nottingham

Mar and Kellie Manuscripts - National Records of Scotland

Mar Manuscripts -National Records of Scotland

Mellerstain Manuscripts, Mellerstain House, Berwickshire

Mundy Manuscripts, Lincoln Record Office

Public Record Office, Kew

Wharncliffe Manuscripts, Sheffield Archives

General reading

Allen, R.J., *The Clubs of Augustan London*, (Archon Books, 1933)

Balen, Malcolm, *A Very English Deceit. The South Sea Bubble and the World's First Great Financial Scandal,* (Fourth Estate, 2002)

Barnes, Diana G., 'Tenderness, Tittle-tattle and Truth in Mother-Daughter Letters: Lady Mary Wortley Montagu, Mary Wortley Montagu Stuart,

Countess of Bute and Lady Louisa Stuart', in *Women's History Review, 24: 4* (Routledge, 2015)

Beattie, Alexander, and Stanley, C.W.N., *Thoresby Hall,* (London, 1964)

Beattie, J.M., *The English Court in the Reign of George II,* (Cambridge, 1967)

Black, Jeremy, *Walpole in Power,* (Stroud: Sutton, 2001)

Bohls, Elizabeth A., 'Aesthetics and Orientalism in Lady Mary Wortley Montagu's Letters,' in *Studies in Eighteenth-Century Culture, 23,* eds., Hay, Carla H. and Conger, Syndy M., (Appalachian State University, 1994)

Browning, Reed, *The War of the Austrian Succession,* (Pergamon Press, 1994)

Bruce, Susan and Smits, Katherine, eds., *Feminist moments: reading feminist texts,* (Bloomsbury Academic, 2016)

Buck, Anne, *Dress in Eighteenth Century England,* (London, 1980)

Bulloch, John Malcolm, *A Pioneer of Inoculation - Charles Maitland,* (Aberdeen University Press, 1930)

Carrell Jennifer Lee, *The Speckled Monster: a historical tale of battling smallpox,* (Johns Hopkins University Press, 2003)

Campbell, Jill, 'Lady Mary Wortley Montagu and the Historical Machinery of Female Identity', in *History, Gender & Eighteenth-Century Literature,* ed., Tobin, Beth Fowkes, (University of Georgia Press,1994)
  - 'Lady Mary Wortley Montagu and the 'Glass Revers'd' of Female Old Age,' in *Defects: Engendering the Modern Body,* eds., Deutsch, Helen, and Nussbaum, Felicity, (University of Michigan Press, 2000)

Chung, King-Thom, *Women Pioneers of Medical Research: biographies of 25 outstanding scientists,* (Jefferson, N.C., McFarland, 2009)

Colley, Linda, *Britons: Forging the Nation 1707-1837,* (New Haven, Connecticut,1992)
  - *Captives: Britain, Empire and the World, 1600-1850,* (London, 2002)

Cowan, Brian, 'What was masculine about the public sphere? Gender and the coffee house milieu in post-restoration England,' in *History Workshop Journal, No. 51,* (OUP, Spring 2001)

Curling, Jonathan, *Edward Wortley Montagu 1713-1776 The Man in the Iron Wig,* (Andrew Melrose, 1954)

Dale, Richard, *The First Crash - Lessons from the South Sea Bubble,* (Princeton University Press, 2004)

Davis, Fanny, *The Ottoman Lady: A Social History from 1718 to 1918*, (Greenwood Press, 1986)

Dennison, Matthew, *The First Iron Lady: a life of Caroline of Ansbach,* (Collins, 2017)

Ehrenpreis, Irvin, and Halsband, Robert, *The lady of letters in the eighteenth century; papers read at Clark Library Seminar, January 18 1969*, (University of California, 1969)

Erskine, Stuart, (ed.), *The Earl of Mar's Legacies to Scotland and to his Son, Lord Erskine 1722-1727,* (Alloa House, 1896)

Fappani, Antonio, 'Lady Montagu ed it co: Ugolino Palazzi,' in *Commentari dell'ateneo di Brescia,* (Italy, 1961)

Feldman, Paula, *British Women Poets of the Romantic Era*, (Baltimore, 2000)

Fernea, Elizabeth Warnock, 'An Early Ethnographer of Middle Eastern Women: Lady Mary Wortley Montagu (1689-1762),' in *Journal of Near Eastern studies*, 40. (Chicago University Press, 1981)

Fothergill, B., *Sir William Hamilton, Envoy Extraordinary*, (Nonesuch, 1969)

George, Dorothy, *London Life in the Eighteenth Century,* (Kegan Paul, 1925)

Gillis, John R., *For Better for Worse: British Marriages, 1600 to the Present,* (Oxford University Press, 1986)

Glynn, Ian and Jennifer, *The life and death of smallpox,* (Wellcome Institute, 2005)

Goller Karl Heinz, *The Emancipation of Women in Eighteenth Century Literature*, (Cambridge, 1983)

Greg, Edward, 'The Jacobite Career of John, Earl of Mar,' in *Ideology and Conspiracy: Aspects of Jacobitism 1689-1759*, ed. Cruickshanks, Eveline, (Edinburgh: Donald, 1982)

Grundy, Isobel, 'Inoculation in Salisbury,' in *The Scriblerian*, 26, (Philadelphia Temple University, 1993)
   - 'Medical Advance and Female Fame; Inoculation and its After-Effects,' in *Lumen, 13,* (London, 1994)

Guerinot, J.V., *Pamphlet Attacks on Alexander Pope 1711-1744: A Descriptive Bibliography,* (London Methuen, 1969).

Halsband, Robert, *Lord Hervey, Eighteenth Century Courtier*, (Clarendon Press, Oxford, 1973)

Harvey, A.D., *Sex in Georgian England: attitudes and prejudices from the 1720s to the 1820s,* (Duckworth, London, 1994)

Haslett, Moyra, *Pope to Burney, 1714-1779: Scriblerians to Bluestockings,* (MacMillan, 2003)

Heffernan, Teresa, *Veiled figures: women, modernity and the spectres of orientalism,* (Toronto, 2016)

Henderson, G.D., (ed.), *Mystics of the North-East including...Letters of James Keith,* (Aberdeen, 1934)

Holden, Philip and Ruppel, Richard J., (eds.), *Imperial Desire: dissident sexualities and colonial literature,* (University of Minnesota Press, 2003)

Hollis, George Truett, 'Count Francesco Algarotti and the Society,' in Allan, D.G.C., and Abbott, John L., (eds.), *The Virtuoso Tribe of Arts and Sciences: Studies in the Eighteenth-Century Work and Membership of the London Society of Arts, Manufacture and Commerce,* (University of Georgia Press, 1992)

Hunter, Joseph, *South Yorkshire: The History and Topography of the Deanery of Doncaster, in the Diocese and County of York,* (London, 1828-31)

James, Francis G., *Lords of the Ascendancy - The Irish House of Lords and its Members 1600 -1800,* (Catholic University of America Press, 1995)

Kinniard, Joan, 'Mary Astell and The Conservative Contribution to English Feminism,' in *The Journal of British Studies.* 19: 53-75, (CUP, 1979)

Leeks, Wendy, 'Ingres Other-Wise,' in *Oxford Art Journal*, 9, (OUP, 1986)

Levine, Joseph, *Dr Woodward's Shield: History, Science and Satire in Augustan England,* (University of California Press,1977)

Lew, Joseph W., 'Lady Mary's Portable Seraglio,' in *Journal for Eighteenth Century Studies*, 24, (Oxford, 1991)

Lonsdale, Roger, (ed.), *The New Oxford Book of Eighteenth-Century Verse,* (Oxford University Press, 1984)

Lowenthal, Cynthia, *Lady Mary Wortley Montagu and the Eighteenth-Century Familiar Letter*, (University of Georgia Press, 1994)

Maclean, Gerald, (ed.), *Britain and the Muslim world: historical perspectives*, (University of Exeter, 2009)

Mahaffey, Lois Kathleen, *Alexander Pope and his Sappho: Pope's Relationship with Lady Mary Wortley Montagu and its influence on his work*, (PhD Thesis, University of Texas, 1963)

Mannheimer, Katherine, *Print, visuality and gender in eighteenth century satire: 'the scope in every page,'* (New York Routledge, 2011)

Mack, Maynard, *The Garden and the City,* (OUP, 1969)
- *Alexander Pope - A Life,* (Yale University Press, 1985)

McDowell, Paula, *The Women of Grub Street: Press, Politics, and Gender in the London Literary Marketplace 1678-1730,* (Clarendon Press, Oxford, 1998)

Mellman, Billie, *Women's Orients: English Women and the Middle East 1718-1918: Sexuality, Religion and Work,* (Indiana University Press, 1992)

Merrill, Yvonne Day, 'The Social Construction of Western Women's Rhetoric before 1750,' in *Women's Studies*, (London, 1996)

Messenger, Ann, 'Town Eclogues,' in *His and Hers: Essays in Restoration and Eighteenth-Century Literature,* (University Press of Kentucky, 1986)

Miller, Genevieve, T*he Adoption of Inoculation for Smallpox in England and France,* (University of Pennsylvania Press, 1957)

Miller, Hildy, and Bridwell-Bowles, Lillian, (eds.), *Rhetorical women: roles and representations,* (University of Alabama Press, 2005)

Ministère des Affaires Etrangères, Sardaigne, (1898)

Monod, Paul Kleber, *Jacobitism and the English People, 1688-1788,* (CUP, 1989)

Moore, James Carrick, *The History of the Small Pox,* (London, 1815)

Moore, Lucy, *Amphibious Thing: The Life of Lord Hervey,* (Viking, 2000)

Nokes, David, *John Gay: a profession of friendship*, (Faber, 2014)

Northcott, Richard, *Francesco Algarotti: a reprint of his essay on opera and a sketch of his life*, (Press Printers, 1917)

Nussbaum, Felicity A., *The brink of all we hate: English satires on Women 1660-1750,* (University Press of Kentucky, 1984)
- *Torrid Zones: Maternity, Sexuality and Empire in Eighteenth Century English Narratives,* (Johns Hopkins University Press, 1995)

Perry, Ruth, *The Celebrated Mary Astell,* (University of Chicago Press, 1986)

Plumb J.H., *Sir Robert Walpole: The Making of a Statesman, The King's Minister,* (Allen Lane, 1972)

Pointon, Marcia, 'Hanging the Head: Portraiture and Social Formation,'
- 'Killing Pictures,' in Barrell, John, (ed.), *Painting and the Politics of Culture: New Essays on British Art 1700-1850,* (OUP, 1988,1992)

Porter, Roy, *English Society in the Eighteenth Century*, (Penguin, London, 1991)

Pringle, Patrick, *When They Were Girls: girlhood stories of fourteen famous women,* (London, 1956)

Razzell, Peter, *The Conquest of Smallpox: The Impact of Inoculation on Smallpox Mortality in Eighteenth Century Britain,* (Caliban Books, 1977)

Reynolds, Myra, *The Learned Lady in England 1650-1760,* (Boston, 1920)

Riding, Jacqueline, *Jacobites: A New History of the '45 Rebellion,* (Bloomsbury, London, 2016)

Rizzo, Betty, *Companions without Vows: Relationships among Eighteenth Century British Women,* (University of Georgia Press, 1994)

Rumbold, Valerie, *Women's Place in Pope's World*, (CUP, 1989)

Salmon, Christine, *Representations of the Female Self in Familiar Letters 1650-1780,* (Ph.D. thesis, University of London, 1991)

Sedgwick, Romney, *The History of Parliament: the House of Commons 1715-1754*, Vol II (London HMSO, 1970)

Sherburn, George, *The Early Career of Alexander Pope,* (Russell and Russell, London, 1963)

Shevelow, Kathryn, *Women and Print Culture: the Construction of Femininity in the Early Periodical,* (Routledge, London,1989)

Shuttleton, David E., (1995), 'A Modest Examination: John Arbuthnot and the Scottish Newtonians,' in *British Journal for Eighteenth-Century Studies*, 18, (Oxford,1995)
- *Smallpox and the Literary Imagination 1660-1820,* (CUP, 2007)

Skelton, Neil, *The Borbach Chantry West Dean, Wiltshire*, (The Churches Conservation Trust, 2005)

Skinner, Andrew W., 'Sir James Steuart: The Market and the State', in *History of Economic Ideas,* 1/1:1-42, (London, 1993)

Smith, Charles Samaurez, *Eighteenth-Century Decoration: Design and the Domestic Interior in England*, (London, 1993)

Smith, J.R., *The Speckled Monster: Smallpox in England, 1670-1970, With Particular Reference to Essex,* (London, 1987)

Spacks, Patricia Meyer, *Reading Eighteenth Century Poetry,* (Oxford. Wiley-Blackwell, 2009)

- 'Female Rhetorics', in Benstock, Shari (ed.), *The Private Self: Theory and Practice of Women's Autobiographical Writings*, (Routledge, London, 1988)

Staves,Susan, *Married Women's Separate Property in England, 1660-1833,* (Harvard University Press,1990)

- *A Literary History of Women's Writing in Britain 1660-1789,* (CUP, 2006)

Stone, Laurence, *The Road to Divorce: England 1530-1987*, (London, 1991)

Stuart, Lady Louisa, *Introductory Anecdotes,* (London, 1861)

- *Gleanings from an Old Portfolio*, ed., Clark, Alice, (Edinburgh, 1895-8)

- *Selections from her Manuscripts,* ed., Home, J.A., (Edinburgh,1899)

- *Letters of Lady Louisa Stuart to Miss Louisa Clinton*, ed., Home, J.A., (Edinburgh, 1901)

Tomalin, Claire, *The Life and Death of Mary Wollstonecraft,* (London, 1974)

Treglown, G.L., and Mortimer, M.C.F., 'Elegant and Elusive: Wineglasses of the Kit-Cat Club', in *Country Life,* 170, (London, 1981)

Uglow, Jenny, *Hogarth: A Life and a World,* (New York, 1997)

Vickery, Amanda, *Women's Lives in Georgian England,* (Yale University Press, 1998)

Voltaire Foundation, *Studies on Voltaire and the Eighteenth Century,* 332, (Oxford, 1995)

Wilson, Adrian, 'The Politics of Medical Improvement in Early Hanoverian London,' in Cunningham, Andrew and French, Roger, (eds.), *The Medical Enlightenment of the Eighteenth Century,* (CUP, 1990)

Acknowledgements

I would like to thank the following for their generous help with this book: Claire Hopkins, Lori Jones, Laura Hirst, Catherine Curzon and all at Pen and Sword Books, Michael Bosson at Sandon Hall, Hugh Matheson, Gregor Pierrepont and Robert Brackenbury in Nottinghamshire, all at Middlethorpe Hall, the British Library, Lynsey Nairn at the Bute Archive, Jane Ingle at Bury Archives, Columbia University Library, Sheffield City Archive, Christies and The Prince's Foundation at Dumfries House, The Master and Fellows of Trinity College, Cambridge, the National Trust for Scotland, Lichfield Cathedral, The Portland Collection at the Harley Gallery at Welbeck Abbey, Tony Sanger from Wortley Cottage Guest House, who kindly drove me through the rain to see Wharncliffe Lodge, Bridgeman Images, Molly Braithwaite, Robert Fraser and my fellow students at City Lit, Evren Essen at the Pera Palace, Istanbul, Linda France, Lauretta Dives for her encouragement, Mark and Morag Jordan for their research support in Brescia and Lovere, James Runcie, Marilyn Imrie, Bill Paterson and Hildegard Bechtler for their patience in Istanbul and their willingness to try an historic *hammam,* Daisy Wyatt, Rupert Gray, Jack Wyatt, Kat Derrenberger and Rufus Rock for their forbearance and Stuart Rock - my photographer, editor, researcher and compañero - without whom this dream would never have come true.

Notes

All comparisons between financial figures in Mary's day and today come from the following website: https://www.measuringworth.com/calculators/ukcompare/

1. Spence, (1975), 2.357.

Introduction

1. E & P, p.95.
2. This imagined dialogue inspired by reading Bulloch.
3. This imagined dialogue inspired by reading CL.1. 208-10.
4. This imagined dialogue inspired by reading Maitland.
5. Voltaire, (1980), Letter 11.
6. CL. 1. 338.
7. Maitland, p.3.
8. This imagined detail is inspired by a reference in CL.3. 5.
9. Maitland, p.10.
10. Ibid., p.11.
11. Henderson, p.58.
12. E & P, p.36.
13. CL. 1. 26.
14. Spence, (1975), 2.356.

Chapter 1

1. E & P, p.9.
2. CL. 3. 27.
3. CL. 3. 277.
4. CL. 3. 20.
5. Skelton, p.6.
6. E & P, p.9.

7. France, p.14.
8. E & P, p.9.
9. Ibid.
10. Ibid.
11. RW, p.110.
12. CL. 1. 42.
13. In 1706 Mary's father, the Earl of Kingston, was made Marquess of Dorchester and her brother William took the title Earl of Kingston. In 1715, though, Mary's father was made 1st Duke of Kingston. We will therefore refer to him as Kingston throughout.
14. CL.3. 36.
15. CL.2. 97.
16. HMS. 250.
17. Ibid.
18. HP. 2. 233-4.

Chapter 2

1. CL. 1. 167.
2. Sheridan, (1775), 5. 1.
3. CL. 1. 5.
4. Ibid., 28.
5. HMS. 74. 2-3.
6. Ibid., 52-3.
7. Spence, (1975), 2. 357.
8. CL.1. 45.
9. Ibid., 53-4.
10. Ibid., 63.
11. Ibid., 107.
12. Ibid., 121.
13. PRO. N.I., MS. D. 652, p.88.
14. CL. 1. 126.
15. Ibid., 138.
16. Ibid., 152.
17. Ibid., 163.
18. Ibid.
19. Ibid., 164.
20. Ibid., 167.
21. E & P, p.83.
22. CL. 1. 148.

23. Ibid.
24. Halsband, (1956), p.26.
25. Mundy, 1/MM/11/5.

Chapter 3

1. CL. 1. 168.
2. Ibid., 186.
3. Ibid., 228.
4. Smith, p.69.
5. RW. p.124.
6. CL. 1. 170.
7. Ibid., 178.
8. Stuart Wortley, p.213.
9. CL. 1. 169.
10. Ibid., 175.
11. Ibid., 200.
12. Ibid., 192.
13. Ibid., 195.
14. Ibid., 192.
15. Addison, (1714), Number 561.
16. E & P, p.74.
17. Ibid., p.215.
18. Mar, p.505.
19. CL.1. 221
20. Ibid., 226.
21. Ibid., 236.

Chapter 4

1. E & P, p.203.
2. Ibid., p.86.
3. Ibid., p.93.
4. HP 2. 233-4.17
5. E & P, p.181.
6. Pope, (1751), p.43.
7. Wal Corr, 14. 242.
8. E & P, p.184.
9. Hunt, 22, 255.

10. E & P, pp.203, 241.
11. Ibid., p.203.
12. Hunt, LO 7417.
13. Pope, (1797), vol. 2 p. 332n.
14. Ibid., vol 2. p.345.
15. BL Eg, 2234.

Chapter 5

1. CL.1. 308.
2. Ibid., 249.
3. Ibid., 252.
4. Ibid., 253.
5. Ibid., 258.
6. Ibid., 260.
7. Ibid., 265.
8. Ibid., 270.
9. Ibid., 272.
10. Ibid., 264.
11. Pope, (1956), 1. 353-4.
12. Ibid., 368.
13. Graham, 2. 35-6.
14. CL.1.296.
15. Ibid., 297.
16. Ibid., 305.
17. Ibid., 308.
18. Ibid., 313.
19. Dumont, pp.273-7.
20. CL. 1. 314.
21. Ibid.
22. Ibid., 458.

Chapter 6

1. CL. 1. 338.
2. Ibid., 406.
3. Ibid., 321.
4. Ibid., 341.
5. Ibid., 337.

6. Ibid., 390.
7. Ibid., 366.
8. E & P, p.209.
9. CL. 1. 394.
10. Ibid., 345.
11. Ibid., 395n.
12. HMS. 81. 126.
13. Ibid., 423.
14. Ibid.,429.
15. Ibid., 432.
16. Ibid., 434.
17. Ibid., 438.
18. Addison, (1941), p.377.
19. CL.1. 332.
20. Ibid., 446.
21. Ibid., 444.

Chapter 7

1. E & P, p.95.
2. Maitland, p.3.
3. E & P, p.35.
4. Ibid., p.36.
5. Voltaire, (1980), Letter 11.
6. Ibid.
7. Hunter, Joseph, p.43 - but not in Stuart (1861) because it seemed a bit high-handed about royalty.
8. Massey, (1724), p.3.
9. Maitland, pp.12, 15, 17.
10. Applebees Journal, 28 April 1722.
11. Wagstaffe, pp 5-6.
12. Grundy, (1993), 1:63-5.
13. Hill, (1724), p.241.
14. E & P, pp.35-6.
15. Grundy, (1999), p.218.
16. Halsband, (1953), pp 390-405.
17. Hill, (1724), p.243.
18. Burges, pp.3-4.
19. Lady Mary Wortley Montagu Monument, Lichfield Cathedral.
20. Goldsmith, Act Three.

Chapter 8

1. Pope (1956), 1. 494.
2. CL. 1. 31.
3. Pope (1956), 4. 423.
4. Wal Corr., 17. 276-7.
5. E & P, p.227.
6. Pope, (1854), p.105.
7. HMS. 81: 112-3.
8. http://www.en.utexas.edu/Classes/Moore/neoclassical/neoPoetry6.htm
9. Mack, (1969), p.31.
10. CL.2.15.
11. Mellerstain MS, 14 July 1722.
12. CL. 2.15.
13. E & P, p.42.
14. CL.3. 27.
15. CL. 2. 12.
16. Ibid. 182.
17. E & P, p.235.
18. CL. 2. 57.
19. https://quod.lib.umich.edu/e/ecco/004780226.0001.000/1:3?rgn=div1; view=fulltext p.15.
20. E & P, p.241.
21. https://www.poetryfoundation.org/poems/44895/epistle-to-dr-arbuthnot
22. CL. 2. 8.
23. Hervey, 941/ 47/2 folio 121.
24. E & P, p.39.
25. CL. 2. 44.
26. Ibid., 50.

Chapter 9

1. CL.2. 2.
2. CL. 1. 446.
3. Ibid., 448.
4. CL. 2. 1.
5. Balen, p.123.
6. Perry, p.392.
7. CL.1. 451.
8. CL.2. 2.

9. Pope, (1956), 2. p.52.
10. Ibid., pp.33-4.
11. CL.1. 453.
12. Ibid.
13. Anon, p.3.
14. CL. 2. 3-4.
15. Ibid., 5.
16. Ibid., 6.
17. Ibid., 8.
18. Ibid., 12.

Chapter 10

1. E & P, p.230.
2. E & P, p.157, trans. p.389.
3. Ibid.
4. E & P, p.163, trans. p.391.
5. HMS, 80. 137-8.
6. Mellerstain MS, 14 July 1722.
7. E & P, p 233.
8. Ibid., pp.230-232.
9. Ibid., p.75.
10. Ibid., p.270.
11. CL.2. 51-2.
12. E & P, pp. 221-4.

Chapter 11

1. CL. 2. 76.
2. Halsband, (1956), p.127.
3. Erskine, pp.176-7.
4. CL. 2. 26.
5. Bute MWM 1/3/1
6. National Records of Scotland, GD/124/15.
7. CL.2. 82.
8. Paston, p.327.
9. HMS, 77. 112-113.
10. *London Evening Post*, 5 March 1728.
11. CL.3. 96.

12. Mar, 4 April 1728.
13. National Records of Scotland, GD/124/15/1337.
14. PRO, C22, E16.
15. https://quod.lib.umich.edu/e/ecco/004809329.0001.000?view=toc
16. Bute LO/4/5.
17. CL. 2. 95.
18. Bute LO/5/1.
19. Greg, p.194.
20. CL.2. 224.
21. CL. 3. 266.

Chapter 12

1. https://www.poetryfoundation.org/poems/44906/the-rape-of-the-lock-canto-1
2. Johnson, (1905), 3. 200.
3. Pope, (1956), 1. 114
4. Pope, (1956), 1. 289.
5. Pope, (1956), 2. 139.
6. Pope, (1956), 2. 77.
7. Gentleman's Magazine, (1784), 54, 895.
8. E & P, p.37.
9. Pope, (1956), 3. 53.
10. https://oll.libertyfund.org/titles/pope-the-complete-poetical-works-of-alexander-pope
11. https://oll.libertyfund.org/titles/pope-the-complete-poetical-works-of-alexander-pope
12. Grub Street Journal, 13 April 1732.
13. https://quod.lib.umich.edu/e/ecco/004809261.0001.000?view=toc
14. Pope, (1956), 3. 352.
15. Mack, (1985), p.588.
16. Pope, (1956), 3. 357.
17. E & P, pp.286, 266, 270.
18. Daily Post & Daily Journal.
19. Hervey, 941/47/4 folio 461.
20. Moore, (2000), p.195.
21. CL. 2. 100.
22. https://quod.lib.umich.edu/e/ecco/004809326.0001.000/1:2?rgn=div1;view=fulltext
23. https://quod.lib.umich.edu/e/ecco/004809329.0001.000?view=toc
24. https://www.poetryfoundation.org/poems/44895/epistle-to-dr-arbuthnot

25. CL. 2. 99-100.
26. https://www.poetryfoundation.org/poems/44893/epistles-to-several-persons-epistle-ii-to-a-lady-on-the-characters-of-women
27. Guerinot, pp.254-8.
28. E & P, p.283.
29. Spence, (1975), p.358.

Chapter 13

1. E & P, p.386.
2. CL. 2. 81.
3. Ibid., 70.
4. Ibid., 82.
5. *Daily Journal*, 18 August 1727.
6. CL. 2. 82-3.
7. Curling, p.43.
8. Cited in Grundy, (1999), p.289.
9. CL. 2. 257,273.
10. Cited in Grundy, (1999) p.321.
11. Llanover, 1. 461-2.
12. Egmont MS. 1820-3.
13. WhM/439/13-14.

Chapter 14

1. E & P, p.134.
2. Ibid., p.295.
3. Ibid., p.296.
4. CL. 2. 237.
5. Frederick III of Prussia, 22. 327, 10 October 1739.
6. Ministère des Affaires Etrangères, Sardaigne, vol. 202, f. 61.
7. Stuart, (1899), p.4.
8. CL. 2. 101
9. Northcott, p.8.
10. CL. 3. 141.
11. E & P, p.295.
12. Ibid.
13. CL. 2.103.
14. CL.3. 98.

15. CL. 2. 103.
16. Ibid., 104-6.
17. Ibid., 107.
18. Bristol MS, 2, 5.
19. Grundy, (1999), p.361.
20. Halsband, (1956), p.159.
21. E & P, p.288.
22. CL. 2. 109.
23. E & P, pp.382, 300.
24. E & P, p.381.
25. CL. 2. 110.
26. CL. 3. 97.
27. CL. 2. 111.
28. John Murray Collection, 29 July 1737.
29. E & P, p.105 n.1.
30. E & P, p.134.
31. CL. 2. 115.
32. Ibid., 116.
33. Ibid., 132.
34. E & P, p.297.

Chapter 15

1. BL Eg., 2234, 25 Feb. 1741.
2. CL. 2.139.
3. Ibid., 140.
4. Ibid., 142.
5. Ibid., 148.
6. Ibid., 149.
7. Ibid., 146.
8. Ibid., 159.
9. Frederick III of Prussia, 22. 327, 10 October 1739.
10. Algarotti, 2. 33.
11. CL. 2. 160.
12. Ibid., 163.
13. Ibid., 166.
14. Ibid., 164
15. Ibid., 172.
16. Ibid., 177.
17. Ibid., 192.

18. Ibid., 196.
19. Ibid., 175.
20. Frederick III of Prussia, 18.15, 3 June 1740.
21. CL. 2. 198.

Chapter 16

1. CL. 2. 240.
2. Ibid., 202.
3. John Murray Collection, 22 Sept. 1740.
4. CL. 2. 206, (translated 510).
5. Wal Corr. 13. 227-8.
6. Ibid., 234.
7. Wal Corr. 14. 38 n.40.
8. Wal Corr. 13. 234.
9. Ibid.
10. Wal Corr. 37. 78-9.
11. CL. 2. 212.
12. Finch MS, 21/10 Feb 1741.
13. CL. 2. 225.
14. Ibid.
15. Ibid., 228.
16. Wal Corr. 30. 10.
17. Spence, (1975), p.357.
18. Ibid., p.361.
19. Ibid., p.361.
20. Finch MS, D5, p.140.
21. Grundy (1999), p.436.
22. John Murray Collection, 29 May 1741.
23. CL. 2. 232. n.1.
24. Ibid., 237.
25. Ibid., 240.
26. Ibid., 240-1.

Chapter 17

1. CL. 1. 41.
2. Ibid., 336.
3. CL. 2, 256.

4. Ibid., 290.
5. Ibid., 309.
6. Ibid., 316.
7. Ibid., 251.
8. Ibid., 306.
9. Harley MS, 18 August 1744.
10. CL. 2. 354.
11. Ibid., 324.
12. Ibid., 353.
13. Ibid., 271.
14. Ibid., 363.
15. Ibid., 189.
16. Ibid., 277.
17. Ibid., 249.
18. Ibid., 269.
19. Ibid., 280.
20. Huntingdon MS, Mo 2838.
21. CL. 2. 275.
22. Ibid., 286.
23. Ibid.
24. Ibid., 287.
25. Ibid., 288.
26. Ibid., 292.
27. Ibid., 301.
28. Ibid., 312.
29. Ibid., 349.
30. Ibid., 352.
31. Ibid., 356.
32. Ibid., 357.

Chapter 18

1. RW, p.104.
2. CL. 2. 379.
3. Ibid., 382.
4. Harley MS, 6 May 1747.
5. RW. p.83.
6. RW. p.85.
7. RW. p.86.
8. CL. 2. 405.

9. Ibid., 466.
10. Ibid., 447.
11. RW. p.90.
12. CL. 2. 461.
13. RW. p.91.
14. CL. 3. 35.
15. RW. p.95.
16. Ibid., p.97.
17. Ibid., p.98.
18. Ibid. p.104.
19. Ibid.

Chapter 19

1. CL. 3. 302.
2. Ibid., 212.
3. Ibid., 127.
4. E & P, p.263.
5. CL. 3. 187.
6. Bute BU/98/5, 30 August 1758.
7. CL. 3. 122.
8. CB MS, f. 21.
9. CL. 3. 183.
10. Ibid., 198.
11. Bute MWM/1/2/3.
12. CL. 3. 113.
13. Ibid., 178.
14. Wal Corr, 20. 226.
15. CL. 3. 28.
16. Ibid., 247.
17. Ibid., 227.

Chapter 20

1. CL. 3. 290.
2. Ibid., 261.
3. Ibid.
4. Bute BU/98/6/267: 7 March 1761.
5. CL. 3. 255.

6. Ibid., 258 & 257.
7. Ibid., 253.
8. Ibid., 279.
9. Ibid.
10. Ibid.,282.
11. Ibid., 281.
12. Stuart, (1901), p.254.
13. CL. 3. 258.
14. Ibid., 272.
15. E & P, p.54.
16. Wal Corr, 10. 5.
17. Finch, 1, 311.
18. National Records of Scotland, GD/124/15/1716/5.
19. Wal Corr. 10. 5.
20. Wal Corr. 5.190.
21. CL. 3. 294.
22. Wal Corr. 22. 56.
23. Montagu, (1818), intro. p.5.
24. CL. 1. 467.
25. E & P, p.19.
26. CL. 2. 12.
27. CL. 3. 302.

Index